Leigh Straw is an academic, historian and writer. She is passionate about telling Australian stories. Her books include *The Worst Woman in Sydney: The Life and Crimes of Kate Leigh* (2016); *After the War: Returned Soldiers and the Mental and Physical Scars of World War I* (2017), for which she was joint winner of the 2018 Margaret Medcalf Award; and *Lillian Armfield: How Australia's First Female Detective Took on Tilly Devine and the Razor Gangs and Changed the Face of the Force* (2018). Leigh is a Senior Lecturer in History at the University of Notre Dame Australia.

ANGEL OF DEATH

Leigh Straw

ABC
BOOKS

The ABC 'Wave' device is a trademark of the
Australian Broadcasting Corporation and is used
under licence by HarperCollins*Publishers* Australia.

First published in Australia in 2019
by HarperCollins*Publishers* Australia Pty Limited
ABN 36 009 913 517
harpercollins.com.au

HarperCollins*Publishers*
Level 13, 201 Elizabeth Street, Sydney NSW 2000, Australia
Unit D1, 63 Apollo Drive, Rosedale, Auckland 0632, New Zealand
A 53, Sector 57, Noida, UP, India
1 London Bridge Street, London, SE1 9GF, United Kingdom
Bay Adelaide Centre, East Tower, 22 Adelaide Street West, 41st floor, Toronto,
  Ontario M5H 4E3, Canada
195 Broadway, New York NY 10007, USA

A catalogue record for this book is available from the National Library of Australia

ISBN 978 0 7333 3966 0 (pbk)
ISBN 978 1 4607 1077 7 (ebook)

Cover design by Hazel Lam, HarperCollins Design Studio
Cover image of Dulcie Markham by News Ltd/Newspix; all other images by shutterstock.com
Typeset in Sabon LT Std by Kirby Jones

For
Kristina Kotua
thank you for your friendship
and
Jack, Lawson and Riley,
my boys. Love always.

Contents

Prologue: Alias Mary Eugene, 6 August 1939   1

1. Waverley runaway: Young Dulcie Markham   15

2. 'I went out for a good time': Prostitution, 1920s and 1930s   35

3. Little Chicago's 'hold-up man': Organised crime in Sydney   59

4. 'Man stabbed in heart': Dulcie loses her first lover   88

5. 'Police seek mystery blonde': Two more lovers gone   109

6. 'Good-bye, sweetheart!' Dulcie's war   135

7. Shot in the face: Another lover dead   159

8. Across the tracks at the 'Rue de la Roe': A Perth sojourn   172

9. Shots in St Kilda: Revenge cuts both ways   188

10. 'I've had enough': A slow change of heart   207

11. A 'model housewife': A quiet life and a dramatic end   221

Epilogue: 'What does it matter so long as you get the money?'   231

Author's note: Writing Dulcie's story   245

Dulcie Markham's timeline   253

Notes   255

Bibliography   287

Acknowledgements   305

p1 null 2⅝⅝ X 3½" deer

Alias Mary Eugene

6 August 1939

It was a cool Sydney evening on 6 August 1939 when, a little before eight o'clock, twenty-five-year-old Dulcie Markham made the fateful decision to go to a party with her lover, Guido Calletti. Only one of them would survive the shooting a short while later.

Dulcie May Markham was the glamour woman of Australian crime, known on the streets as 'Pretty Dulcie'. With soft, finger-waved blonde hair immaculately styled around the contours of her face, her ocean-blue eyes striking against her 'peaches and cream' complexion and bright red lipsticked lips, she looked like a movie star and dressed like one too. She wore deep-red dresses to inquests and courtroom appearances, and brighter, flashier frocks for working the streets and brothels. She was one of Australia's most famous prostitutes, but had impeccably bad taste in men.

Her lover that night in August 1939, Guido Calletti, was a notorious gangster with a long criminal record, known to knife or shoot his rivals. One-time leader of the Darlinghurst Push – a gang of youths – he had been put away many times for assault and for consorting with known criminals. Born into an Italian-Australian family in Eastwood, north-east of Sydney city, Guido seemed destined for prison from a young age. He lived by his fists and sometimes came off second best – by 1939 his nose had been broken several times. As a kid, he was sent to a number of reformatories, but they did little to curb his path into crime. He became a con man, pimp and extortionist and, fascinated by the rising criminal underworlds of Sydney, wanted a piece of the action in the 1920s. During the heyday of Sydney's Razor Wars from 1927 to 1931, which turned the city into the most violent place in Australia, he was vicious and homicidal. He became a notorious gangster, with a long list of police detectives and criminal rivals intent on keeping him out of the crime business.

Dulcie Markham was more popular in Sydney's crime scene than Guido, and her notoriety far exceeded his. She kept close company with many gangsters in Sydney, and extended this to Brisbane and Melbourne in the 1930s. Leading magistrates and police detectives were convinced she was the real criminal operator behind the men with whom she claimed merely to associate.

Walking along Brougham Street to the party in August 1939, Dulcie was well suited to the area – a notorious crime spot nestled within Woolloomooloo and Kings Cross. Brougham Street runs off William Street – a main thoroughfare down into Kings Cross from Hyde Park – and continues down from Kings Cross towards the harbour through Woolloomooloo. It is also a stone's throw from Darlinghurst, aka Razorhurst. When organised crime developed in Sydney following World War I, these were its main areas of operation. Regular police raids on the rundown terrace houses turned up stolen goods, drug stashes and crooks on the run from the law. They also revealed people like Dulcie Markham, whose killer smile matched her deadly reputation.

Parties in houses on Brougham Street, like the one to which Dulcie and Guido were headed, were hard-drinking, loud-mouthed get-togethers combining illegal gambling with prostitution and often cocaine dealing. 'Cockatoos' – lookouts for the police – were placed in the front rooms or on nearby street corners to give the call-out if a local constable was doing the rounds. Such parties were a risky affair after the introduction of new consorting laws in the late 1920s, which gave NSW Police the power to arrest anyone associating with a known criminal. If found guilty, they faced up to six months in prison.

Many of the old terraces and boarding houses along Brougham Street were demolished in the 1970s with the works for the Eastern Suburbs Railway and council efforts to rejuvenate the area, but redevelopment and renovations to the remaining terraces were slow in changing the street's seedy reputation. Sex workers still walked around looking for business on Brougham Street and nearby laneways into the 1990s. In his history of the suburb, Australian author and playwright Louis Nowra recalls how people would drive in reverse along the one-way street, often when drunk, not having the patience to drive along Cowper Wharf Road to enter it the right way.

The terrace at 16 Brougham Street was a standard one for the time. The front verandah gave straight onto the street, and the front door, to the right, led into a hall extending past a bedroom and along to the lounge area. There were stairs up to the next level, a kitchen flowing on from the lounge, and a toilet and other amenities outside. The backyard was flanked by a high quarry wall. The terrace balcony was mostly shaded with striped fabric that gave the occupants some privacy from the street – especially, as would come to light in the investigations, when the room behind it was used for prostitution.

It was the kind of house where you would find members of the Brougham Street gang. They were notorious in Woolloomooloo and Kings Cross, and long-standing rivals of Dulcie's lover, Guido. The police had been successful in breaking most of the gangs with the consorting laws, and while the worst of the Razor Wars violence was well and truly over by 1939, the Brougham Street gang continued to menace locals. They used standover tactics to maintain their hold over gambling, drinking and drugs in the area, taking a cut from the earnings of other criminal businesses operating nearby, and offering protection in return. It was thuggery cloaked in a form of protection from other crooks.

Guido's old scores had not been settled as Dulcie approached 16 Brougham Street. A man with a long memory, he was a violent ticking time bomb intent on reclaiming his hold on Kings Cross. While he planned to confront his rivals at the house party, his guest, Dulcie, was looking for a good time.

In the hours leading up to Guido's arrival at the house, birthday celebrations had been in full swing for one of the guests, Peggy Patterson. Her friends Flora Horton, Maude Beale and May McDonald put on lunch and drinks for her, and all became tipsy with the festivities. They kicked on past lunch and were joined by other women and two labourers, George Allen and Robert Branch, both members of the Brougham Street gang. Lunch turned into dinner and the party roared on.

It was a gathering of many criminal identities where everyone had an alias. Robert Branch was also Robert Jackson, George Allen used the name George Cave, and May McDonald also went by May McIvor. Her husband, John McIvor, also used McDonald as an alias.

The mood of the party changed immediately when Guido showed up. Drunk and uninvited, he brought along friends from an earlier football match, where they had also been drinking. While at the game, he had pulled out two firearms; he hadn't fired at anyone, but he had worried his friends all the same. Guido was gearing himself up to take on members of the Brougham Street gang. He was up for a fight.

There was conflicting evidence about whether Dulcie and Guido arrived together. Maude Beale would later state that Guido arrived first and Dulcie walked in shortly after with one of his mates. While Guido was unwelcome, Dulcie seemed at ease in the house, wandering through to the back and striking up a conversation with some of the women there, including May, Peggy and Maude.

This was Dulcie's neighbourhood. She knew the streets stretching up from the wharves to the Woolloomooloo end of Palmer Street well. In her line of work, it was important to know the safe houses. There was a degree of acceptance of prostitution in eastern Sydney, particularly around Darlinghurst, Kings Cross and Woolloomooloo. Residents knew which houses also functioned as brothels, and women working the streets were, according to one former local, Mary Baker, not 'looked down on'. As Mary recalled: 'They kept their business to themselves, and people didn't interfere in other people's business. You said good morning or good afternoon to anyone, irrespective of what people did, as long as they didn't interfere with you.' Some of the women helped out in the neighbourhood and looked after children while their mothers went to work. Dulcie's work was more accepted than the criminal company she kept. It was Guido who put her at risk of harm in Brougham Street.

Guido Calletti certainly had a way with beautiful women. Though average in appearance and height (just over five feet six inches), he was confident and tough, and caught Dulcie's eye. Their friendship dated back a decade earlier, to 1929, when Dulcie was new to the streets of eastern Sydney. Back then, Dulcie was in love with another young crook, Scotty McCormack, and Guido had his sights set on popular prostitute Nellie Cameron. Nellie worked for notorious brothel madam Matilda 'Tilly' Devine, and her lover at the time was Frank Green, Tilly's standover man. Guido won Nellie from Frank and they later married in Melbourne. A love triangle developed, and by the late

1930s, Guido was living apart from Nellie and sleeping with Dulcie, who was also estranged from her husband of the time, Frank Bowen.

Guido wasn't the only one looking for trouble in the Brougham Street terrace that evening. His friend Clarence 'Clarrie' Riley, a low-level crook who also worked as a machinist at the Haymarket end of George Street in downtown Sydney, turned up at the house to take on Robert Branch. When Clarence suddenly rushed at Robert and punched him in the face for not paying him money owed, a scuffle broke out and Guido raced in to assist. That's when things went horribly wrong.

Guido pulled out one of his guns and threatened to shoot Robert Branch. Clarence moved aside as Robert grabbed Guido and shouted for someone to get the gun. Something hit the main light in the hallway – one witness later said it was a chair – as Guido and Robert jostled for control of the gun. George Allen was there too by now, meaning Guido was outnumbered, while Clarence ran along the hallway towards the front door. That's when the shots rang out.

It was sheer pandemonium. Peggy Patterson hit Allen across the head with a bottle and he threw her back into the kitchen. Dulcie ran to Guido as he staggered backwards, having been shot twice in the abdomen. It was a shocking scene, with some scrambling to escape the house and others stunned at the sight of the mortally wounded Guido crumpling to the ground, bloodied and yelling in excruciating pain. As Dulcie crouched on the ground, cradling Guido's head in her lap, she screamed for someone to call an ambulance, well aware that gunshot wounds to the stomach were bad news. He didn't live much longer.

*

True, Guido had gone to the party looking for a fight with the Brougham Street gang, but he also should have known better than to get involved with a woman as deadly as Dulcie, who during her lifetime would develop a unique reputation in Australian crime history. Guido was neither the first nor the last of her lovers to die in violent circumstances.

Popular *Daily Mirror* crime reporter Bill Jenkings – nicknamed 'Ace' because he was often the first journalist at a crime scene – met Dulcie several times outside courtrooms and when they both lived in Bondi. Bill, who was on good terms with Dulcie, claimed she 'saw more violence and death than any other woman in Australia's history'. This was surprising for a crime reporter like Jenkings, not least because Dulcie didn't look like a notorious crook. 'Flickering her long eyelashes' in court, she distracted reporters with her 'deep blue eyes' and 'manicured fingernails artistically poised'. She enjoyed the attention and the performance she brought to courtrooms.

Dulcie started out as a teenage streetwalker around eastern Sydney before working in brothels and becoming involved in the underworld mainstays of drugs, gambling and sly grog (illicit alcohol sold from unlicensed premises). Violence was a part of life in the Australian underworlds, but it was the intimate nature of the violence that captured media interest in Dulcie. Gangsters found it easy to fall in love with her but harder to stay alive. Newspapers wrote that she 'had a closer view of violent death than probably any other woman in Australia'. At least a dozen of her lovers and husbands were stabbed and gunned down, and she also witnessed or even, police would allege, encouraged other murders. In the Australian underworld, she was called the 'Black Widow', and newspapers branded her the 'Angel of Death'.

Dulcie Markham's story played out like a Hollywood movie and she was the star attraction. Her highly charged sexual image could just as easily have translated into a 1930s or 1940s film noir role. Had she taken a different course in life, and not run away from home and become a prostitute, perhaps she could have been an actress. In her real-life story, Dulcie is a beautiful, captivating and complex character regularly featured in sensational crime stories and horrendous murders. The story of her life is one of love and loss, vengeance and violence, and offers a warts-and-all insight into what it was like to live and work in Australia's underworlds from the 1920s to the 1950s. She kept company with some of the most violent criminal identities in Brisbane, Melbourne and Sydney.

Dulcie was called a femme fatale. She ensnared her lovers, many of them married men, and kept husbands and boyfriends at the same time, one or two at once in Brisbane, Sydney and Melbourne. In newspaper stories and courtroom testimonies, she was the underworld beauty who led her lovers into dangerous and deadly situations. They didn't like sharing her with others, though they were perfectly fine with profiting from her sex work. Jealousy over Dulcie was behind many of the underworld shootings in the 1930s and 1940s.

We know some striking stories of the women involved in the Australian crime scene in the first half of the twentieth century. They include Dulcie's contemporaries, crime bosses Kate Leigh and Tilly Devine, who have captured much of the crime limelight over the years. They are unique in the Australian crime landscape as female leaders. Between them, they ran two of the most violent gangs and controlled the sly grog, cocaine and prostitution rackets in Sydney.

Dulcie Markham was not an underworld leader, but her criminal story reaches much further than Sydney, spanning three Australian cities in a way that neither Kate nor Tilly could achieve. She crisscrossed between these cities, while the police and press scrambled to find out what would happen next. Dulcie saw Australian organised crime from the inside, through its most tumultuous and violent years. Establishing a multicity criminal reputation, this smart operator played the crooks and police alike.

Detectives called her a 'gangster's moll' and a notorious 'gun moll', and reporters repeated this in their newspaper stories. Dulcie hated the description, telling reporters: 'I've been sketched in the newspapers, feet apart, hair flying loose, and holding a smoking gun. But I'm no gun-girl. I've never handled a gun.' She had a point. Dulcie has a story in her own right, and there is a real person behind the provocative, titillating newspaper stories.

Dulcie's story is the third intersecting part of my Australian women and crime trilogy, after *The Worst Woman in Sydney: The Life and Crimes of Kate Leigh* and *Lillian Armfield: How Australia's First Female Detective Took on Tilly Devine and the Razor Gangs and Changed the Face of the Force*. Kate Leigh was a leading crime boss, Lillian Armfield was Australia's first female detective, and Dulcie Markham was caught between their worlds: Leigh wanted to manage and profit from Dulcie's popularity as a prostitute, and Armfield tried to reform her. I was drawn in to Dulcie's story because she kept popping up in my research into Kate and Lillian. I wondered what was it like to be one of Australia's most popular prostitutes, one whom both the police and the crime bosses sought to control.

Who was Dulcie Markham, the woman with the movie-star looks dubbed Australia's 'Angel of Death'? Just how deadly was she and how much of this was press sensationalism? Why were so many of her lovers killed and was there really a curse following her, as she once believed? Who was she when she was out of the spotlight?

Dulcie is alluring, captivating and mysterious. One of the most enthralling women in modern Australian history, she left behind a remarkable story.

CHAPTER 1

Waverley runaway

Young Dulcie Markham

Dulcie May Markham let out her first screams at the world on 27 February 1914 at Crown Street Women's Hospital, on the corner of Crown and Albion streets in Surry Hills. Built in 1893, it was the largest maternity hospital in Sydney and provided care for some of the poorest and most marginalised in the city.

Drama was part of Dulcie from the beginning. Her father, John William Henry Markham, gave his occupation on her birth certificate as 'Theatrical Artist'. He himself was born in Melbourne to John Henry Markham, a builder by trade, and Catherine Pembroke. They were originally from country New South Wales, and young John probably grew up around Gundagai, and in Dapto near Wollongong.

John Markham was twenty-one and living in Surry Hills when Dulcie was born. His parents would later live and die in Sydney.

Dulcie's mother, Florence 'Florrie' Millicent Parker was nineteen when she married John Markham on 28 January 1913. Her parents, George and Millicent Parker, were originally from South Australia, and George worked as a painter. John and Florence were living together in Surry Hills before the wedding, each giving the same address on the marriage certificate. They were married in the manse of the Congregational Church in Waterloo, a neighbourhood a few kilometres south of the centre of Sydney. The Gothic Revival church still stands today on Botany Road. As George had died the previous year, Millicent gave her away. The groom's parents were also present.

When Dulcie was born a year later in February 1914, Florence Markham gave her occupation as 'Home Duties', but her young life had been more dramatic than this. Dulcie inherited a strong streak of juvenile delinquency from her mother. Combined with the theatrical side from her father, it was a fascinating genetic mixture that would reach full fruition in the years ahead.

Eighteen-year-old Florence Parker appeared at Central Police Court on a stealing charge in November 1911. She told the police her name was 'Millie' and denied the charges. She was employed as a 'domestic' at a house on

Riley Street, Surry Hills, and the owner alleged she had stolen 'several articles of wearing apparel'. Millie left this employment and when the articles reported missing were found at her new lodgings in Abercrombie Street in inner-city Chippendale, the magistrate was in two minds as to what to do with her. He told her he didn't want to send her to prison with hard labour at such a young age, so stipulated that she pay a surety for a lessened sentence of good behaviour for twelve months.

What the magistrate did not know in showing this leniency was that Millie had appeared before the courts only two months beforehand. Using her real name, Florence, she faced the magistrate at Glebe Police Court on a charge of 'idle and disorderly', laid after police found her hanging around the convent reformatory on Buckingham Street, Surry Hills. St Magdalen's Refuge, which could hold up to 104 inmates, was established in 1903 by the Sisters of the Good Samaritan and had a fearsome reputation. One sensationalist newspaper story referred to the inmates as 'Laundry Captives'. Escapees talked about severe discipline, cane whippings and working long hours for no pay. Florence was trying to help her friends get out when she came to the attention of a police constable who had seen her wandering the streets at all hours of the day. The magistrate told Florence he was concerned about the company she was keeping and worried she was 'going downhill very fast'.

The magistrates saw many 'wayward girls' like Millie Parker. If these young women couldn't be reformed, they commonly faced being sent to a reformatory home such as St Magdalen's Refuge. Catholic reformatories, some of which tried to get girls to find God and become nuns, felt little better than a form of incarceration to the teenagers sent there. The regimen was strict, the hours of domestic labour were long, and the walls of the convent loomed over them like a prison.

Florence's parents appeared in court to vouch for her and offer their assurances to the magistrate that she could be reformed. Florence's mother, Millicent, told the magistrate her daughter came from a good home and she herself supported the family as a collar machinist. When questioned about the family's ability to control their child, Millicent said she could. It was also revealed that Florence was soon to be married to a 'respectable young man'.

That young man was John Markham. Perhaps with the intention of creating a new life for herself and heeding the advice from magistrates, Florence Markham seemingly kept a low profile and took on the role of wife. Knowing that her previous run-ins with the law had been reported in the newspapers, and living now as the Sydney-born Florence Markham, she could distance herself from the youth offender Florence Parker, referred to in the courts as a South Australian.

John and Florence Markham had moved on from Surry Hills by the time Dulcie was born. They took her home as a newborn to Salisbury Street, Waverley. Dulcie's first house, built only three years beforehand in Federation style, stood on a 386 square metre block, spacious in comparison to the cramped, overcrowded terraces of Surry Hills.

Waverley was an up-and-coming residential suburb when the Markhams moved in, having benefited from the extension of city tramlines through to it from the 1880s. Shops and houses started lining the tram routes, and the area became more commercial as well as residential. By the 1910s, places like Woolloomooloo, Darlinghurst and Surry Hills were bursting at the seams. One city alderman, in a speech celebrating the extension of the tramline to Bronte Beach, said the new line would 'give the people of Woolloomooloo and other congested districts an opportunity to take a tram ride and get a wash'.

As a Salisbury Street kid, Dulcie grew up close to Bondi, Tamarama and Bronte beaches. Neighbourhood children enjoyed summers on the sand and wandering the streets nearby. Before the Beaumont children disappeared from Glenelg in South Australia in 1966, Australian kids frequently wandered down to the beaches or caught buses there and back. Years later, when Dulcie had established her notorious reputation, reporters would comment with surprise that some of Sydney's prostitutes, including

Dulcie, liked regular activities such as bodysurfing. Given her childhood close to the beach, it's not surprising that Dulcie would leave the crime streets of eastern Sydney for some downtime in the surf. One of her great adversaries, the renowned female police officer, Lillian Armfield, also took to the Bondi waves on her days off.

By the time Dulcie was born, the public school on nearby Bronte Road had been extended with two extra classrooms to accommodate the growing number of children in the area. The local council was also considering plans to build new cottages and shops, and a School of Arts was formally opened by the Labor premier, William Holman, in March 1914.

Waverley attracted young families and artistic types but it could still be a rough place with its fair share of sensational crime cases, like so much of Sydney in the early twentieth century. Street fights erupted on occasion, and in one particular fight in 1909, a young man escaped from a beating by a mob of youths only to die at home with a fractured skull. That same year, another young man was charged after being caught fighting in a paddock off Ebley Street. In 1913, a man was charged with attempted murder for shooting his fiancée in a laneway in Waverley, after he returned from a trip overseas to find she had married someone else.

Dulcie would later tell reporters that by her teenage years she was 'more than ordinarily pretty', and claim to have won beauty contests in New South Wales and Queensland. While there is no existing evidence of this, and Dulcie could well have made it up, it's not inconceivable based on her beautiful looks, striking figure and deep blue eyes. She was a Waverley pin-up girl.

When Dulcie was six, her sister Florence Ena was born on 13 July 1920. It wasn't, however, the much-awaited, joyous birth of a new child for the Markhams. According to one family story, Dulcie and her sister didn't share the same father, and on her birth certificate, Florence's father is recorded as 'unknown'. John and Florence Markham were now living apart, but the cause of the marriage breakdown is unclear. In 1927, under the listings for 'Marriages Dissolved' in Sydney's *Daily Telegraph*, there is reference to a 'Florence Markham v Harold Markham' divorce case. This may have been Dulcie's parents, but if so, the use of Harold is odd.

Little is known of Dulcie's younger years because of the fragmentation of her family life, and she didn't leave behind much of a record of her childhood. The silences around her father also continued in the years ahead. There is an interesting case in 1927 of a John Henry Markham, who was the same age as Dulcie's father, being charged with stealing. Arrested under warrant, he was sentenced to three months in prison. Later, in 1931, the same John Markham was apprehended for obtaining money under false pretences and served another three months in prison. Regardless of whether this John Markham was Dulcie's father, her home life had broken down before her tenth birthday. It was a fractured family, and her nephew only learned about his aunt's notorious life after his mother, another Florence, passed away in the 1980s.

With an absent father and a mother busy with a younger child, Dulcie ran away from home early in 1929, when she was fifteen. Had Florence passed on some of her earlier behaviours and personality to her eldest daughter? From the late nineteenth century onwards, social campaigners and professionals – doctors, social workers, religious leaders and the police – researched these links and were concerned that criminal traits could be passed on from parent to child. A child's upbringing was paramount to concerns for their later welfare.

Genetic inheritance or not, Dulcie became one of the many runaway girls in Sydney who came to the attention of the Women's Police, female police officers who worked to find runaway girls and prevent their entry into Sydney's underworlds. Nevertheless, in 1929, Dulcie took her first steps onto the streets that would create her reputation as the 'Angel of Death'.

*

Lillian May Armfield had been in the NSW Women's Police for more than a decade before young Dulcie Markham came to her attention as a runaway girl in 1929. Moving from country New South Wales to Sydney and, in 1915, becoming one of the two first female police officers in Australia, Lillian knew the streets where runaways shouldn't go, where they would encounter everything from opium dens and fraudulent fortune-tellers to cocaine peddlers and sly-grog profiteers.

Now in charge of the Women's Police, from her very first days in the job Lillian had been tasked with finding runaway girls. It would take many decades before female officers – in these years a very small group of fewer than ten women working closely together – were amalgamated into the wider police force, so in the early years they were expected to assist with investigations relating directly to girls and women. Remarkably, of the 200–300 girls who were reported as runaways each year in Sydney, Sergeant Armfield and her officers returned all but a dozen to their families or sent them to girls' homes. Lillian believed she made a difference by working the crime-ridden streets of eastern Sydney with what she called 'womanly sympathy'. She later told a newspaper reporter: 'You'd be surprised the number of girls who come to the city without knowing anyone or where to go to live or get a job.' They had usually fought with their parents and taken off to the city with little thought for how they would support themselves. One young girl ran away from home leaving a note for her guardian to 'forget' they had ever known someone by the name of Peggy.

News of a missing girl often started with a phone call to a police station from concerned family. One prominent Macquarie Street doctor frantically notified police of his daughter's disappearance in 1940. Lucy Craig walked out of a building in the city centre one day and her parents hadn't heard from her since. The great fear, worse than Lucy becoming another runaway, was that she had met with foul play. Fourteen months later, after various police investigations and scouring local flats, the Craig family clearly still believed their daughter could be located, offering a sizable reward of £200. Three years after she was last seen in Kings Cross, however, all they had were some reported sightings and her personalised handkerchief found at a railway station. Lucy was never found.

A missing girl might also come to the attention of the Women's Police by way of the Child Welfare Department. Florence Markham reported Dulcie missing in the early months of 1929, but in April 1929, a warrant for Dulcie's arrest was requested by Alphonse Joseph Turner of the Child Welfare Department after she was 'charged with being an uncontrollable child'. Incorrectly called 'Dulcie

Marken', she was now officially listed as a runaway. Her description in the notice is interesting: 'fifteen years of age, 4 feet ten inches high, thin build, fair hair and complexion, blue eyes; dressed in a dark dress, and a white straw hat'. A dark dress offset by a white hat creates a striking image of a young Dulcie. It was a taste of things to come.

After being notified of a missing girl and with a warrant issued from a magistrate, Lillian Armfield and her officers in the Women's Police were responsible for locating Dulcie Markham. They placed notices in the Sydney newspapers and began each day with a routine of scouring the streets for missing girls. Lillian Armfield called it the 'dawn patrol' and it would rescue hundreds of girls each year from its inception in 1915. Policewomen watched trains arriving at Central Railway Station, which brought in runaways from outer suburbs and country towns, and down at Circular Quay kept an eye on the ferry passengers. Officers talked to girls and young women travelling solo and quizzed them about where they were staying and working. They also watched crowds leaving movie theatres in an effort to locate runaways. Many slipped into the city undetected, or wandered its many winding, secluded alleyways in order to hide from police. Boarding houses were added to the daily patrols, and the female officers came to know many of the landlords, some of whom were willing to report a missing girl renting one of their rooms.

Boarding houses were common in the inner eastern neighbourhoods of Sydney. Up to twenty per cent of adults lived as boarders or lodgers in the early twentieth century. The rent was cheaper than in other establishments leased out at the time. While the middle class was leading a garden city movement by moving further out from the inner-city areas, often to the North Shore, to a house with a garden and more space, the poorer working classes remained close to the city in the eastern Sydney urban neighbourhoods associated with crime, overcrowding and poverty. If they couldn't afford the terrace rents, they opted for the boarding houses. A third of Sydney's population lived in the inner city in 1911, but by the 1930s this had been reduced to around sixteen per cent.

Sydney's housing crisis widened the gaps between the wealthy and the poor. City councillors inspected inner-city and eastern Sydney housing, including terraces and boarding houses. They found that there was a serious lack of appropriate housing, and that rents continued to climb beyond what ordinary workers could afford. In 1918 it was estimated that anywhere from 150,000 to 200,000 people were living in 25,000 houses in the eastern suburbs. At least six to eight people lived in each house, but town planners believed another 500,000 people could be accommodated. This meant, on average, each house could contain up to twenty people.

Working-class houses in eastern Sydney, either one-storey cottages or two- to three-storey terraces, along with the boarding houses, were filled to capacity. Three or four families would be living in the same terrace, often with single lodgers too. Residents shared the kitchen, bathroom and outside toilet, and crowded the hallways in the hurry of the morning and evening. In these congested spaces the bugs scurried around and the cockroaches took up residence.

The City of Sydney's Oral History Project has revealed some interesting insights from locals about what it was like to grow up in Sydney's working-class neighbourhoods. Anne Ramsay, who grew up in Redfern, was born in 1914, the same year as Dulcie. Some of Anne's earliest memories were of 'the dirt and the squalor', and the hard times everyone went through working and trying to pay the rent. Anne recalled joining other kids as a lookout for a group of young men who played two-up in an attic. They would be bought off with some food or coins, but only if they kept quiet and didn't tell their parents or the patrolling police. The local kids would also make their own fun. Anne and her friends would take her mum's old tin trays and race down steep hills on them. When she arrived home she would be 'belted' for the holes in her pants.

Anne also recalled the closer relationship the police had with the locals. While there was a working-class wariness of police work and its intrusions into everyday life, the constables used their patrols to become acquainted with the locals. They were also sensible in getting to know the young kids so that they could work on developing respect. The flipside of this is that the constables knew the kids and could quickly pull them into line. Anne Ramsay remembered Christmas parties the police put on for local kids at the Redfern barracks of the NSW Mounted Police. The police would put the small kids on the horses and the older children would walk them around; the police 'were friends' to the kids.

The local kids also knew how to look after one another, and the places and characters they should avoid. As Anne Ramsay remembered: 'We weren't allowed out on our own. We had to have some of the kids with us and mostly there was always an elder one with us but we weren't allowed out very much on our own.' Yet Anne was still a naïve child, despite the places she wandered to with friends. When asked about crime figure Kate Leigh's brothels in Surry Hills, Anne said: 'I just thought she was having a lot of people going to her place, that's all.' Anne wasn't allowed inside Kate's places, so her naïvety remained.

These were the streets Lillian and her officers patrolled methodically, looking for missing girls. They walked down to the wharfs at Woolloomooloo and wandered back through the streets to Kings Cross, Darlinghurst and Surry Hills. They often found young girls sitting in doorways or in alleyways, without enough money to find a place to stay.

Dulcie was a little harder to find than some of the other runaways. Whereas there were dozens of girls who left country towns and ran off to the city, Dulcie grew up only a few kilometres away from eastern Sydney where police often found runaways. Dulcie was coming in from Waverley to Woolloomooloo, via Paddington.

We might imagine what it was like for Dulcie for a moment. From her home on Salisbury Street, regardless of the route she took, it was at least an hour's walk to the city. This was a long time for a teenager not to be spotted by passers-by, but Dulcie would have been doing her best not to be seen. She would have taken back roads and perhaps sat in parks for a short while before heading off again. While it was quicker to take Oxford Street, she was better off cutting through Centennial Park.

Eastern Sydney and its neighbourhoods were not entirely unknown to Dulcie. Her grandparents lived in Surry Hills and her parents had lived in the area before moving out to Waverley after their marriage. But even a young girl born at the Women's Hospital on Crown Street would have recognised the difference from Waverley. The main streets through eastern Sydney, including Oxford, William, Bourke and Crown streets, were also the stamping ground of crooks, prostitutes and anyone generally dodging the law.

While these main thoroughfares were busy back in the 1920s, people coming to Sydney stayed clear of the rundown, working-class parts of the city's east. Oxford Street was not a tourist destination. Visitors kept close to the Quay and inner-city commercial streets.

The police were not just concerned that Dulcie was an 'uncontrollable child', as if she were only misbehaving. While the newspapers estimated that more than eighty per cent of runaways were boys and girls between the ages of 14 and 17 – children much like Dulcie – the great fear for girls was that they could be lured into prostitution.

Girls and young women who wandered about the streets were looked upon with suspicion. Police and charity workers stopped them and asked about their family situation and if they were working. If they weren't working, or could give no evidence that they were, the police could get them off the streets with a charge of idle and disorderly, living without lawful means of support. The police already had a warrant to arrest Dulcie as an 'uncontrollable child', but this could be upgraded to a vagrancy charge.

The *Catholic Press* newspaper was particularly worried about young girls ignoring the advice of the churches about threats to their innocence on the streets. It warned its readers in September 1915 of strangers and brothel madams in the business of corrupting young women, and advised young girls not to get into a carriage or cab with a stranger. If they did, they might be lured into a strange house, which would then be revealed as a brothel. For their own good, young women were advised to stay off the streets at night and to carry identification in their purses.

Dulcie had to consider that her mother might not want her back or, believing she couldn't control her, send her to a girls' home or somewhere like Callan Park Hospital for the Insane in Rozelle, which regularly took in 'wayward girls' and young prostitutes. Dulcie needed money and a place to live. Rent wasn't cheap in the city, and she needed to stay where the landlord would keep quiet, which more often than not meant extra payment.

Even had she wanted it, Dulcie would have struggled to obtain regular employment without family support and personal or prior work references. Residents of eastern Sydney could find work in the city or down on the docks, but they also worked shifts in the medium-sized industrial sites and factories dominating the landscape of Darlinghurst and Surry Hills. Sargents Pies on the corner of Burton and Bourke streets was a large local employer and became an iconic building in Darlinghurst. Historian Joy Damousi has shown that factories became important early sites for female administrative leadership. In its infancy in the early twentieth century, the role of the female factory inspector provided women with opportunities to consider and push for better industrial conditions for female workers and, for some, to bring about greater social change. Factory inspectors such as Annie Duncan argued for the need for new female professionalism. Campaigns and work by such women were about making the most of the opportunities available at the time.

There were greater opportunities for women during World War I. With the male workforce reduced due to enlistments, women took up work in domains previously closed to them. There were more female bricklayers and factory workers, but also more women in regular female work, in printing, clothing and food production. Even the female police officers who were trying to find Dulcie had benefited from the war. The introduction of special constables and the Women's Police came not only after pleas from social workers and women's groups to have women working on cases involving women, but also because the NSW Police Force experienced its own manpower shortages. Two hundred and twenty NSW police officers served in the war; forty-six of them died on active service.

While women were working in wider professional areas than in the nineteenth century, women's work in general was restricted across the country. They were accepted into teaching and health work, but wider professional qualifications were severely limited, and women had to leave paid work when they married and had children. Professional work was also class-based. Working-class families could rarely support sons, let alone daughters, into university or training schools. The women's movement from the late nineteenth century had a strong middle-class membership. Young working-class girls and women were still more likely in the 1920s to get work in factories or in shops.

Dulcie had no interest in working in a factory or in a shop, and she couldn't afford to obtain further qualifications. She did the best with what she had been given in life, which proved to be very useful in the underworlds of Sydney. She was smart, tough and strikingly beautiful. This was exactly what most worried the officers of the Women's Police in their search for Dulcie. There was work that would take advantage of the teenager's looks and charm, and pay more than she could hope to put together with factory work. Dulcie was in direct danger of being lured into prostitution.

Lillian Armfield and her small band of officers searched for Dulcie in the eastern Sydney streets and the brothels known for their young girls. Over the course of the 1920s, Lillian had watched the rise of organised crime under the control of powerful women in Sydney. Brothels became a central part of this business, and one woman in particular staked a claim to being Sydney's 'Queen of the Underworld'. Tilly Devine was always on the lookout for new talent, and Dulcie could earn her good money pulling in the punters on her looks alone.

CHAPTER 2

'I went out for a good time'

Prostitution in the 1920s and 1930s

While the female police officers were doing their best to bring Dulcie into custody, she had other plans. Speaking in 1940 of how she started out in Sydney's underworld, Dulcie confidently and unashamedly told newspaper reporters: 'I was pert, more than ordinarily pretty, and fellows took a lot of notice of me.' It was exactly the kind of attention Lillian Armfield didn't want Dulcie receiving, having seen too many girls 'go wrong', as she described it, and ruin their chances at a better future. But she met her match with the pretty and feisty Dulcie, who shrugged off help and was, in Lillian's opinion, 'completely incorrigible'.

Dulcie didn't see it that way, recalling, 'I went out for a good time.'

In the view of 1929 society, however, Dulcie was headed for a 'fall'. Prostitution, the 'great social evil' of the time, was seen as a 'fall' from femininity. In the first months of 1788, British Lieutenant Ralph Clark looked out at the arrival of female convicts in Sydney and described them all as 'damned whores'. Not all of the female convicts were or had been involved in prostitution, but it developed in the inner-city streets and then extended further inland with the gold rushes in the eastern colonies from the 1850s and Western Australia from the 1880s.

Some of the most outspoken opponents of prostitution came from within evangelical religious movements. Church leaders preached the need to 'save' prostitutes in order to prevent the further degradation of society, arguing that young men and husbands were being led into immoral lifestyles by streetwalkers and brothel-keepers. These women purportedly preyed on men's 'weakness for sex', took their money and kept their secrets. Church leaders also told of broken marriages and the spread of venereal diseases. One church minister told a Christian convention in 1898: 'There is perhaps not another city on the face of the earth in which vice has more completely established her dominion than the capital of New South Wales.'

Prostitutes, whether soliciting on the streets or selling sex in brothels, worked for an 'immoral purpose'. Social reformers were trying to clean up the streets, particularly working-class neighbourhoods, in their campaign to rein in the loose morals of unprotected womanhood. The 'common prostitute' – the woman soliciting on the streets in a public space – drew considerable attention, too, from city planners and business owners. It was bad enough that some women had 'fallen' from respectability, worse that their *un*respectability was on show in public.

Other, more politically motivated Sydneysiders wrote to the newspapers of 'poverty's prostitution'. One letter to Sydney's *Labor Daily* in May 1929 argued that 'the ever-increasing number of girl prostitutes upon streets of Sydney' was attributable to the 'curse of capitalism'. Two months later, the same paper published a letter blaming the social system for working-class children leaving home in their teens to get work and escape parental control. Again, the political perspective of the newspaper's readers is clear, the writer stating that prostitution could only be cured with 'the abolition of capitalism'. Political views aside, Australian social, medical and legal opinions took seriously the argument that poverty was driving girls and women into prostitution.

Social workers tried to offer prostitutes places to stay away from the brothels and off the streets. The

Sydney Rescue Work Society created an establishment it called the Open All Night Refuge for Women. Social reformers campaigned for better government regulation of prostitution, and a deputation from the Public Morals Association met with the government's chief secretary in March 1905 to discuss immorality in the city.

All of this depended on the eye of the beholder. The prostitute viewed selling sex as work and, if desired, could turn it into a profession; church leaders and their congregations saw prostitution as an immoral act contravening God's codes of behaviour; legislators had to consider how to regulate it on the advice of police authorities, who were under pressure to contain it.

By the twentieth century, Sydney's prostitutes were concentrated on what the police called the 'Barbary Coast', which according to one detective, Ray Blissett, stretched along Elizabeth Street in the city, 'up through Surry Hills to Campbell Street, Riley Street and over the hill down into Palmer Street and Crown Street'. Crime and brothel bosses made a fortune by combining sex with knock-off booze and drugs.

Ray Blissett knew these streets well from years of policing them, and had established a formidable and respected reputation in the police force. Born in Boolaroo near Lake Macquarie in 1908, Ray started out as a bullock driver. He was a country lad – the nearest large town was

Newcastle nineteen kilometres away – and also worked picking fruit. His mother lost two brothers in World War I, and in his younger years he worked closely with his parents. He went to school two days a week and had a job in a grocery shop with his father. As a teenager, Ray started thinking about a job in the police force and joined in 1928, aged twenty. Originally posted to the training centre in Redfern, he worked long Friday shifts at Central Police Station and took up a spot at Glebe Police Station. In those days, according to Ray, 'you could stick your head out of the police station window and pull in a thief any time'.

Sydney author Larry Writer describes Ray Blissett as the 'muscle' of the NSW Police Force from the 1930s. One of Ray's colleagues told Writer he witnessed Ray throw a baton at an offender on the run in 1930. The blow knocked the man out cold and Ray made his arrest. Ray's colleagues knew they were in good hands when working with him; he could sort out a gang of thugs on his own.

John Frederick 'Chow' Hayes, one of Australia's most violent criminals, had a high opinion of Ray Blissett. Hayes started out as a petty criminal and developed a long list of offences, including charges for assaulting police officers. Naturally distrustful of the police, given his criminal background, Hayes nevertheless liked Blissett: 'He'd be one of the few fair dinkum coppers I met in my life. Everything he'd say in court would be exactly what took place – no verbals or any of that rubbish.'

Ray Blissett became a member of the Consorting Squad and developed his own understanding of how Sydney's world of prostitution worked. There were the amateur streetwalkers, the girls in the brothels and what Ray called the 'flasher types of molls'. They would wait around in King Street in the city and take their clients out to the brothels on Yurong Street in Darlinghurst, which then ran between William and Oxford streets. Streetwalkers could wander down the major thoroughfare of William Street from business in the city centre. It was a difficult beat for detectives like Ray Blissett, who would often have to step in when prostitutes were battling it out for clients.

Martin Place in the city centre was a notorious spot for open fights between prostitutes. Before the mall was created in the 1970s, Martin Place was a main road. Cars snaked along it and parked at its sides, while pedestrians weaved their way around the traffic, some heading to work. It was a good street for business but not always of the corporate kind. Thoroughfares with back streets and alleyways running off them are great for the sex trade. In the 1930s and 1940s, working girls targeted businessmen knocking off for the day and then waited – if they weren't moved on by the police – for the drunken punters coming out of pubs nearby and staggering along Martin Place to catch a tram down George Street or hop on a train out to the suburbs.

The back streets and alleyways around Woolloomooloo and Kings Cross were harder to police. A prostitute could work her way up to the Cross, avoiding the main streets and slipping along the smaller, quieter ones. Lillian Armfield often saw prostitutes picking up business on the streets and taking clients into brothels masquerading as regular houses. Running off the main streets of William, Bourke and Macleay in Darlinghurst, Woolloomooloo and Potts Point were a number of smaller streets met by laneways and places. Despite the demographic changes to the area today and expensive cars replacing barrows and old work vehicles, the laneways and the houses lining them still create a crowded, darkened feel in the evenings, and someone could still hide in the shadows, as Dulcie did when looking for work.

While the police could move on or arrest girls and women for soliciting in the streets, usually charging them with vagrancy, it was harder to find them in brothels. Police raids of suspicious terraces often turned up a number of prostitutes, but Women's Police officers sometimes had better access to the brothels, which were a key part of their daily patrols to locate missing girls. Some of these buildings were well known as brothels, while the landlords of others maintained the facade that they were lodging houses. Often they were a combination of both, with people renting rooms in a terrace house that kept a couple of rooms free for prostitution. The police, however, were more inclined to turn a blind eye to the brothel business than they were to women soliciting in public. It was out of sight out of mind, unless their business spilled out onto the streets or there were complaints from the neighbourhood.

Brothels were also located in the centre of Sydney, mainly along George, Pitt, Castlereagh, Elizabeth, Liverpool, Phillip and King streets. Beyond the open-air soliciting in the Domain and Hyde Park, the sex business was increasingly confined by the early decades of the twentieth century to notorious streets in Woolloomooloo, Darlinghurst and Surry Hills, including Campbell, Palmer and Riley streets. Woolloomooloo's brothel reputation went back to the nineteenth century. Clara Moffatt, charged in 1893 with keeping a brothel on Riley Street, had a number of teenage girls working for her. By the 1920s, these same places were being called 'dens of depravity', and people were regularly charged with keeping houses of ill-repute.

Brothels enjoyed a spike in their business after the Police Offences (Amendment) Act of 1908 criminalised street prostitution. In response, the NSW Police Force had begun lobbying for further changes to the law, to curb prostitution and brothel-keeping. Police wanted soliciting to be punished with up to six months in prison. Men living off prostitution and landlords of houses of ill-repute were to face up to twelve months' imprisonment. Brothel-keeping, police argued, should also be punished with twelve months' imprisonment. Police were increasingly successful in driving most women off the streets, but this regulation of prostitution also turned it into a 'deviant underworld'.

Joan St Louis worked as a professional prostitute in Sydney and Melbourne in the 1930s until she picked up work in a brothel on Hay Street, Kalgoorlie, in 1941. By 1942 she was working in a brothel in the infamous Roe Street precinct of Perth, and came to know all the leading madams in Perth, Sydney and Melbourne, becoming one herself during World War II. In an interview later in life, she provided a vivid account of what it was like to work in a brothel and take up prostitution as a profession. Through her insights, we can imagine the world Dulcie stepped into in the late 1920s.

Joan St Louis left Tasmania to live with her aunt in Sydney when she was fifteen years old. She couldn't find work and decided to 'become a professional prostitute'. By seventeen she was married to her first husband, a barman who supported her work. She didn't know why she chose prostitution; she said it was 'just one of those things'.

The regularity and normalcy of this life comes through in the elderly Joan's recollections. It was very busy on pay weekends, and in a brothel there might be up to thirty clients a night, shared between four or five workers. A very quick session was worth five shillings, half an hour was double that, and a full hour cost a pound. In today's money, that hour would be worth more than $70. The women also had the opportunity to work all night at a much higher rate. The workers were usually aged between their early twenties and late forties; anyone younger than twenty-four, at least in Joan's brothels, would be advised to come back later.

The brothels where Joan St Louis worked in Sydney, Melbourne and Western Australia were always 'very nice, very comfortable' with good carpets and beds, 'everything that was needed just like an ordinary house'. This served a double function. The workers felt better in familiar, homely surroundings, as did the clients.

While there was no leisure time, except for reading, the women working in the brothels generally felt looked after. They gave up to half of their earnings to the madam in exchange for food, protection and money to pay the fines if they ended up in court. There was generally a large staff servicing the brothels, too. Along with the workers there would be housemaids, a laundress, a night woman, a yardman and a cook. There was a large staff with all the 'girls to cater for'.

On an average day, brothel work would start with breakfast before the first customers were allowed from

10 a.m. Lunch would be served between 12.30 and 1.30 p.m. before work continued until 5.30 p.m. After dinner, the work would go on into the evening and through the night shift. The average brothel worker would take in their business in the evenings and during night shift, but those looking for more work and pay would operate all day.

There was a certain level of protection in the brothels. The workers could refuse a client and they had to be paid upfront. According to St Louis, the women were the 'cleanest bunch of girls you could ever wish to meet' and protected themselves: 'you examined him (the client), washed him, had intercourse, washed him again, and washed yourself'. Given the number of customers they had, particularly during the years of World War II, they didn't pose a significant health threat. The greater threat, according to the madam, was the amateur prostitutes wandering the streets, who were unprotected and not given the health checks required to work in the brothels. Contraception was not at all widespread in the 1930s and 1940s, but in a matter-of-fact way, Joan said: 'grass doesn't grow on a well-worn track'.

When asked her profession during the war, Joan answered that she provided an 'essential service'. She didn't live in the brothels, adding that it was safer to live elsewhere. There was little association between the different brothel houses, and the madams all tried to keep to themselves and watch over their own workers. The police tolerated the business but they put heavy restrictions on the prostitutes, not wanting them walking the streets.

The women generally got on well, aside from the 'bickering'. A madam had to be a 'born diplomat' or she couldn't keep the peace and run the brothel successfully. There were sometimes fights between the girls, not so much over professional jealousy as over some being too lazy to make money. St Louis organised her business very carefully. She eventually had two brothels and separated her workers according to age – younger women in one house and older women in the other: 'There was no contrast [between the women] … See a man will walk into the house and if they all look around about the same age he doesn't stop to think that they might be forty or twenty-five or thirty …'

Or fifteen in Dulcie's case. And one leading Sydney madam knew the young runaway's value in the prostitution business. It was only a matter of time, as the female police officers knew, before Dulcie would cross paths with the woman who claimed ownership over the brothel business in Kings Cross and Woolloomooloo, but it was in the heartland of her crime business, Palmer Street, that she discovered Dulcie Markham.

Very little got past Tilly Devine, and one of the things she enjoyed most was getting one over on the female special constables.

*

These days, terrace houses in Palmer Street, Darlinghurst, in what agents describe as a 'classic city-fringe location', sell in the millions of dollars. The suburb is a vibrant hub of restaurants, bars, pubs, community gardens and park spaces. In 1929, it was a *violent* hub, best known for its criminal underworlds trading in booze, drugs and sex. One of the most infamous houses was number 191, and its owner was the 'Queen of Underworld'. She ruled the street with a foul mouth, ready fist and the help of loyal standover men who enjoyed the profits that came from protecting her and her many businesses.

Tilly Devine was a standout on Palmer Street in the late 1920s. Everyone familiar with the area and the stories in the newspapers knew who she was. A relatively short woman, standing at five feet four inches, with fair hair and piercing blue eyes, she was quite beautiful in her younger years and was known in prison as 'Pretty Tilly'. Her beauty was matched by her fearsome reputation for fighting – in her brothels, on the streets and outside courtrooms. During one argument, she put the heel of her stiletto into a man's forehead.

Tilly was born Matilda Twiss in Camberwell, London, in 1900. She worked as a teenage streetwalker before meeting James Devine, a young Australian soldier, during

World War I. Jim had worked as a shearer in Queensland before enlisting in the AIF, but his service to his country was shady at best. He was repeatedly detained during the war for being absent without leave and was declared an 'illegal absentee' by May 1918. By that time, he had married sixteen-year-old Tilly. After he returned to Australia in 1919, Tilly followed close behind and arrived in Sydney on a war-bride ship. Their young son, Frederick Twiss, was left in London to be looked after by family.

The Devines rented a flat in Paddington and worked together in prostitution, theft and extortion around wider eastern Sydney. Jim took up work as a hire-car proprietor, but the police knew the cars were never hired out. They were used to ferry Tilly and other prostitutes to and from jobs around the city streets. By the mid-1920s, Tilly owned a number of brothels, and both she and Jim were peddling cocaine. In her first years in Sydney, she was arrested for prostitution nearly eighty times.

Tilly Devine developed a reputation for violence based on her ruthless standover tactics. One of the most infamous of them involved a razor attack in 1925. Tilly confronted Sydney Corke outside a hairdressing shop on Crown Street over a gripe that he was later not interested in sharing in court. He was a smart man. He knew the retribution that would come from Tilly and her husband, 'Big Jim' Devine. Tilly attacked Sydney, pulling her arm back, razor in hand,

and moving to slash him across the face. He managed to get his hand up to shield the blow but the cut was deep. As blood spurted out between his fingers, Tilly was said to have walked back along the street singing out, 'I am the notorious Tilly Devine.' She was sentenced to two years in prison for the assault. Sydney Corke never regained full use of his hand.

Tilly also owned the house next door to her infamous brothel at 191 Palmer Street. The terrace, listed in recent years as a three-bedroom, two-bathroom renovated family home, is now worth around the $3 million mark. Back in 1929, when Dulcie was looking for work, it was bursting with prostitutes and local thugs plotting out their business in sex and cocaine.

In Tilly's brothels, business was conducted in the basement, ground floor and upstairs bedrooms, but she let out a room to a regular renter in case of police raids. As Tilly's biographer Larry Writer states, she could claim that she and her girls were 'landladies'. The doors and windows were reinforced with steel, and a loaded gun was kept at each establishment. Darcy Dugan, one of Sydney's most notorious bank robbers and escape artists, who worked for Tilly in his younger years, recalled the 'gaudy wallpaper and furnishings' in the Palmer Street brothel. There was a reception lounge area that 'smelled of stale cigarettes and human sweat', where 'three heavily made-up women in flimsy, frilly dresses lounged on an enormous settee, smoking'. It left a lasting impression in Darcy's mind as his introduction into the brothel business in Sydney.

Tilly Devine and 'her girls' often sat out the front of the brothels looking for new talent. A keen businesswoman, Tilly had already snared the beautiful Nellie Cameron in 1926. Nellie, born Ellen Kelly in 1910, was the daughter of Colin, a horse driver, and Lillian. Colin enlisted in the AIF in October 1916 when Nellie was six years old. On a number of occasions during the war, Colin suffered from nephritis – kidney inflammation – a pre-existing condition that had prevented him from being accepted into the AIF before 1916. By then, the Australian Army, needing more men, had eased eligibility restrictions.

Nellie saw her father again when he was invalided home in March 1918 to their house in Summer Hill. Like so many other men who returned from the war and found it difficult to settle back into civilian life, Colin Kelly could not maintain his household and commitment to his family. Lillian Kelly filed for divorce in 1922 on the grounds of desertion, and remarried the same year, to Robert Cameron. She and Nellie moved to the wealthy North Shore, where Nellie's stepfather provided her with a private-school education. It didn't last. Nellie ran away from home.

We can't know what drove Nellie to run away to Darlinghurst, but it would have been hard for her to welcome her father home at eight, only to see the effects the war had on him, and then at twelve experience her parents' divorce and her mother's remarriage. Using her stepfather's name, the sixteen-year-old became Nellie Cameron and began associating with known criminals around eastern Sydney, taking up prostitution and being hired by Tilly Devine. One story has her stepfather trying, unsuccessfully, to find her in eastern Sydney. Nellie remained close to Tilly and became one of the most popular prostitutes in Sydney from the late 1920s.

Nellie was soon joined by the other new girl in eastern Sydney, who was starting to establish herself as a prostitute around Woolloomooloo. According to local stories, Tilly was sitting out on her front porch when young Dulcie wandered past. Tilly would have known about Dulcie before she saw her, with other prostitutes and Tilly's standover men keen to tell her about a beautiful teenager doing some good business on the streets; news travelled fast in Darlinghurst and Woolloomooloo. Dulcie got work in Tilly's brothels early on in her career.

Dulcie would still have been trying to dodge the female police officers Tilly despised so much. Tilly was known to hiss, 'I hate you,' at these officers when she passed them on the street. She offered her girls protection and promised she would look after them. Tilly's grandson, Richard Twiss, who emigrated to Sydney with his family in 1955 when he was a child, talked to the *Sunday Telegraph* in 2011 about running errands between brothels for his gran: 'She sent them to Ireland and Scotland if they needed a rest or they needed to get away from the law.' Tilly herself was also convinced of her good work, telling reporters in February 1932: 'I might drink and swear, and have a run in with the police now and then, but I'm not really bad.' The other side of the coin, however, was not lost on the police who knew her. When Tilly passed away in 1970, one former chief of the Consorting Squad said she was 'highly respected by the girls she employed' and was kind if they were loyal, but she wasn't past using violence 'if it was necessary'.

Despite their best efforts, the Women's Police had to admit that even they couldn't reform some of the runaway girls who had ended up in a brothel. Some were, according to Lillian Armfield, 'real trimmers', and couldn't just be sent back to their parents. When Lillian's guidance failed, she had to resort to charging the girls with vagrancy or putting them into state care as neglected children. When this didn't work, all the police officers could do was ensure that if any of the girls got into trouble in their line of work, they felt they could talk to female constables and seek some protection.

In soliciting for sex in the street, Dulcie would have to have been very careful. While being a teenager posed a significant threat to her safety, not least the sexual violence inflicted on vulnerable streetwalkers, she needed to be careful not to cross any of the brothel madams, especially Tilly Devine. Rivals were swiftly dealt with and the violence was extreme.

Sex and violence in the neighbourhoods of eastern Sydney could become normalised for girls and young women, especially those living between the streets and boarding houses. For those women directly involved in prostitution at the lower level, it was brutal; their sexual services were sold for large profits by the underworld leaders.

Maria Tinschert witnessed at first hand the violence inflicted on sex workers in the late 1920s and 1930s. Often the attacks she witnessed were carried out by other prostitutes and madams. Maria's own family life was horrific enough; she was sexually and mentally abused by her parents. Her mother, Violet Goodfield, was a prostitute who associated with Tilly Devine and the other leading underworld figure of the day, Tilly's bitter rival Kate Leigh. Violet pushed Maria into the sex business as a child prostitute at the age of only ten. The family lived in Chullora, in Sydney's west, but Maria's mother worked in the brothels around eastern Sydney. Some days she would spend hours in the wine bar at Central Railway Station while Maria sat quietly outside. One time, she completely forgot Maria was there and caught the train home, leaving the young girl to wait for her father to collect her. There were no apologies.

Maria saw the rivalry, standover tactics and violence inside the brothels. Sometimes it shocked her with its sudden ferocity. On one occasion, Maria was sitting in a house in eastern Sydney while her mother, Violet, was dressing in another room. A young woman arrived and one of the other women called out to Violet. In an instant, not liking what the young woman had said, Violet slashed her across the face and neck with a razor. While the young prostitute ran away from the house, bleeding profusely, Violet continued dressing and acted like nothing had happened.

When she wasn't working in one of Tilly's brothels, Dulcie had to negotiate this landscape of prostitution and ownership by the madams. Back in the late 1920s, workers from the Woolloomooloo wharves provided good business for prostitution, as did visiting seamen on trading vessels. Sex workers could also look for business down at the water's edge and coax their clients back up to one of the brothels.

According to Detective Ray Blissett, who came to know Dulcie well in Woolloomooloo, she worked the streets over the hill in the 'Loo away from the main business of Tilly Devine. Chapel Lane in Darlinghurst was one of her popular places to pick up clients, and she also worked in the smaller brothels on Cathedral Street, Woolloomooloo. Even today, 'adult entertainment clubs' still operate on Cathedral Street, including one which is covered at the front for client privacy with bushes and a large tree. Now, as it did then, Cathedral Street cuts from the city through the main part of Woolloomooloo and ends at its intersection with Dowling Street, where the famed Old Fitzroy Hotel still stands. Author and playwright Louis Nowra, in his history of the area, describes the pub today as a place that accepts people who wouldn't usually be accepted in the trendier parts of eastern Sydney. More than some of the other gentrified areas of eastern Sydney, Woolloomooloo, as Nowra points out, retains some of its former seedy reputation. There are no-go areas where drug dealers operate, but the suburb seems to deal with its 'volatile diversity'.

In Dulcie's day, there were also 'houses of ill-fame' not large enough to be known as brothels but that used rented rooms in the terraces for prostitution. One sex worker who worked around the 'Loo and the Cross from the late 1970s told me a few years ago that there were often many girls packed into a terrace at a time, sleeping in a rented room or out on the balcony on shabby mattresses. Even when they were not working in a brothel, the sex workers moved around regularly between houses, often to avoid police attention and also to keep an eye on each other.

The conditions could be tough. Late nights on the streets left women exhausted and sleeping wherever they could. Young sex workers listened to stories being told by older women in the business about how not much had changed since the 1920s and 1930s; women were always packed in close to each other in safe houses and regularly moved around.

Prostitutes in Dulcie's day were well known to locals, and kids grew up regularly seeing the women about. One local, Judy Chambers, looking back on growing up on Cathedral Street during the Depression years, recalled prostitutes with their 'red hair and red fingernails' sitting on the front verandas of terraces operating as brothels. Dulcie was a standout in these places, even at the age of fifteen. Though her hair was fair in her younger years, she told newspaper reporters she turned her 'locks' even lighter to a 'rich, almost golden white'. This, she said, was to suit the 'preferences of gentlemen' when she first started out in prostitution.

*

Special Sergeant Lillian Armfield reached an important conclusion about the runaway girls she was tasked with finding – 'it was my experience that very few girls are bad beyond redemption' – but she now had to deal with girls who were of a different generation from her own and were looking for greater freedom. Lillian herself was a single woman showing considerable independence working in a male-dominated profession, but she was conservative about the kind of life an independent woman should live. She also distinguished between independence for young women and girls, believing that teenage girls should stay at home until old enough to get respectable work. Lillian found, however, that runaways and young prostitutes were becoming bolder, and a growing number resisted her help. One teenager, bailed up by Lillian in front of her parents and told to get off the streets and out of prostitution, refused home discipline and told Lillian: 'Oh, don't be so old-fashioned.'

Florence Markham continued to place notices in the newspapers, and contacted police for months after Dulcie ran away from home early in 1929. Every now and then she would get word from family or friends that they were still looking for her, but it was hard to find someone who didn't want to be found.

Dulcie's notoriety, however, was on the rise from the middle of 1929. She was still listed as a runaway and known for soliciting around the 'Loo and Kings Cross and in some of Tilly's brothels. Lillian Armfield would later recall a young Dulcie boasting that 'it was easy to get a hundred pounds a night at one of the brothels'. She made no excuses for her work and wanted none of Lillian's advice or help.

Dulcie's new life took her right into the middle of some of the most violent years of crime Australia has seen, when Sydney was in the grip of the Razor Wars, and powerful women were on the rise. This was exactly why the female police officers wanted Dulcie off the streets and away from manipulation by formidable underworld figures. But Dulcie had made her decision: she wanted in on the game.

Within two years of running away to eastern Sydney, however, Dulcie found out just how violent living and working in the underworld could be. It began with her catching the eye of a young gangster called Scotty.

CHAPTER 3

Little Chicago's 'hold-up man'

Organised crime in Sydney

Within months of running away from home, Dulcie became a 'gangster's girl'. The world of prostitution was closely linked to the gangs in Sydney in the 1920s. Young crooks ran errands for the brothel madams and provided protection. They became, as historian Robin Hammond describes it, 'the foot soldiers of organised crime'. Some of the young standover men also wanted in on more of the action, rather than passing over the profits to the crime bosses. When they nosed in on prostitution on the streets they were called 'bludgers' for living off the earnings of the streetwalkers. Dulcie met and fell in love with one of these bludgers, a young 'hold-up man' as the newspapers would later call him.

Cecil William Bethel 'Scotty' McCormack was a country lad, born in Orange, New South Wales, on 2 May 1909. Scotty developed into a good-looking boy, and by the time Dulcie met him in 1929, he was five feet three and a quarter inches tall with brown hair, blue eyes and a soft complexion. Dulcie was at the start of her criminal career but Scotty already had a long record.

Scotty made his first appearance in the Children's Court in January 1923 when he was fourteen, charged with stealing. He was sent to Gosford Farm Home for Boys, which like most of the homes for young offenders at the time was a formidable place. Rather than rehabilitate young offenders through welfare programs, the idea was to reform them, usually through strict daily routines. Gosford Farm Home was officially opened in 1913 but boys had been living in tents on the grounds since 1911 and helped to construct the main home building. It was located on a 700-acre site on Mount Penang, seventy kilometres north of Sydney.

A few months after Scotty arrived at the Gosford home, details of a recent inquiry into conditions there were finalised. The new superintendent was now expected to 'foster a greater indulgence in sport amongst the boys', and technical education was to be introduced. From 1923 to 1945, it was known as the Gosford Training School but remained a difficult place of reform. Detained against their will, each year, dozens of boys escaped and had to be tracked down by police. In the first six months of 1939, more than forty boys escaped, some of them using violence to do so. One fifteen-year-old attacked an instructor with an eighteen-inch piece of pipe as he tried to abscond. He failed, and the instructor, though suffering heavy blood loss, survived.

When notorious Sydney criminal Chow Hayes did time at the Gosford home at the age of sixteen, he became friends with Scotty McCormack. He was two years younger than Scotty but was already known to police for petty crimes, and had family links to the Redfern Mob youth gang. He later described the home to writer David Hickie as 'a real bastard of a place' and a 'breeding ground for crims'. There was little chance of reform, according to Hayes, who claimed that all of the boys sent there 'later became heavy criminals and many ended up being killed in underworld activities'.

Scotty also became friends with sixteen-year-old Harry Pidgeon, who had been sent to the Gosford home in August 1923 on a stealing charge. Harry was born in England but arrived in New South Wales as a baby. Later, perhaps to hide his true identity, he told authorities he arrived in Australia in 1921 with a 'batch of Barnardo boys' and could then only speak his native Welsh language. Harry had been working on a station at Bourke in rural New South Wales when he was charged with stealing and sent to the home. Three inches taller than Scotty, Harry also had brown hair and blue eyes. They were similar in build and looks, though Scotty was the more handsome of the two. When Harry and Scotty left the home, they took up as thieves in eastern Sydney.

The mug shots for Harry and Scotty reveal the reality of what it was like loitering about the streets and working in gangs. Their ill-fitting outfits are the same: trousers with a belt (Harry is wearing braces to hold up his trousers but it's not clear if Scotty is too, as his jacket covers more of his shirt), crumpled shirt, jackets and hats. They were young low-level crooks with little money to live off beyond what they could put together from labouring work and selling stolen goods.

There is no record of why Harry and Scotty ended up in Sydney after leaving the home, but they may have hatched a plan to get work in the city together. A large city like Sydney offered young offenders more opportunities and, as they would have hoped, more anonymity than the country towns they grew up in. Scotty also knew Chow Hayes would look after him on the streets when they all got out of Gosford.

McCormack and Pidgeon were back before the courts in June 1925, facing break and enter charges at the Central

Criminal Court in Darlinghurst. They had broken into a house in inner Sydney and another in Leichhardt, and allegedly stolen clothing, other goods and money. Scotty was charged with stealing, attempted break and enter, and break and enter. Harry was up on two charges of stealing and break and enter. They were both sentenced to twelve months' imprisonment in Long Bay Prison. Scotty was only sixteen years old.

Scotty wasn't long out of prison before he was again picked up by the police and fined for using indecent language in December 1926. It was a regular charge in eastern Sydney, where young crooks often faced off with the local police. Scotty McCormack was now set on a course that would take him into the violent streets of postwar eastern Sydney. It's hard to imagine his life being any different once he had gained a criminal record at fourteen and been sent to the Gosford home. Underworld Sydney offered Scotty a place to belong as a young gang member.

Gangs were an essential ingredient in the rise of organised crime in Australia in the early twentieth century. The gangs in the two largest cities, Sydney and Melbourne, functioned through structure and organisation alongside violent coercion and discipline. In the world of organised crime, gang activity offers key benefits: instrumental (drugs and crime), symbolic (power, prestige) and social (belonging, cohesion). In eastern Sydney, gang leaders could appeal to young people by offering a place to belong and an opportunity to make money. Impoverished teenagers were vulnerable to such appeals. As the slum neighbourhoods deteriorated further, gang membership increased. In and out of homes and regularly in trouble with the police, Scotty McCormack appreciated the protection a gang offered and the opportunity to belong somewhere.

Street gangs – 'push gangs' as they were called in Australia – operated in the poorer neighbourhoods of the major cities from the late nineteenth century. Their members – larrikins and larrikinesses – were anti-authoritarian and enjoyed creating a public nuisance. They were not always poor, however. The 'pull of the push' also appealed to young unskilled workers who wanted to create a different identity for themselves outside the social expectations of the proper, moralistic members of society. The push gangs were incredibly violent. Police constables were warned not to take them on alone, and shopkeepers were regularly pestered by them. They fought openly in the streets and were referred to in the press as the 'larrikin menace'.

The most notorious push gangs in Sydney were the Rocks Push, the Surry Hills' Forty Thieves, and the Big Seven in East Sydney. There was a religious divide between the gangs – Protestant and Catholic – and young boys would often fight it out in the streets over religions that had been at loggerheads for centuries. Gang street battles – over religion, money, stolen goods and territory – were common in Surry Hills from the 1880s. While poverty was not always a prerequisite to gang life, many young people joined the pushes to escape the slum conditions of working-class Sydney.

Young people working in the gangs crossed paths with more serious criminal groups. By the mid-1920s, criminal leaders were organising their business so that it would infiltrate and control cross-sections of society from the streets to police operations, legal work and politics. Push gang members were offered introductions into the world of organised crime as drug runners and 'cockatoos' at brothels and sly-grog shops. They were asked to offer protection to prostitutes and scour the streets for crooks on the run from underworld retribution.

Whether it was the lure of the 'bad boy', the empowerment in belonging to a group, or an unconventional view of what a modern girl could be, Dulcie Markham began associating with leading gang figures from her very first weeks away from home in 1929, making the most of her good looks and sexual charm. Female decoys were an important part of the push gangs' thieving business. The thieves' woman, as she was also known, had a clear role in the gang: to lure men into dark alleyways, where the male members of the gang would descend upon them, attacking them and stealing anything of value. On many occasions, victims were found by police or passers-by, half-naked and bleeding in laneways. Female decoys were named and shamed in the press as companions of thieves and undesirables, and depicted as preying on supposedly unsuspecting men.

Dulcie Markham was the perfect female decoy, an attractive addition to any gang – a sixteen-year-old dressing much older than her years and with a confidence that belied her youth. Dulcie was willing to lure men away from pubs and parties with the offer of sex. Then, in a quiet spot away from prying eyes, where her male companion would be distracted with the expectation of sex with her, the rest of the gang arrived and relieved Dulcie of her duties.

It is confronting to consider a sixteen-year-old offering sex to strangers, even without the gang violence that went with it. While the gang offered protection to the underage Dulcie, she was still alone with a stranger for however long it took her associates to turn up. This is exactly what the female constables tried to prevent each day when they conducted their 'dawn patrol' looking for runaway girls and teenagers living on the streets or seen near brothels. Male members of the gangs knew the value of the female decoy to their work, so they were unwilling to let them leave easily. It was even harder to rescue a decoy when she fell in love with a member of the gang.

Scotty started out working with gangs in Surry Hills, notably the Palmer Street gang, taking orders for goods they wanted stolen to sell off for large profits. By 1929 he combined theft with work as a barrowman. Calling out about their wares, their horse-drawn wagons full of fruit and vegetables, barrowmen were a common sight and sound about eastern Sydney. Some also used the barrow as a front for watching houses and noting the routines of their residents. Scotty was joined in the barrow business by another young crook who became one of the city's most notorious gangsters, Guido Calletti. Scotty and Guido had an agreement that if one of them was sent to prison, the other would maintain the fruiterer business.

On the run from her mother and trying to keep a low profile on the streets, Dulcie met Scotty McCormack in eastern Sydney and they moved in together. Knowing the world of Sydney's Razor Wars that surrounded Dulcie is essential to understanding how violence became normalised for her. As crime reporter Bill Jenkings said, she saw more violence than anyone else – and it started when she was fifteen.

*

Sydney's newspapers were turning out front-page stories in the late 1920s declaring that gang violence was turning

67

the inner eastern neighbourhoods of the city into a 'Little Chicago'. The scandal sheet *Truth* called for 'thugdom' to be ousted from Darlinghurst, and newspaper reporters, having given the area, including the surrounding suburbs Woolloomooloo and Surry Hills, the moniker Razorhurst, were portraying it as 'a plague spot, a blotch upon the good fair name and honour of Sydney'. It was a place of 'thugs' and 'parasites' where 'drink and depravity reign supreme'. While press sensationalism exaggerated some of the details, for the locals there was no denying the gun battles, knifings and razor violence. Even if they didn't witness the public acts of violence between rival gangs, they could hardly avoid seeing the tell-tale regular police raids on terraces doubling as brothels and gambling dens.

In the back streets off William Street today, at the bottom end of Darlinghurst, where so much of this violence occurred and underworld feuds ended in a bloodied mess, you can wander up Crown Lane to a quaint terrace that has been turned into a wine bar called Love, Tilly Devine, with exposed bricks and an intimate charm on two levels. The darkened laneway is not what it once was: in the first half of the twentieth century, Crown Lane offered a ringside seat to Sydney's violent organised crime.

In the twentieth-first century, organised crime is local, national and transnational. Globalisation over the last few decades has added to the international reach of organised crime in a way that was impossible a century ago. It has increased the worldwide business in drugs, human trafficking and terrorism, for example. Policing organised crime is now a multilayered, cross-agency operation that involves investigating criminal activities and networks across national and transnational boundaries. In response to policing agencies developing high-level investigative tactics to break traditional organised crime, crime groups have adapted making by their networks more flexible and dynamic – and less organised. They also seek ways to operate within legitimate industry practices.

When Dulcie Markham struck out in Sydney's crime scene, however, organised crime was more traditionally structured. Criminal groups did have international links – mainly in terms of drug importation – but they were not as well developed as they are today. The mainstays of organised crime business were localised, and centred on prostitution, sly grog and extortion. Once the nightclubs began to take off, especially in Kings Cross, crime leaders started controlling gambling, prostitution and drugs. Their standover tactics ensured a loyal group of people protecting them as leaders, and kept competitors at bay.

Organised crime in 1920s Sydney was mainly structured around the business of two key leaders. While other crime figures would try to stake a claim to controlling business in Darlinghurst, Surry Hills and Woolloomooloo, Kate

Leigh and Tilly Devine ran the show. Each held their own areas of power: Leigh was best known in Surry Hills and Devine controlled business in Darlinghurst and parts of Woolloomooloo. While they contested certain streets (Palmer and Riley, sometimes William Street) and vied for greater involvement in Kings Cross, control was measured within their mapped-out territory. The gangs were an essential part of their business in cocaine, sly grog and prostitution.

Kate Leigh and Tilly Devine were ruthless and successful criminal operators. They developed their businesses over a number of years, increasing their connections and criminal know-how. By 1929, when Dulcie was a young newcomer to eastern Sydney, Leigh and Devine were well established. Their rise to power from the early 1920s had caught the police completely off-guard. It wasn't that they were unknown to police – both already had impressive criminal records and were on the police radar for sly-grog selling and prostitution. Detectives simply found it hard to believe that women could have such a hold over the rise of organised crime. Crime was regarded as a male domain, and women were not expected to be at the centre of the rise of organised crime in Australia.

In the years leading up to the notorious Razor Wars, women were far more likely to be charged with drunkenness, soliciting, vagrancy or offensive behaviour than with more serious crimes. Female offenders only accounted for around ten per cent of all people charged with petty crimes at the time, but there was plenty of public commentary about women behaving badly. Even in Perth, a much smaller city than Sydney or Melbourne, with no developed organised crime scene, newspapers and letters from the public stressed anxieties about women transgressing gender and social expectations. Religious campaigners in 1916 declared Perth a 'city of drunken women'. Public drunkenness was a criminal offence at the time.

Historically, three in four criminals are likely to be men. Women were not seen as serious competitors in male domains, especially in crime. With their lower social status – women were still regarded as the weaker sex – it stood to reason they would not be seen as a major threat in the criminal world. The prevailing Victorian social and judicial view that women were less culpable than men in relation to crime meant they were seen more as troubled than troublesome.

Kate Leigh and Tilly Devine showed the Sydney detectives just how outdated their expectations were. As Larry Writer states, these two women were the first female organised crime bosses anywhere in the world.

Kate Leigh was a wayward girl, similar to Dulcie, and got her start in crime by associating with gangs in Surry Hills. Born Kathleen Mary Josephine Beahan in Dubbo in country New South Wales in 1881, as a child she was called 'Bonny' and known for her striking blue eyes and good looks. She learned to fight from a young age and became unruly in her teenage years. Local police accused her of associating with known criminals and prostitutes around Dubbo and Narromine. When Kate's parents said they could no longer control her, she was sent hundreds of kilometres away to Parramatta Industrial School for Girls.

If the police and welfare officials in Dubbo had thought the industrial school would reform Kate, they were sorely mistaken. The heavy-handed, sometimes abusive school regime broke the spirit of many girls who were sent there from the late nineteenth century. (And, as a recent inquiry has shown, physical and mental abuse continued there until the 1970s.) But it didn't break Kate Beahan. She was sixteen when she was sent to Parramatta, and when she was released two years later, in 1899, the institution had done enough to harden her determination not to conform and to ensure no one else would control her life.

Not long after her release, pregnant and trying to find work and a place to stay, Kate moved in with James Lee, and the pair married in 1902. Their daughter, Eileen, was born the year before. The Lees used the anglicised 'Leigh' version of their surname, and Kate was best known as 'Leigh' even after the marriage fell apart. In 1910, Kate told a courtroom her estranged husband was addicted to opium and had deserted his family. She would marry twice more, and those marriages fared even worse than the first.

By the 1910s Kate was associating with known gang leaders and criminals in Darlinghurst and Surry Hills. In 1915 she was bundled off to Long Bay Prison on a perjury conviction after giving a false alibi for her lover, Samuel Freeman, in the attempted murder of a postal worker four days before the Eveleigh Railway Workshop heist of the previous year. He and his mate, Ernest 'Shiner' Ryan, were also charged and found guilty of the heist. Freeman spent more than 20 years in prison and Ryan a decade. Kate Leigh served less than her five-year sentence and was determined never to compromise herself for a man again. (Her third marriage was to Shiner Ryan in Fremantle in 1950, at the end of her long criminal career.)

Kate Leigh established a formidable criminal empire in the 1920s based on sly grog, prostitution and then cocaine dealing. Kate maintained control of her empire through violent standover tactics to put others out of business, and through a network of associates who were directly involved in sourcing, buying and selling the booze and drugs. She maintained her power through the loyalty of workers willing to avoid incriminating their boss by taking the fall themselves. By the end of the 1920s, she and Tilly Devine were two of the most notorious crooks in Australia and were fierce rivals.

Across Australia during World War I, after decades-long temperance campaigns, state governments legislated early closing times for pubs. In most cities it was 6 p.m. but Western Australia stretched it out to 9 p.m. Restrictions on drinking were fuelled by social and political concerns over drunkenness and its effects on the streets (gang violence was one consideration) and in families. The liquor laws meant that unlicensed drinking was criminalised and sly-grog shops were regularly raided by police.

Sly-grog shops had been a part of the Australian drinking scene for a long time. Colonial newspapers wrote about them in the 1820s, and they featured on the goldfields during the rushes of the 1850s. They also popped up across the rural landscape on pastoral properties. Station hands and shearers would often drink poor-quality liquor in rundown shanties. Sly-grog sellers also featured in popular literature. Henry Lawson's 1907 short story 'The Blindness of One-Eyed Bogan' mentions a 'hard-looking woman' who was 'just the sort' to keep a sly-grog shop. The new legislation of the early twentieth century placed far greater restrictions on unlicensed drinking, but its most important side effect was giving criminal operators an opportunity to provide a service to those still wanting to drink after pub closing times. Sly-grogging became an important source of criminal income until the 1950s, and one that had widespread public tolerance.

In 1919, Kate Leigh, Australia's most notorious sly-grog seller, entered into the business of selling alcohol from unlicensed premises. She paid off brewery workers to offload some of their beer at her houses in Surry Hills, and sold the bottles at a higher price, making a profit from local demand for alcohol. Sly grog used to be passed through a hole in the wall of the Shakespeare Hotel on Devonshire Street, Surry Hills, and taken to Kate's terrace house nearby.

The urban layout of eastern Sydney supported Kate Leigh's business. Badly lit alleyways ran along the back of her houses, allowing many customers to come and go undetected. Kate's Devonshire Street property also had a second door to the left of the front entrance, through which she could sneak drinkers into the back room. If customers used the back door, they had to tap and ask if 'Mum' was in.

The police knew where the sly-grog houses were, but although they often raided them, the businesses profited from the corruption of some of the police officers. Mary Baker, who grew up in eastern Sydney in Dulcie's day, recalled:

the police were usually cap in hand [i.e. hand in
glove] with the sly grog owner. And they were either
paid not to raid them, or if they were going to raid

them, they would ring up the owner of the sly grog
shops and say, we're going to raid you tonight,
you'd better not have any liquor in the premises. So
the liquor used to be all hidden or something. But
sometimes the coppers used to run a double cross
and they'd turn up after they'd warned ... they'd still
turn up and raid.

Both Kate Leigh and Tilly Devine recognised that organised crime as it was emerging in Sydney in the 1920s functioned best through a world of networks through which they could allocate tasks to their workers, who in turn operated in gangs to maintain the business and protect their bosses. Kate and Tilly also used police connections to inform on each other. Detective Ray Blissett said Kate Leigh was one of the best informants the police had at the time, and enjoyed giving information about Tilly. Kate also benefited from political corruption. She supported local politicians by helping out at elections and, when she needed a favour, she was quick to remind them of that support.

Violence and coercion kept most of the locals in their place and added many more to the ranks of the rising crime groups. Organised crime functions through the maintenance of such a social structure. Crime leaders not only want to make money, they also want to control the system that makes this possible. Maintaining power in the early twentieth century meant controlling the space and territory that allowed illicit activities to flourish.

Territory is an essential part of organised crime, and allows it to function within particular locations defended by gangs. This was especially true in early twentieth-century Sydney. Crime territory was established with clear boundaries, and this 'turf' was essential to the lucrative business in drugs, prostitution, sly grog and gambling. Eastern Sydney was the heartland of these businesses.

Knowing the territory and those who have the most control over it is not enough to get into organised crime. Entry is generally heavily restricted and usually occurs via an intermediary acting for the leader or leaders. In the early twentieth century, the leaders controlled the gangs of young crooks like Scotty McCormack and his mate Guido Calletti. These young men had to be prepared to contribute in a variety of ways to the business of their bosses. They could be required to run drug packages around the city, drive cars and trucks to collect booze and stolen goods, and act as tough standover men. They would also work on the doors of houses doubling as brothels or illegal gambling venues. The gangs were suspicious of outsiders, especially rival crooks from Melbourne, and so preferred locals either from around eastern Sydney or the inner west. It was a smart tactic, too, because locals would know the streets and hideouts, and bring with them their own connections that might add to the make-up of the criminal group.

At the same time Scotty McCormack was making a name for himself as a 'hold-up' crook, the gangs launched a war against each other that would last for years. The intensity of the violence turned eastern Sydney into one of the most dangerous places in Australia.

Norman Bruhn, a Melbourne crook and newcomer to Sydney, tried to cross Kate Leigh and Tilly Devine but suffered dire consequences from taking them on. Bruhn, a ruthless gangster who often slashed rival thieves and cocaine traffickers with a razor in alleyways, arrived in Sydney in 1926 and got involved in prostitution and selling cocaine. Eight months after making the trip to the harbour city, he was shot in Charlotte Lane, Darlinghurst, in June 1927. He lingered in Darlinghurst's St Vincent's Hospital before succumbing to his wounds, having never given up the name or names of those who had fired at him. Both Kate and Tilly were content that Norman Bruhn was out of the way and control of the crime business remained in their firm grasp. The consensus seems to be that either Kate or Tilly had ordered the shooting by one of her gunmen.

While the newspapers created sensational stories about violence on the streets threatening respectable life in Sydney, the general public were rarely targeted by underworld violence. In their efforts to protect their territory and the business associated with it, organised crime leaders use violence strategically, to take out rival leaders or standover men in order to deal with direct criminal competition by disrupting business. Sydney's warring gangs mainly administered the violence against each other.

Kate Leigh was supported through the years by a number of men who had risen through the ranks of the youth gangs to become standover men. Gregory Gaffney, known to police as 'Gunman Gaffney', was forever getting caught either carrying revolvers or shooting at rivals. He was imprisoned in March 1928 for being caught with a loaded gun in Foveaux Street. Kate Leigh also used Walter 'Wally' Tomlinson as a standover man. Tough and loyal, he became Leigh's lover. When Gaffney was released from prison, he worked with Tomlinson to secure Leigh's hold over drugs and sly grog.

Tilly Devine's gang included Frank Green and Sid McDonald. Known as the 'Little Gunman', Green was a violent standover man paid by Tilly to add muscle to the protection of her brothels. He was one of Nellie Cameron's lovers but was too much of a tearaway even for her. Sid McDonald was a good-looking young thug from Queensland who featured in a number of gun battles. He had a mop of hair on the top of his head but cut the rest in close at the sides. Along with Frank Green, he kept close to the Devines and was quick to reach for his gun to solve disagreements.

Nellie Cameron's other lover, Guido Calletti, also worked for Tilly Devine. While he at times flitted between the two underworld leaders – usually depending on which he owed money – he was more closely associated with Tilly.

The gangsters lived and died by the gun and razor. Several fights and ambushes took place between rival gang members during the heyday of the Razor Wars. When Gregory Gaffney ambushed Frank Green and Sid McDonald on 17 July 1929, they retreated to the Devines' house in Maroubra. Tilly and Jim Devine had moved out of eastern Sydney at the time, and used their new home as a retreat from the worst of the violence in Darlinghurst and Surry Hills. They needn't have bothered; the violence followed them there.

Gaffney and Wally Tomlinson went after Green and McDonald on that July evening, but Gaffney was shot dead by Jim Devine. Unsurprisingly, the underworld code of silence held and Devine was found not guilty, mainly in the absence of witnesses who would testify for the police prosecution.

Only a few months later, in November 1929, Wally Tomlinson and his good mate, ex-footballer Barney Dalton, along with another friend, Edward Brady, were walking along Crown and William streets when shots rang out nearby. Wally was shot in the chest and arm. Dalton suffered a gunshot wound to the heart and died soon after at St Vincent's Hospital in Darlinghurst.

Wally Tomlinson wasn't talking to anyone, least of all the police. Thomas Kelly, the man who had driven the injured men to the hospital, told reporters that locals had witnessed the shooting and a crowd of 200 people was there by the time he drove off. A short while later, however, with his injuries proving severe and placing him in a critical condition in hospital, Wally Tomlinson was ready to talk. He named Frank Green as one of the shooters. But then Tomlinson changed his mind; he didn't know who had fired the shots. Green was acquitted of Barney Dalton's murder in June 1930.

Frank Green survived longer than anyone would have predicted or wanted. By the 1950s he was living in a shabby place in Paddington and his thuggish days seemed to be behind him. He no longer had any power in Sydney's underworld. He was a drunk who regularly argued with his lover, Beatrice Haggett. On the night of 26 April 1956, he and Beatrice had an argument. She was tired of his constant nagging and accusations that she was having an affair. During the course of the row, Beatrice grabbed a carving knife and thrust it into Frank's chest, just below the collarbone. He died shortly after. Quizzed about whether she would attend Frank Green's funeral, Kate Leigh laughed and told reporters she had no intention of going but would happily 'dance on the bludger's grave'.

Business and exchange in organised crime are maintained by discipline and control, violence and intimidation. Frank Green and the other gangsters used by the crime bosses to maintain order were controlled by Devine and Leigh, and held accountable for keeping everyone else in line. These thuggish standover men would stop at nothing to protect their bosses and the business. Henry 'Jack' Baker was another standover man and one of Kate Leigh's lovers. He stood by her through various underworld feuds and fights, and protected her houses with his fists, claiming in court that Kate had a 'heart of gold'. He took a bullet to the chest in 1938 from Chow Hayes after trying to prevent Hayes from accessing one of Kate's establishments. Jack Baker survived, but carried the bullet in his chest for the rest of his life.

Organised crime drew in and sustained all of these disparate personalities through another key characteristic: power and profit. Young lovers Dulcie and Scotty were undeterred by the violence they witnessed living and working in eastern Sydney. They were drawn to the power and profit that organised crime offered. In 1930, their place in the hierarchy was low so, for the time being, they relied on each other to profit from crime. Scotty McCormack bludged off Dulcie's business in sex, and she benefited from his protection and money from stolen goods.

Pressure was firmly on the shoulders of the police to do something about escalating violence in eastern Sydney. By 1925, the police had had enough. After years of trying to 'clean up the streets', they launched an 'aggressive offensive' on youths on the streets and in the city's parks. It came not long after a young man was almost beaten to death by a gang in Prince Alfred Park near Central Station. The push gangs were also now popular further out from the city, including Botany, Waterloo and Alexandria. There was a deep antipathy between the gangs and the police. Police officers investigating the gangs referred to their members as 'rats' who, when alone posed no threat but when with their group 'will fight anything'.

The NSW Police Force was successful in getting legislation passed that extended the Vagrancy Act and gave officers greater powers of arrest. The consorting legislation also allowed police to prosecute anyone associating with known criminals. The thinking was that if criminals could not meet and consort with each other, the police could strike a blow to criminal business. Leading officers told the press and public that the new powers would clean up the city by ridding it of 'gangs of ruffians'.

One of Guido's great adversaries was Detective William 'Big Bill' Mackay. At more than six feet tall, Bill Mackay was a tough Scottish immigrant – the newspapers called him 'burly' – who had learned to police on the rough streets of Glasgow. His hardline approach to police work pushed many of his officers to breaking point. Equally liked and disliked in the police force, Mackay was a formidable adversary to Sydney's gangsters. At the height of the Razor Wars, he was detective inspector at the Central Intelligence Branch (CIB) and led the police offensive against the gangs. During a raid in January 1928, he came to blows with the occupants of a house on Riley Street, Darlinghurst. Mackay sent many of Sydney's crooks packing, either south to Melbourne or north to Brisbane. Guido Calletti was one of the victims of Mackay's crackdowns, going down for various charges. For his efforts, Mackay won the King's Police Medal in 1932 and became commissioner of police three years later.

Despite the early measures to tackle the razor gangs from 1927 onwards, the newspapers continued to pressure the police to do more. *Truth* newspaper called for greater police accountability in January 1930:

And what are the police doing? How are they using those wider powers, specially given them by Parliament, to rid Sydney of its shameful underworld?

So far, the indications are that very little, if anything, has been done. When the Consorting law became operative most people imagined that police activity would at once become noticeable; ... that relentless drives among the dens of the underworld would be made, and hundreds of dangerous gangsters roped in; ... that Black Marias would be working overtime carting underworld denizens to their proper quarters – Long Bay prison; ... that there would be a scurry among 'coke merchants' and sly-grog sellers, a helter-skelter among the 'ladies of the block,' and a hurried exit from those night clubs that harbor criminals of the lowest and most desperate character.

But those things remained only in the imagination!

Upon those officers of the force who, backed up by 'Truth,' succeeded in persuading the Chief Secretary that the Consorting Clause was necessary, devolves the responsibility of justifying their representations. 'Truth' persistently and insistently urged the Government to give the police the powers they said they required, because the community was promised a drastic clean-up if they could only get those powers.

Now the police have them. And it is for them to use them with the effect they promised.

The newspaper was critical of the efforts of police to put the new powers to greater effect. It argued the city needed to be rid of 'desperadoes and thugs and spielers and unwholesome women', and if the police could not manage this, questions needed to be raised about their success as 'detectors of criminals and preservers of law and order'; and that perhaps the police did not 'want to clean up the underworld'. These are harsh words from newspaper editors and reporters not entrusted with policing and prosecuting Sydney's criminals.

It is interesting to note that the shootings and stabbings of leading gang figures all took place within a fifteen- to twenty-minute walk of the Sydney city centre. This is part of the reason the newspapers wanted the area cleaned up. Sydney's underworld was mere blocks away from the state Parliament building on Macquarie Street, but the trains, trams and government cars allowed politicians to bypass these parts. Wealthier Sydneysiders living in larger properties further out of the city could do the same. While at work, though, the state politicians were close to the very poor in eastern Sydney who needed their assistance. Crime was a direct result of the impoverished living conditions and impaired opportunities available to people in the places being compared to Chicago.

In 1929, Big Bill Mackay launched the Consorting Squad, which included Ray Blissett. The squad was made up of detectives from the CIB who enquired into the 'different trouble spots and troublemakers'. They were a mobile squad with 'no control over their movements'. They were also known as the 'basher gang'. If anyone objected to the 'thumping', they'd lock them up for swearing at the officers, charging them with using indecent language.

Scotty McCormack was already on the police radar as a troublemaker by the middle of the 1920s. He carried a gun and a razor, picked fights with rival gangsters and had a reputation as a thug for hire, but it wasn't the police who ultimately brought Scotty down and gave Dulcie her first experience of intimate violence. Scotty wasn't entirely trustworthy, even to his mates. After putting money together for another one of Guido Calletti's court cases in 1930, Scotty kept the donations for himself. And while Scotty was busy ripping off the underworld, another young crook had his eyes on Dulcie and was biding his time until Scotty slipped up.

CHAPTER 4

'Man stabbed in heart'

Dulcie loses her first lover

Scotty McCormack left for Melbourne with Dulcie early in 1930, trying to avoid the regular police crackdowns on the gangs. It didn't work. The Sydney detectives informed their Melbourne counterparts and he was arrested in an East Melbourne house on 1 February 1930. The newspaper story following his arrest describes him as a 'convicted housebreaker' living 'with a woman from New South Wales'. Scotty and Dulcie returned to Sydney, where he was subsequently charged with 'habitually consorting with criminals'. In August he was charged with assaulting a police officer and sentenced to six months' imprisonment at Brookfield Prison Farm near Tumbarumba, though Dulcie would later talk about him having also been at Long

Bay. Scotty seems to have been in and out of prisons and prison farms over the course of 1930. As far as protecting Dulcie went, Scotty was unreliable.

Dulcie was still registered as a missing girl on the police lists supplied to the newspapers. Of the 408 missing girls and women located in the year leading up to October 1930, 34 remained unaccounted for. 'Dulcie Markham, 16' topped the list of those still missing, but she was now using the alias Mary Eugene, to distance herself even more from her former life and avoid being sent a girls' institution. While Scotty was away in prison, Dulcie, as Mary Eugene, remained a favourite among the gangsters, and started carving out her own place in eastern Sydney.

Dulcie quickly set about finding a different place to stay and securing regular work to pay the rent and bills. She was only weeks away from turning seventeen and had to be cautious without the protection Scotty offered her, sporadic as it was. Dulcie moved to a 'residential' at 706 George Street, Haymarket, working for Kathleen (Catherine) Scurrie (Scurry). The locals and police knew it doubled as a brothel. Dulcie would later reveal in her evidence to police: 'There is accommodation for eighteen or twenty people at the residential … I paid my way there.' Sydney crook Chow Hayes later described how you could enter the brothel via a narrow stairway.

Kathleen Scurrie appeared in court only months before Scotty McCormack was sent to gaol, in a case for a malicious wounding that allegedly took place at her George Street terrace. Waterside worker Herman Wulf went to see his wife, Elizabeth, who was working as a housemaid there, assaulting her and cutting her across the face with a penknife. Kathleen stepped in to help Elizabeth out, hitting Herman across the head with a jug and taking the knife from his hand. Elizabeth refused to give evidence against her husband and pleaded with the magistrate to release him, arguing it was the drink that turned him violent. Judge Curlewis, who would preside over many cases relating to the violence in eastern Sydney at the time, commended Kathleen Scurrie on saving Herman from a 'worse crime'. It wasn't the first time Herman Wulf had been charged with assaulting his wife, but Curlewis seemed perplexed that a man who had fought at Gallipoli could show the cowardice of committing such a crime unless 'there was something wrong in his head'. Wulf was released on the condition that he did not drink or assault his wife within the next five years.

Perhaps Elizabeth Wulf was not merely a housemaid; maybe she also worked as a prostitute in the house. Whatever the case, Kathleen Scurrie certainly knew how to look after the women who worked for her. This is just what the teenage Dulcie needed in 1930.

Dulcie became friends with Kathleen's son, Alfred Dillon, whom she called Fred. They occasionally went to the pictures, sometimes with his mother, but Dulcie was later adamant that it was only a friendship, saying in courtroom evidence: 'I don't think that every man who takes me to a Picture show is going to put a wedding ring on my finger.' Others in Sydney's underworld speculated, however, that Alfred was 'sweet' on Dulcie and made the most of Scotty's prison term.

When Scotty was released in December 1930, he found Dulcie and won her back. He eventually encouraged her to leave the George Street house and work back in Darlinghurst and Woolloomooloo, where he could keep an eye on her and profit from her sex work. He didn't need Alfred's mother taking her cut, and he was suspicious of the friendship young Dillon claimed to have with her. Kathleen lost one of her most popular workers.

Around 7.45 on the evening of 13 May 1931, Dulcie met Scotty on the corner of Kings Cross Road and Victoria Street at the bottom end of Darlinghurst. Dulcie was with him for a short while before heading off to the 'Kings Cross Picture Show'. Scotty was planning to play billiards with friends. He had also arranged to meet Chow Hayes later that evening.

Dulcie kissed Scotty and walked off to the pictures. It was the last time she saw him alive. A different Fred,

Fred Ryan, then joined Scotty on the street corner. He was a 'flower seller', which was about as convincing as Scotty working as a barrowman. Scotty told Fred he had an appointment in Kings Cross and the pair, having had a drink in the saloon nearby, wandered along the street up to the Cross.

Close to the Strand Hotel, on the corner of Crown and William streets, Scotty and Fred came across two other men. Alfred Dillon and his friend Matthew Foley were on the corner of Crown Street, watching Scotty approach. Foley had only arrived in the state weeks before from Fremantle, Western Australia. He would later testify that Alfred and Scotty had words with each other as they walked past a doorway. When Alfred put his hand on Scotty's shoulder, Fred Ryan stepped in to separate the pair. Foley said that his view of what happened next was obscured by Alfred Dillon's back. At a sudden sound of breaking glass, Dillon took off along Bourke Street and Foley ran towards his home along Forbes Street. Scotty McCormack had been stabbed.

It was a quick, brutal attack that left Scotty in agony. Bruce McGill, an engineer, was driving along William Street just after the stabbing, close to 8.30 that evening, when someone called out to him to take a man to hospital. He couldn't make out the man, just a 'huddled up form in the back of the car'. The someone was Fred Ryan, who jumped into the front passenger seat before McGill sped to St Vincent's Hospital. Fred wasn't sticking around to check on his mate. He told McGill to tell the hospital staff the injured man's name was McCormack, and ran off as the car pulled up near the hospital.

Police arrived at St Vincent's soon after, while other officers scoured the scene of the crime, after the evidence from McGill and calls from locals near the intersection of Bourke and William streets. Police made further inquiries in the surrounding area, and Matthew Foley and Alfred Dillon were implicated in the attack. Meanwhile, Scotty McCormack was pronounced dead at the hospital.

Dulcie's friend Gracie Davis found her at the cinema and told her Scotty 'has had a fight and he has been taken to the Hospital'. Dulcie hurried there, but it was too late. She followed Scotty's body to the morgue and identified it.

The story broke in newspapers soon after as a 'shocking crime' on William Street. Reporters collected details from the police and nearby locals to put together a picture of what had happened. Police revealed they were looking for at least two men. One had allegedly held Scotty 'while the other thrust a knife through his heart'. The newspapers spared few details about the violent nature of the murder. Horrified readers were told in the *Sydney Morning Herald* that Scotty was attacked with a steel weapon 'weighing a pound and with a blade 10 inches in length'. The *Daily Examiner* in country New South Wales reported that the stiletto weapon pierced both of Scotty's lungs. It was later found by police in a drain near the scene of the crime. Other newspaper articles were keen to point out Scotty's violent reputation, calling him 'one of the most vicious gangsters who ever gained headline publicity … for his exploits in the local underworld'.

Scotty's old mate from the Gosford Farm Home, Chow Hayes, had been worried when Scotty didn't turn up to meet him the previous evening. He found out about the murder the next morning when he read the newspaper.

It didn't take the police long to piece together Scotty's movements that evening. Alfred Dillon and Matthew Foley, now prime suspects in his murder, were quickly apprehended. Foley maintained he hadn't seen Scotty fall, or any sign of a weapon. He also claimed not to know Scotty and not to have seen him before. Alfred Dillon was scared too. He had already been threatened. His mother told detectives that on the night of the murder, two men called at her shop on George Street demanding to see Alfred, and telling her: 'We want his body; he has killed one of our mates.' Dillon was already known to police, as they would record in the inquest depositions, describing him as 'an associate of Prostitutes and thieves'.

At the inquest, further details were revealed about the minutes following Scotty's stabbing. Interesting evidence was presented by a friend of Dulcie's, Ruby Reardon, who had been living with Dulcie in Kathleen Scurrie's home. The crime reporters described Ruby as 'slim, self-possessed, dark-eyed and red-lipped', much like her friend Dulcie. Shortly after Scotty's stabbing, Ruby bumped into Alfred Dillon, who greeted her on the corner of Palmer and Stanley streets. In her statement to the police, Ruby claimed that Alfred told her to go home or she would get 'pinched' by the police. A short while later she came across two officers who arrested her for vagrancy.

Ruby was adamant that she had only spoken briefly to Alfred and he had not mentioned Scotty McCormack: 'He just bumped into me,' she said, 'on the corner opposite the church.' In court, Ruby claimed that Alfred hadn't revealed that he had seen Scotty and 'went for him' and 'he dropped', as she had previously told police. Ruby also retracted her earlier evidence that Alfred had told her to keep quiet as, in his words, 'this means life or death to me'. She claimed she was drunk when she talked to the police, saying 'my memory would not be as fresh then as it is now'. Sensationally, Ruby told the courtroom she was put in a cell on the evening of Scotty's death and told by detectives her vagrancy charge would be withdrawn if she signed a statement about meeting Alfred Dillon. Either Ruby Reardon had been intimidated by the police into giving up Dillon or she feared underworld retribution.

Dulcie Markham, publicly identified as Mary Eugene, had also been tracked down by the police. Their investigations revealed she knew both Alfred and Scotty. There was some speculation in the newspapers, at the time and in the years that followed, that Dulcie had been with Scotty at the time of the stabbing. None of those who had been placed at the scene by the police, however, identified Dulcie as being there.

Dulcie Markham made her first public appearance as a member of Sydney's underworld on 15 June 1931. It was a memorable first act in what would become a long criminal career.

Dulcie walked into the City Coroner's Court looking like a movie star gracing the set of a film. She wore a stunning dark-red dress with a hat of the same colour pulled close to her head, framing the blonde shoulder-length locks around her face. Her lips were also a shade of red, and she presented as a youthful beauty smiling at the crowd of onlookers. Court reporters described her as 'exceedingly pretty' and 'sprightly'. In this solemn place where details of murders were pored over for answers and dead bodies lay in the morgue at the back, Dulcie cut a sensational figure. Her blood-red dress fitted the occasion perfectly.

Also in the Coroner's Court were other eastern Sydney crooks, keen to know how the new girl on the streets would respond to questions from the police. While the detectives hoped Dulcie would name Alfred as the attacker, local thugs and associates of both Alfred and Scotty were hoping the underworld code of silence would be upheld. While the crime leaders were intent on distancing themselves from the internal squabbling that dominated much of the violence within and between the gangs, this was the world Dulcie lived in every day. She had vital information that the detectives wanted.

Young Dulcie was identified by the court as 'Mary Eugene … a single woman' residing at '45 Craig End [i.e. Craigend] Street, Darlinghurst'. By the time Dulcie was living on Craigend Street, the inner-city suburb was carrying all the scars of rapid development and overcrowding in the terraces lining its streets. For Dulcie, Craigend Street was perfectly located close to the main thoroughfare of William Street, intersecting the prostitution golden triangle of Darlinghurst, Kings Cross and Woolloomooloo.

Dulcie told the court she knew Alfred Dillon and Scotty McCormack. When Scotty was released from prison, he had tried to get work to support Dulcie: 'He was trying to get a Position. I was going to live with him when he got a Position and he was going to keep me …' She admitted he had a temper and told of how only a few days before his death, Scotty had 'quarrelled with some Germans down in the Loo'. He had his coat ripped and suffered a small knife wound. Dulcie also denied that Alfred had any reason to be jealous of her relationship with Scotty: 'My attitude toward Dillon would not give him any cause to be jealous of McCormack.' As a seventeen-year-old girl giving evidence at an inquest, Dulcie sounds quite considered and mature. She gave little away in her statement to the court. All she had done was go to the pictures that night, leaving Scotty to meet up with someone, but he had not told her who it was. She knew nothing about the attack – or, more likely, was keeping quiet about it.

A number of police officers also gave evidence at the inquest, including Detective Sergeant (later Inspector) Alexander Kennedy, a known identity in the criminal courts. Well regarded in the force, Kennedy came from a long line of policemen. His great-grandfathers had been sergeants back in England, as had his great-uncles. Alexander's father had also served as a senior sergeant in New South Wales. In 1933, Alexander's own son, Harold, joined the force. Kennedy had investigated numerous criminal cases before crossing paths with Dulcie in the McCormack case. After joining the police in 1906, he spent thirteen years in Maitland, near Newcastle. In the late 1920s, he took up a plain-clothes position in the city and was in charge of the detectives at Darlinghurst Police Station.

At the conclusion of the inquest, on 17 June 1931, the coroner found no evidence that Matthew Foley had directly been involved in the killing of Scotty McCormack but was more convinced that Alfred Dillon had committed the crime. He was committed for trial.

Alfred Dillon's mother, Kathleen Scurrie, appeared as a witness at the September trial of her son. The newspaper reporters spared little in describing her in the witness box: 'Her rotund little figure was clothed in fashionable style. With an effort, she stopped herself from swooning when she first entered the witness-box, but thereafter her evidence was given between spasms of sobbing.' She confirmed she was running a 'residential' at 706 George Street and also claimed Scotty McCormack came to her place demanding money. When questioned about whether her son, Alfred, had been frightened after Scotty McCormack was killed, she said he had been calm. In an impassioned plea for her son, she sobbed and told the Crown prosecutor that she had to stand up for her child because no one else would.

When the accused, Alfred Dillon, took the stand, the *Truth* reporters were there to capture the moment: 'Wearing a neat blue suit, and with fair hair brushed carefully back from a forehead that jutted over closely-set eyes, Dillon, sharp-featured and wiry of build, then entered the witness-box.' He gave evidence that he helped his mother run the residential. His story matched Matthew Foley's, and he described going home on the evening Scotty McCormack was killed. He talked to 'two girls outside the front door' and then went inside and up to his mother's bedroom. He had a cup of tea with her and another woman called Mrs Anderson. He told the courtroom: 'I had no quarrel with McCormack, and I did not inflict any injuries on him. I did not see him that night.' He added in reference to the stiletto murder weapon, 'I have never had that instrument in my possession.'

Under cross-examination, Alfred claimed to have known Scotty only by sight, having had only the slightest of interactions with him, mainly nodding his head. Quizzed about whether he had a quarrel with him, Alfred maintained 'there was no need to'. This was hard to believe, given that Scotty had allegedly gone to Alfred's George Street home and threatened his mother for money, as Kathleen had mentioned in her testimony.

Asked if he knew Mary Eugene, Alfred said he did and that she had lived with him for three or four months. In that time, however, he didn't 'keep company' with her and they had only ever gone out to the pictures. He had also not seen her with Scotty, and she had moved out two or three months before his death. Alfred also claimed he only knew Ruby Reardon by sight, even though he told the court she stayed at his place, and denied having shouted to her on the night of Scotty's death, 'Yes, we got him.' He then told the courtroom he was nervous that night when questioned by the police because he didn't want to be blamed for something he hadn't done. He admitted to knowing that Scotty had been stabbed but not that he had died: 'two chaps came to my mother and said that McCormack was stabbed, and that I was going to be blamed'.

Sensationally, in this trial, the jury could not come to a verdict. Another trial was set and Alfred Dillon was remanded in custody. The second trial was less successful for him. It was reported in the newspapers: 'Amid a hushed silence, beneath the glitter of electric light Dillon heard his fate ...' The *Sydney Morning Herald* told its readers that the jury had shown some leniency in convicting the twenty-one-year-old of manslaughter instead of murder. The magistrate, however, was less willing to continue the leniency. In passing his sentence he said: 'it seems to me that the circumstances of the case do call for a very severe penalty. I do not think I can reduce the amount of the sentence below a very long term.' Alfred Dillon was sentenced to thirteen years' prison.

Kathleen Scurrie sobbed for her innocent son, as she described him. Alfred Dillon was released in 1937, having served only half his sentence, and moved to Western Australia to start a new life. *Truth* would allege that he was joined by a young woman who had waited for him to be released.

*

Dulcie Markham was no longer simply a runaway girl. She had now made a startling entry into a murder case and ensured the reporters would remember her the next time they heard a story about Mary Eugene. Her role extended beyond her court appearance. In the months after Scotty's death, she took on the part of grieving lover. In public, she wore a black wig and toned down her usually colourful clothing.

There's more to this story, too. Dulcie was a young woman coming of age at an interesting time. Violence and death aside, her appearance at the inquest into Scotty's death revealed a young woman crafting a public identity.

Dulcie was born into a world where women's flesh was carefully guarded under floor-length dresses with long sleeves. Their hair was generally long and politely bundled up under large hats. Women were expected to be demure, refined and delicate. As Thomas Keneally writes, 'late adolescence was supposed to be a period of meek near-invisibility' in Australia when Dulcie was born.

Dulcie's late adolescence coincided with a period of challenges to the old strictures. The flapper entered the world stage in the years following World War I and represented a deep shift in female identity, dramatically influencing teenagers like Dulcie, who were looking to make a statement and defy societal expectations. In the aftermath of the war and the trauma and loss it left behind for survivors and their families, it was fair to say society entered a reactionary period. With everything that had been lost, young people were enjoying their youth and the future that lay ahead.

Flappers experimented with colours and designs, and basked in what was seen as youthful androgyny. The boyish shaping of dresses, with dropped waists to create straight contours, flattened the chest and hid hips. Dances of the time, many a variation on the Charleston, were best demonstrated in short, light dresses with no sleeves so that young women could move their arms more freely.

While the flapper was more widely popular in the 1920s – the Roaring Twenties – she was in fact a product of the emergence of the late-nineteenth-century 'modern girl'. Professor Linda Simon's work on flappers traces them back to the 1890s, when young prostitutes in Britain were called 'flappers'. They were not exactly the jazz babies of the 1920s, but they were young women pushing the boundaries and using dress and manners to stand out. In the United States in the 1910s, there was some discussion about a 'flapper' being someone caught in between, neither a girl nor a woman. She was a 'troubling adolescent girl' by social standards of the day. In Sydney in the 1910s, Dulcie Markham's mother, Florence, was one of these troubling adolescent girls. With her fierce independence, she pushed the boundaries of social mores for young women. Young girls, it was said at the time, were most likely to take up this identity when they were sixteen or seventeen, and would get over it by about twenty. Dulcie ran away from home at fifteen and made her first court appearance when she was seventeen.

Internationally, the flapper was most creatively brought to life by American writer F. Scott Fitzgerald. A voice for the youth of the 1920s, Fitzgerald picked up on the burgeoning identity of the flapper and made her a central character in his short stories and novels. Fitzgerald modelled some of his characters on his wife, Zelda, one of the most famous flappers of her time. These literary characters had far-reaching resonance with girls and young women. Fitzgerald's early works, *The Beautiful and Damned*, *This Side of Paradise* and *Flappers and Philosophers* transformed the flapper into a literary symbol for the lost generation of the 1920s. She was powerful, complex and contradictory.

The flapper also found her way into Australian popular culture by way of the 'flicks' and public dancing. While the Australian flapper identity was in some respects less grandiose than in the United States, and lacked a Fitzgerald to capture its essence in an Australian context, it nonetheless influenced the attitudes and dress of girls and young women, particularly in Melbourne and Sydney.

Flappers were not popular with everyone, as some letters to the newspapers suggest. One letter to the editor seemed overly concerned about Sydney becoming a 'city of knees'. Fearing flappers were everywhere, they wrote in 1926:

> *They have possession of the city – nobby-kneed chickens to plump, pert seventeeners. There are many other grades of 'flappers' – the women to 40, who want to call back youth with paint, powder and pointed knees. Sydney is almost a city of knees now, so far as the feminine portion is concerned. This, too, in the middle of winter! If women, in obedience to Fashion, will display their knees now, covered only with silk stockings, when summer comes what may we expect?*

One Hurlstone Park resident wrote to the *Sunday Times* in Sydney in 1929, asking that the 'modern girl of Sydney' be taught a 'lesson in behavior'. The writer alleged locals were faced with constant 'rudeness from flappers of anything between fifteen and nineteen' on trains and buses, and in shops and on the streets:

> *Last Monday afternoon I was riding in a Coogee tram with my wife, who was wearing a fur coat. Two young flappers sitting opposite, with plenty of silk-stockinged leg displayed, and lips plastered*

horribly with rouge, seemed to find something funny
about the coat. They made continual nudges at
each other, and winked, and tittered like the young
idiots that they are. When I asked them, courteously
enough, to behave themselves, one of them stuck
her nose in the air and replied, in insulting language.
This is not the first time my wife and I have been
subjected to rudeness from impudent girls ...
Perhaps if these girls devoted more time to thinking
and less to jazz and boys and movies, we should see
a change for the better in their ways. The trouble
is that the girls of to-day are brought up in an
environment of too much freedom. No restraint is
put upon their behavior – and the result is that they
are rude, crude, impertinent, shallow, and silly.

Flappers were not deterred. One reportedly told a journalist in 1928 she liked being a flapper because 'people don't mind what you do while you are a flapper. They make allowances, and say; "Oh, she's only a flapper." I tell you, I like it.'

Imbued with what Judith Mackrell calls a 'spirit of audacity', the flapper threatened social codes because she claimed the right to live a life beyond marriage and motherhood. There was a good measure of 'brashness and defiance' associated with flapper identities, bringing with them a shift in female consciousness – women could be individuals in their own right.

Young Dulcie Markham emerged from Scotty's death as a modern flapper. She became Mary Eugene, and with her new street identity pushed the boundaries of female respectability, particularly as an 'uncontrollable' teenager. She drank, swore, dressed to stand out, and went to parties. And if all of this was not scandalous enough, Dulcie was a prostitute and gangster's girl.

Dulcie entered the 1930s with her own provocative look, dyeing her hair to suit, as she later said, the interests of 'gentlemen'. While commentators at the time, as Keneally writes, complained that girls took up 'the moral tone of the man of the world', Dulcie was already seeing more of the world than most girls her age. It is interesting, too, that when her first love, Scotty, was stabbed, Dulcie, a young, modern flapper, was enjoying the latest entertainment – she was at the 'flicks'.

Yet for all her youthful bravado in turning up at Scotty's inquest dressed to stand out and smiling at the court reporters, Dulcie was still very young and had suffered the loss of her first love in violent circumstances. It was a dramatic entry into Sydney's underworld for a teenager. Facing a vagrancy charge years later, Dulcie was questioned in court about her criminal associations. The police prosecutor, no doubt looking to provoke her, asked her about the staggering number of deaths to which she was linked. When he asked about Scotty, she shouted back: 'I was only fifteen then!'

*

In the months following Scotty's murder trial, the police increased their consorting patrols, and few of the underworld identities were beyond police action. Brothel madam Tilly Devine was twice convicted for consorting in 1931. Dulcie was also a target of increased police patrols. She was charged with consorting in August 1931 and placed on a bond for good behaviour for twelve months. It lasted a month; she was charged with vagrancy in September and sentenced to seven days' hard labour in prison. By November, Dulcie was being presented to the courts as a 'known prostitute', once again facing a soliciting charge. The magistrate suspended her sentence, again on good behaviour, but stretched the length to eighteen months. She remained somewhat 'good' in 1932, only facing charges for using indecent language.

By 1933, Dulcie had had enough of the police and court attention in Sydney. She left for Melbourne, and began what would be a long love affair with a city that came to know its own version of 'Pretty Dulcie's' curse.

CHAPTER 5

'Police seek mystery blonde'

Two more lovers gone

The distance between Sydney and Melbourne is close to 900 kilometres, and in Dulcie's day the journey was not something to be taken lightly. The express train from Albury to Melbourne, the *Spirit of Progress*, didn't start running until 1937, so in 1933 it was a long train journey. Wealthier crooks in Sydney took taxis between the cities – Kate Leigh once travelled across the country in a taxi – but Dulce Markham didn't have that kind of money. There's a chance she travelled with a friend to Melbourne, as she had with Scotty in 1930. This interstate journey would set a course she would follow throughout her life: when her involvement in the underworld got too 'hot', she would leave for another city.

Melbourne was like a home away from home for young Dulcie. It had its own underworld, with movable loyalties and young gangsters looking to make a name for themselves. Melbourne's crime scene had been gaining national notoriety in the 1920s while Dulcie was growing up in Waverley. It was the city that made Leslie 'Squizzy' Taylor. Born in Brighton, Melbourne, in 1888, he was sent to a boys' home in his teens. Squizzy became the leader of the Bourke Street Rats – a push gang similar to those in Sydney – and started racking up convictions for assault and pickpocketing. He was arrested for robbing a bank worker in 1916, but got off when he produced a convincing alibi. By the end of the war, he was involved in the sly-grog business and was dealing in stolen goods. He was also at the centre of a number of underworld shootings and became a leading player in the cocaine trade.

Squizzy Taylor's colourful life ended as dramatically as he had lived it. He was killed in a shootout in St Kilda in October 1927. His assailant was John 'Snowy' Cutmore, leader of the Fitzroy gang, who had gone to Sydney in the early 1920s after falling out with Taylor over a robbery. When Cutmore returned to Melbourne in 1927, probably to avoid a charge or warrant issued for him in Sydney, Taylor told him he was no longer welcome in Melbourne.

A violent showdown took place in Cutmore's mother's house. Cutmore was also shot, and died alongside his rival.

As murder and theft cases continued to come up in newspaper stories throughout the 1920s, and rival gangs contested control of the crime business, the general public grew more worried about a spike in crime in Melbourne. The *Weekly Times* fretted about Melbourne's potential to end up like other cities, with 'Pest spots of immorality, commonly as sordid as they are vice-promoting'. The newspaper argued, however, that while these things 'deface every city', Melbourne was not as bad – although it shouldn't throw caution to the wind. There were in the city and inner suburbs 'patches where crime flourishes … Receivers are numerous and prosper with a flagrant contempt of authority …'

There was some concern in the Victorian police ranks about the risk of rising crime in the city centre. The superintendent of police warned businesspeople to be careful carrying money on them after the close of business each day. As *The Age* reported in August 1927, criminals were targeting people in the city and becoming a menace, increasing the work of detectives:

It is their habit, it was explained, to study carefully the movements of shopkeepers who unwisely carry the Friday's takings to their homes from their

business premises. When a favorable opportunity
presents itself these persons are waylaid, and after
being brutally assaulted in some badly-lighted [sic]
locality, are robbed of their possessions.

The police force, the newspaper argued, needed to be strengthened. There were suggestions for the introduction of a police 'flying squad'. This would be similar to the squad formed by the London Metropolitan Police Force in 1919. Made up of a dozen detectives, the squad was tasked with investigating and conducting surveillance on known crooks. By the 1920s and 1930s, the Met squad had developed a fearsome reputation for prosecuting high-level robbers. In Australia, the flying squads were introduced into detective work to conduct raids wherever required. Sydney had its own version from the late 1920s, to tackle the razor violence and then, from the middle of the 1930s, illegal betting.

While Melbourne might have been viewed in the press as becoming a rival to Sydney's organised crime scene, the reality was a little different. The police were right to be concerned about a select few gang members and crime figures, but the criminal statistics revealed another story. Myths abounded about crime bosses and criminals roaming the streets, but in the years between World War I and the Depression, the notorious law-breakers of the time were a very visible minority. They might not have endeavoured, according to historian Chris McConville, to create criminal empires, but their criminal activities did establish the mainstays of crime business in the city: prostitution, sly grog, fraud, gambling and drugs.

The Melbourne crime scene was still a ruthless and violent place to live and work. The crims held particular territory and fought for control of the main crime businesses. So much so that by the later 1930s, Melbourne was on its way to holding the Australian record for violent robberies. By the end of the 1930s, Melbourne had a higher per capita crime rate than London.

Prostitution in Melbourne came under attack in the 1891 Crimes Act, in which streetwalkers were prohibited from harassing or approaching people in public. Brothels were then banned under the Police Offences Act of 1907, but complete prohibition was ineffective. While brothels were closed down in the 1930s, the business continued on, scattered in the city and inner suburbs, in buildings posing as boarding houses and using gambling as a front. La Trobe, Spring, Lonsdale and Exhibition streets in the city formed the main block for prostitution. By the 1930s, St Kilda had also established a reputation for streetwalkers and brothels. It was in St Kilda that Dulcie made a name for herself later in that decade.

In her first year or so in Melbourne, Dulcie tried to keep a low profile. She found work in a few brothels but was still soliciting on the streets. When her friend at the time, Henrietta Gwynne, tried to bail her out from Fitzroy Police Station on the evening of 8 November 1933, Gwynne ended up in trouble herself. She asked Ernest Harridence, a justice of the peace, to assist at the station. Dulcie had been charged with having no lawful means of support – a vagrancy charge used against streetwalkers – and the JP checked that her friend, Henrietta, was being honest in saying she had a bank book for a local bank and would cover the bail of twenty pounds to get her friend out of the cells. She also argued that she and Dulcie were living off sufficient means in a house in Young Street, Fitzroy. Dulcie got out but Henrietta was caught using a defunct bank book. She was later ordered to pay the outstanding bail or serve time in prison if she defaulted.

As she had been in Sydney, Dulcie was once again on the police radar as a prostitute. She tried to keep her work off the streets, so renting a house with other women was essential to maintaining an income. They could pose as regular renters while at the same time using their rooms for sex work. The other lodgers might kick up a fuss if there were rowdy parties or customers made too much noise, but they were more inclined to protect their neighbours than give information to the police.

Nellie Cameron, fellow Sydney prostitute, teenage runaway and one of Tilly Devine's girls, was in Melbourne at the same time as Dulcie. She had gone to Melbourne with her lover, Guido Calletti, both of them trying to avoid outstanding arrest warrants and consorting charges. They were married at a Registry Office at 101 Gore Street, Fitzroy, on 20 February 1934, giving their address as 116 Lansdowne Street, East Melbourne. At the same time the pair were married, Dulcie was living and working in Fitzroy. It might have been a large city, but to have Sydney's two most notorious prostitutes and gangsters' favourites living in it at the same time raises the possibility that Dulcie and Nellie kept up their association in Melbourne.

Melbourne introduced Dulcie to a city that would sustain her business in a few more years, but for the moment she was restless and keen to try her luck wherever she could. She returned to Sydney but was arrested for soliciting in January 1935, her conviction suspended on the condition that she 'be of Good Behaviour for 6 months'. She behaved herself for just over six months, when she was again convicted with soliciting and breach of a bond on 16 July 1935. Dulcie spent twenty-one days at Long Bay Prison. When she was released, she added one more city to her expanding criminal portfolio: Brisbane.

*

Queensland already had a long-standing reputation for prostitution before Dulcie arrived there. As colonisation spread in the nineteenth century and immigration increased, prostitution found its way into Queensland life. Mackay, Cairns and Thursday Island were major centres for prostitution from the 1880s, where girls were shipped from Sydney to service the workers, particularly on the cane fields. The capital, Brisbane, was busier and targeted in government and police crackdowns. The trafficking of prostitutes occurred from the late nineteenth century, but was more coordinated by the 1930s, according to 'Gangland' crime authors James Morton and Susanna Lobez:

> *By the 1930s there was an interstate traffic between Chinese syndicates, with one Sydney-based consortium recruiting young girls for £2 each, housing them and plying them with 'Oriental wine' and drugs, before sending them off to Queensland or New Zealand to be 'housed' in Chinese-owned premises there.*

It is remarkable that Dulcie Markham, only fifteen when she started selling sex in Sydney, was not trafficked. Perhaps her early protection from Tilly Devine and gangsters like Scotty McCormack helped.

By the twentieth century, Brisbane's main prostitution precinct was the East Ward, where prostitutes worked in the run-down buildings, brothels, laneways and corners along Charlotte, Mary and Margaret streets. While the city centre was a busy spot for selling sex, prostitutes also looked for business on the streets and in the brothels along South Bank. Spring Hill was another popular prostitution precinct outside the city centre. Brisbane's plethora of public houses also brought in the prostitutes. There were – and still are – pubs on many street corners where girls and women would loiter for customers and, at times, hope for the offer of a free drink.

The streetwalkers wore elaborately coloured clothing to attract customers: 'ruby velvet with cream lace, or peacock-blue satin with cream lace, black satin, white and cream silk, and white hats with long, drooping feathers'. We already know how beautiful Dulcie was when she appeared at Scotty McCormack's inquest in 1931, aged only seventeen. After her entry into the Brisbane sex business, Dulcie perfected her 'look'. As one Brisbane newspaper would detail, her beauty, clothing and the way she carried herself 'were attractions which many a gay pavement Lothario found difficult to resist'.

Brisbane added to Dulcie's list of lovers. Underworld figure Francis 'Frank' Bowen, described in the newspapers as 'the prettiest boy in gangland', was a perfect match for her. Frank had a record in both Sydney and Melbourne, and used Brisbane as a place to lie low, inasmuch as a crook, especially one in the company of a known prostitute, could do that.

Dulcie and Frank were living together at 271 Grey Street, South Brisbane, in March 1936. The two-and-a-half-storey building, built in the late nineteenth century for publican Michael Foley, was heritage-listed in 1992 and has now been incorporated into the Collins Place redevelopment that includes shops, restaurants and apartment blocks. Grey Street, the main road in the trendy, cultural South Bank area of Brisbane, is regarded today as a premier lifestyle area. Back in the 1930s, and for the next few decades, 271 Grey Street was a townhouse rental property. Dulcie lived there with Frank and a number of other couples, single renters and families.

They were married on 4 March 1936 at 'the house of Mr W.H.W. Lavers, 240 St Paul's Terrace, Spring Hill, Fortitude Valley'. Lavers was a minister, part of the Joyful News Mission. He and his daughter, Sister Grace, were known for their social and evangelical work, particularly with the poor. On their marriage certificate, Frank was listed as a salesman and Dulcie as a domestic.

The domestic cover didn't fool the local police. Dulcie was arrested on 27 March 1936 for being drunk and disorderly. She was staggering along Albert Street with a number of men when a police officer came across her and hauled her off to the city cells. Police headquarters was only a block away in the 1930s, housed in the Treasury Building, and bordered by Queen and George streets. But the police station the young constable had come from was on Roma Street, which in those days intersected with Albert Street. Dulcie screamed abuse at the officer all the way to the station. When she got to the cells, she 'became violent' and broke the bucket in her cell. Considering it was used as a toilet by the inmates, you would hope it was empty. In court two days later, Dulcie was fined for using obscene language and had to pay the value of the bucket. She didn't let up in court, and continued mouthing off at the police officer.

Two months later, Dulcie Bowen was back before the courts on an even more serious charge: impersonating the Under Secretary for Justice by sending a telegram in his name. It was all to do with a permit for a sideshow stall at Kingaroy. Dulcie claimed her husband, Frank, was a showman and she often travelled to country areas with him. The telegram in question had been made out for a Jim Lewis and was to be used to organise a permit for his show. Police would allege this Lewis character was in fact Dulcie's husband and he was using another name in order not to get caught.

The court reporter watched Dulcie's performance closely. A 'platinum blonde with deep blue eyes', she flickered her long eyelashes when questioned and sat 'artistically poised'. She was a young woman who knew how to 'exploit her charms'. The magistrate was unconvinced by Dulcie's story; she was fined for sending the 'bogus' telegram and in default would face three months' imprisonment. She paid the fine.

Dulcie was now splitting her time between Brisbane, Sydney and Melbourne. Little is known of the more personal details of her relationship with Frank Bowen, but it seems Dulcie was independent enough to travel to other cities and meet up with Frank while he was lying low in Sydney. Her relationship with Frank was not exclusive. In Sydney, she carried on relationships with gangsters Guido Calletti and Arthur Kingsley Taplin in 1936. Guido had known Dulcie since 1929 and had been friends with her murdered lover, Scotty McCormack.

Dulcie was increasingly unwelcome back in her hometown of Sydney. Blonde, beautiful and already well known to the constables and detectives around eastern Sydney, she found it hard to keep out of their way. In September 1936 she was charged and convicted with soliciting, and sentenced to three months in prison if she could not keep up good behaviour for six months. The judge also added the condition that Dulcie 'keep away from Kings Cross & Woolloomooloo'.

*

Dulcie's relationship with Arthur Taplin in the late 1930s continued her duel with death. A tall, attractive young man, he fit her type: Arthur was hot-headed and well known to the police, with form in Sydney's underworld. Back in June 1933, twenty-year-old Arthur had been charged with assaulting a police officer. He tried to bring a summons against the same officer, claiming he was in fact the one who was assaulted. The altercation had taken place at a city fish bar where Taplin had supposedly handed over dodgy coins to pay for his meal. When the owner of the shop asked another customer to check the coins, Arthur, as he would do many times, overreacted and assaulted the man. A fight broke out and a glass panel in the front door to the fish bar was broken. What Arthur didn't know was that the man on the other end of his attack was an off-duty police officer.

The drama continued in court. When Arthur was placed in the dock to give his statement, he tried to punch Constable Sutherland. Finally calming down, Arthur told the magistrate he defended himself in the fish shop thinking 'he was being set upon by a larrikin and had only retaliated'. The young labourer also alleged that the officer had rushed at him at Central Police Station while he was being placed in the cells, and that other police had dragged him away. Arthur Taplin's summons against the constable was dismissed; he was found guilty of assaulting the officer and fined.

A month later, in July 1933, Arthur had again came to the attention of the police, this time on the far more serious charge of attempted murder. Police alleged he had shot at Cedric Alan Marr in Darlinghurst. He was caught on the run in Brisbane – possibly trying to get to Dulcie, whom he already knew, and use her place as a safe house – and charged with the shooting. He was arrested and taken back to Sydney on a train in handcuffs, but he had already said too much. He didn't deny the shooting and said he had been 'silly'.

Arthur Taplin was identified in court as a barman and labourer, but his gang associations were also known. On the evening of 17 July, Arthur had been drinking with friends, and they went back to his house to get his pass for a train to Brisbane. In custody, he would tell the police he was trying to set up a new life in Brisbane, getting away from his 'old associations', but on leaving his house a man had confronted him and his friends. There was conflicting evidence, because Taplin also said his friends had picked a fight with a man waiting for a tram in Darlinghurst. That man was Cedric Marr. Arthur lost his cool, pulled out an automatic pistol and told the man, 'Tommie, out of this, or I will fix you.' The man ran away down Josephson Street, Paddington, as Arthur fired two shots at him. Cedric Marr remarkably survived the attack unharmed. That's when Taplin went on the run to Brisbane. (The case also showed the changing nature of police work. One constable giving evidence about the bullets was identified as coming from the 'photograph and ballistic department of the C.I.B.')

Described in court as 'an associate of the worst class of criminals', Arthur was revealed to have already served five years in prison for slashing a woman. He was now found guilty of intent to murder Cedric Marr and sentenced to three months in prison. He did his time and on his release travelled back to Melbourne, where he knew an old friend would find him work and help out. That friend was Dulcie Markham and she began calling herself Dulcie Taplin.

Dulcie was on the police radar in Sydney throughout 1936 and 1937. She was using her Taplin alias but the police knew exactly who she was, though listing her under 'Mary Eugene' in their records. She was charged with consorting in February 1937 and expected to be on good behaviour for twelve months. She again left for Melbourne. Living off the proceeds of Dulcie's work, along with his pay from the bar, Arthur started ingratiating himself into the underworld scene. Outside his bar shifts, he wanted in on the gambling and sly-grog scene.

Although Dulcie was now also using the fantastically outlandish name Tosca De Marca, the Melbourne detectives were alerted to her presence by their colleagues in Sydney, and in July 1937 she was arrested in St Kilda and charged and convicted with vagrancy. She was fined and given two weeks to leave Victoria.

After Dulcie left Melbourne, Arthur Taplin carried on in his thuggery and became a target of underworld violence. On 15 December 1937, a brawl broke out between Arthur and another man, Harcourt Lee, in a bar at the Cosmopolitan Hotel (now gone) on the corner of Swanston and Little Bourke streets. Thirty-eight-year-old Harcourt produced a gun and shot Arthur. As Arthur fell to the ground, Harcourt hid the gun in a hole in a wall at the back of the pub and absconded. Arthur Taplin was unarmed.

When detectives interviewed Harcourt Lee the next day, he alleged that Arthur had threatened him over beer. Harcourt said he was a hairdresser by profession and had simply been having a beer in the pub. Working behind the bar with other employees, Taplin allegedly confronted Lee and said, 'A man ought to blow your brains out. I have a gun.' He then came at Lee with a beer pot and reached into his pocket, a move that looked like he was reaching for a gun. Harcourt pulled out his own revolver and fired. Police put out alerts for any witnesses to come forward. They were also looking for Arthur's lover, Dulcie, whom the detectives believed to be his closest associate.

Arthur Taplin lingered in the Royal Melbourne Hospital for almost a week. As the newspapers would report, he maintained the underworld code of silence, even knowing he was dying, and 'flatly refused the police any information that may have helped them'. He didn't make it to Christmas, passing away on 21 December.

On Boxing Day, *Truth* newspaper in Brisbane published a breathless story about Dulcie Markham. In what it called a 'sensational daylight shooting and killing of a well-known Sydney underworld character', police were hot on the trail of 'Dulcie Eugene', a 'girl' (she was now in her early twenties) who was unable to avoid the 'questing finger of notoriety placed on her movements'. In her 'remarkable young life' in the spotlight, she was now known, the paper declared, as 'Australia's most beautiful bad woman' and a 'golden-haired adventuress'. Dulcie's femme fatale identity was now well established.

Dulcie was back in Sydney when Arthur Taplin was murdered. She was also up to her old tricks. She was arrested on a number of occasions in 1938 for offensive behaviour, indecent language and assaulting a police officer. She paid the fines and went right back onto the streets, associating with other known criminals.

One of them was Scotty's old mate Guido Calletti, but their love affair wouldn't last long. Guido was shot by rival gang members during a party at 16 Brougham Street on 6 August 1939. Twenty-five-year-old Dulcie had now lost three lovers to violent deaths in a matter of years.

When local CIB detectives arrived at Brougham Street soon after Guido was shot, the house was a shambles. The hallway rug was crumpled up from the quick exit of people after the shooting, and the lounge and kitchen were cluttered with chairs and items strewn across the tables. It had certainly been a big day for the birthday celebrations, judging by the number of booze bottles on the kitchen floor.

In stark contrast to the scene at the house, Dulcie was cool and calm, giving her name as Mary Eugene. They asked her questions but she refused to say anything else. Years before, as a teenage runaway, she quickly learned the underworld code of silence: don't tell the police anything. She acted like a woman who had been in similar situations before, and the detectives, taking in her stunning blonde looks and the company she kept, quickly realised who she was. They questioned her, but she remained stony-faced and silent. They told her they would be in touch; she would be asked to give a statement at Central Police Station.

Detective Sergeant Milton Dimmock was one of the first on the scene. He came from a family of police officers, including two brothers who would reach the rank of sergeant and detective sergeant. Dimmock died of a heart attack in 1954 after years of investigating serious criminal cases. Now, he leaned down over the mortally injured Calletti and asked who shot him. The officers heard the same answer as after so many underworld shootings: Guido sputtered out through blood and pain, 'I don't know.'

The occupant of the house, May McDonald, was also questioned. She hadn't run like the others, and while she didn't say who had fired the shots, she told the detective in no uncertain terms: 'All I will say is Calletti got what he was looking for.' He had been told to leave the house twice, hadn't, and May had little sympathy for what followed. Hours later, Guido Calletti was dead in St Vincent's Hospital, and the suspects, George Allen and Robert Branch, were still on the run. Guido Calletti was thirty-six-years-old.

His funeral was the largest underworld Sydney had seen to date. Guido's body was laid out for a public viewing on 8 August in Darlinghurst mortuary. The newspapers claimed 'five thousand people filed past the body' and brought more than 200 wreaths with them. People crowded the nearby streets and police were brought in to allow traffic to pass. They were also there as professional crowd control, and to watch if any potential witnesses showed up to pay their respects.

Mourners wept over Guido's body inside the funeral parlour. One of his friends hugged him close and shouted, 'He was my mate and they shot him.' Dulcie threw herself over the coffin and wept for minutes, but left before the police could ask her any more questions. Nellie Calletti (née Cameron) sent a cross wreath four feet tall for her husband but refused to come to Sydney for the funeral. Someone threw Guido's football jumper over the coffin as it was carried out of the funeral service. His mother, father and three brothers were there too, his mother telling the reporters he had only just buried his grandmother on the day he was shot dead.

There were claims in some newspapers that the press was adding to the 'hysterics' around Guido Calletti's death. *Smith's Weekly* said the funeral reports glorified gunmen like Guido and that this 'child-delinquent, reformatory graduate, petty larcenist, garrotter, associate gunman' could have had a death left 'unwept, unhonoured and unsung' were it not for the 'sensation-mongering daily Press'. The *Smith's Weekly* had no time for Sydney's underworld: 'gangdom is the rat-pit of humanity. The bigger the gangster, the bigger the rat.'

The detectives didn't think much of Guido either. Around fifteen of them mingled in the crowd at the funeral, hoping to hear someone give away clues to Guido's death. They were still looking for thirty-four-year-old George Allen and thirty-one-year-old Robert Branch. They also wanted to take a statement from Dulcie; they had been unable to find her since she left the crime scene, and she disappeared from the funeral before they could get to her.

Guido Calletti was buried in the Catholic section of Rookwood Cemetery west of the city, closer to some of his extended family. The cemetery itself is one of the oldest in Australia, operating from 1867, and the Catholic section was well respected. In the years to follow, crook and cop alike would be buried in Rookwood Cemetery. It was the final resting place for many of those directly linked to Sydney's crime wars.

The detectives got their breakthrough on 9 August. Tipped off about the whereabouts of Allen and Branch, officers hid in bush near a cottage in Cowan, some 40 kilometres north of the city. Robert Branch was arrested at daybreak, but George Allen ran into the bush. He was later found in Eastwood.

Peggy Patterson, the young woman who had seen the shooting unfold in the Brougham Street house and who had only minutes earlier been celebrating her birthday, was brought into Central Police Station to identify the two men in a line-up. With Detective Sergeant Delaney looking on, Peggy went pale and started trembling when the pair walked out. She was too frightened to identify them formally as the shooters, but police would claim her reaction was enough of an indication that they were.

Dulcie was next on the police list. Detectives appealed through the newspapers for more information about her whereabouts, declaring that her evidence was 'important and relative to the inquiry'. In the meantime, they built their case for a trial around other witnesses, particularly Peggy Patterson. Though too frightened to name Allen and Branch while they could see her at the police station, she had provided the detectives with an account of what had happened, and who was there when Guido was shot.

The inquest played out like so many others featuring an underworld murder. A guilty verdict rested with a key witness who was being intimidated to keep silent about what they saw.

May McDonald appeared as one of the main witnesses, given the shooting took place in her house. She wasn't concerned about testifying at the inquest because she didn't like Guido Calletti and wanted to place more blame on him for inciting the shooting. According to May, one of Guido's mates who arrived with him at the house said, 'We'll do the lot, Guido,' to which he responded, 'Yes, we'll fix all of you —.' May's husband, John, also testified that Guido pulled out a gun and tried to shoot Robert Branch.

Maude Beale gave evidence about what she had seen that evening but it differed from her original statement of events. Claiming she wanted 'to tell the truth', she said she saw Guido drunk outside her house before she went to May's place. He showed her a gun and when the shots were fired later at the Brougham Street house, she didn't see who fired them. Police detectives hadn't found a gun on Guido, despite the story that he had brandished two firearms at the earlier football match, raising suspicions about the validity of the witness statements.

The police case was nevertheless successful. The coroner denied bail for Allen, and Branch was remanded in custody on further charges. Both were now to stand trial in November for the murder of Guido Calletti.

Peggy Patterson was the key witness at the trial. She had already given away too much to the police, reacting to the presence of Allen and Branch in police custody. Everyone else present at May McDonald's house that August evening had refused to say who shot Guido Calletti. Clarence Riley was running to the front door, Dulcie and the other women were out the back and came in when the shots were fired, and anyone else there and not named by witnesses or found by the police was keeping a low profile. The underworld was in lockdown.

Peggy sobbed her way into the courtroom as a Crown witness. She took the stand and retracted her earlier statement from the inquest. She now claimed to have been too drunk to remember what happened. She had faint recollections of the Brougham Street party but would not name Allen and Branch as the shooters, and 'refused to answer certain questions'. She also sensationally claimed that she was afraid of the police and said she had lied in the evidence given to the inquest. Now, at the trial, Peggy sobbed when describing being frightened of the police, saying: 'They persecuted me and persecuted my people.' Peggy claimed not only not to know Guido but that he wasn't even at the Brougham Street house the day of her birthday party and the shooting.

Senior Crown Prosecutor McKean, unconvinced by Peggy's case against the police, moved to have her treated as a hostile witness. McKean knew exactly what was going on and had seen it many times before. Someone had put the hard word on Peggy and forced her to change her statement in an effort to protect Allen and Branch. Sydney's underworld had got to Peggy before the trial started.

The prosecution case fell apart. Their star witness, Peggy, had been compromised. Prosecutor McKean announced to the courtroom he could go no further, saying Peggy had joined a 'conspiracy of silence that will be the end of the Crown case ... The administration of justice has been obstructed.'

The magistrate, Justice Davidson, turned to the jury and said that the court's hands were tied: 'What has been said in another Court cannot be used as evidence here, except to test credibility.' He praised the police for having 'done their duty', and criticised Peggy Patterson who had failed, at the very least, to 'do her part' for justice. On Monday 27 November, George Allen and Robert Branch were acquitted and left Darlinghurst Court free men. Peggy Patterson could also breathe a sigh of relief. She had maintained the 'conspiracy of silence'.

The inquest and trial unfolded without Dulcie Markham. As she would do many times over, she went into hiding, trying to avoid having to give evidence to the detectives. As she later said of Guido's death: 'He was a swell guy. I went to his funeral, and then went into smoke.'

Dulcie didn't exactly go 'into smoke'. Using her alias Mary Eugene, she was arrested in Lithgow, a mining town about a hundred and forty kilometres west of Sydney, in October. A warrant had been issued for her to attend Guido's inquest, which, as the police prosecutor said, 'explains why Eugene was at Lithgow'. She was drunk and verbally abusive to the officers making the arrest, and was taken back to Sydney to face further charges.

She avoided having to appear at the inquest but now faced being called as a witness at the trial. This also didn't happen once detectives in Sydney questioned her about the ransacking of a hotel room back in Lithgow. The room's occupants had gone to a wedding and come back to find a number of items stolen from the room. Dulcie admitted to the theft charges and was sentenced to one month in prison, along with fines for drunkenness and using indecent language.

Dulcie was in prison when the murder trial concluded. By the time the police caught up with her, they may have thought they had better witnesses and that she could have been a hostile witness. As it turned out, Peggy Patterson was.

May McDonald thought 'Calletti got what he was looking for', but it was more than just bullets. Death followed Dulcie around the Australian underworlds. The next time she would be connected to a murder, her lover was the accused.

CHAPTER 6

'Good-bye, sweetheart!'

Dulcie's war

Two weeks after Dulcie wept over Guido Calletti's coffin, Prime Minister Robert 'Bob' Menzies announced that Australia was headed into another world war. It was Sunday 3 September 1939, and only twenty-one years since the end of the World War I. Back then a five-year-old Dulcie could not have known the cost of that war. The effects of World War I – the nation's 'baptism of fire' – had far-reaching consequences beyond repatriation. From just over 400,000 enlistees (most of them volunteers) from a population of less than 5 million, 60,000 Australian men were killed and a further 156,000 wounded, gassed or taken prisoner. The mental and physical costs of the war for the returned servicemen and their families would extend into the 1930s and beyond. Bob Menzies knew all of this as he sat down at the microphone to deliver his announcement to the Australian people.

Menzies was confident of the decision to join the war, later insisting in his memoirs that his announcement 'expressed the overwhelming sentiment of the Australian people ... in 1939 neutrality for Australia in a British war was unthinkable unless we were prepared to add secession to neutrality'. Joan Stingemore, a young teenager in Fremantle, later recalled what all this meant to her, her family and friends:

> *Since August we'd been waiting for it. We all knew*
> *it was going to happen. [My family] had a radio;*
> *the neighbours that didn't ... came over and waited*
> *for the announcement. There were mums, and there*
> *were dads that had been to the First World War.*
> *They had their sons with them. There were [also*
> *kids my age and younger]. The people my age all*
> *thought 'Oh great!'; you know, 'this is exciting.' Of*
> *course, I didn't understand yet what there was to*
> *worry about.*
>
> *The boys, 17 and over, were jubilant.*
> *The dads who'd been to war already and the*

mums who'd had to [sit at home waiting once
before] they looked very very sad.

In the wake of the prime minister's announcement, close to 1 million Australians fought in World War II. The nation raised a second Australian Imperial Force (again, as in World War I, largely voluntary) and added to this with a militia force expected to protect Australia's borders and offer home defences. They would come to include many people from remote Indigenous communities who were expected to protect Australia's shores from invasion – ironically, given their own experience of colonisation and its aftermath.

From the last months of 1939, Australians were sent off to fight with and support Britain in warfare across Europe, the Middle East and the Mediterranean. Just as they had done in World War I, Australian airmen, sailors and soldiers honoured the wartime pledge to support Britain in what was for Australia a distant war.

Mothers, daughters, sisters and girlfriends shouted farewell to their loved ones from the docks, waving for as long as they could as the ships steamed out of sight.

*

Dulcie Bowen (still also calling herself Mary Eugene)

yelled her own 'Good-bye, sweetheart!' But in true Dulcie fashion it was inside a courtroom, surrounded by police, as she watched her lover being led away and committed for trial for the murder of another underworld criminal.

The war had a dramatic impact on Dulcie's working life. It increased her business in sex, and this power allowed her to align herself with higher level underworld figures, who promised her protection for a cut of her earnings in prostitution. One of them, Frederick James Anderson, was a ruthless Sydney crook making a name for himself in Melbourne during the war. The twenty-six-year-old Anderson was living with Dulcie when another crook crossed him in the underworld gambling business.

Despite police crackdowns on street betting in the 1920s, gambling continued in betting houses known to police and, some believed, protected by corrupt officers. There were still raids on private houses where bookmakers ran their businesses, and in one case in 1932 a young bookmaker chased by police through Hawthorn Town Hall threw the betting slips and account books to friends as he ran past them. The popularity of starting price (SP) bookmakers continued, and it was this illegal business that featured in twenty-nine-year-old John Charles Abrahams' night out with friends in 1940.

John Abrahams spent the evening of 15 June 1940 playing cards with friends at a house in Fitzroy. He then passed the rest of the night at his sister's boarding house in Collingwood. It also housed a room for gambling, where John and his friends laid bets through the night. Collingwood is one of the oldest suburbs of Melbourne, and in the 1930s and 1940s it was rundown, much like the eastern Sydney neighbourhoods Dulcie had run away to in 1929. Families were packed into slum housing close to being condemned by the local council. Crime was rife in these parts, as youngsters looked to the gangs for more opportunities and a place to belong. Youth crime fed into working for the gambling bosses, running errands for them and being on the lookout for police.

One of John Abrahams' mates, James Maloney, was well known in the Melbourne boxing scene as 'Red' Maloney. A welter-weight champion, he had taken up boxing as a teenager, giving his earnings from the ring to his mother to look after him and his seven siblings. According to his trainer and to his mother, he was easily led and kept bad company when drinking, resulting in a long criminal record. In February 1939, he was sentenced to two months in prison for assaulting a taxi driver. Not long after his release from prison, he was again in court, this time facing a charge of robbery with violence, after it was alleged that he and three other men assaulted and robbed a man in a laneway off Fitzroy Street. The case went to trial but Maloney was acquitted. Red was also known in Fitzroy for running illegal gambling houses. He notched up a number of charges and convictions for this, along with others for assault and robbery, and in 1935 had been called a 'city pest' by one magistrate.

Melbourne's illegal gambling businesses were protected by gunmen hired by the bookies, and although these operations were usually small and decentralised, the competition was red-hot and violent. Standover tactics were employed, and the young gunmen were usually spoiling for a fight. The fallout from an argument John Abrahams had in June 1940 would prove just how fatal the underworld gambling scene could become.

When John left his sister's house on the morning of 16 June with Red Maloney, he was confronted by a man with a gun and shot at close range in the throat. He collapsed to the ground while Red tried to stem the blood loss; John never regained consciousness.

Nine hours later, Melbourne detectives had enough information from witnesses and pulling in their regular informants to go after Dulcie's friend Fred Anderson and charge him with murder. Fred Anderson had been playing cards with the victim the night before. He was arrested in a house in Murdock Street, Brunswick, along with a young woman who was then charged with vagrancy and told police her name was Mary Eugene. It was alleged that Fred Anderson had travelled from Sydney to Melbourne six weeks before the attack. When Dulcie managed to have the vagrancy charge appealed, she told the courtroom that Fred kept her with a regular weekly allowance.

Frederick Anderson told the police he was a caterer, but this couldn't have been further from the truth. Known in the criminal circles of Sydney and Melbourne as 'Paddles' because of his big feet, Fred Anderson was an up-and-coming crook around Sydney, and was moving in on the Melbourne crime scene. Young standover men were often brought down to Melbourne to take care of rivals, in the hope they could return quickly to Sydney without police working out their Melbourne connections. By the 1930s, however, the detectives in Melbourne and Sydney were working together more closely, aware of the crossover in organised crime but each still keen to force the crooks out of their own city into the other.

At the July inquest into Abrahams' murder, Fred Anderson was committed for trial. A distraught Dulcie added her own drama to the proceedings at the Coroner's Court. Now a brunette, she called out 'Good-bye, sweetheart' to Fred Anderson as he was led away. Court reporters watched and recorded the scene as police officers rushed over to Dulcie and bundled her out of the courtroom. Yelling 'offensive remarks', she was eventually brought back in, but still struggled with the officers. The coroner didn't proceed any further, and Dulcie was last seen by reporters, 'weeping bitterly on the shoulder of a woman friend'.

In a rare media moment, Dulcie spoke to reporters, talking a little about her life and offering some insight into how she saw herself. Dulcie told the Melbourne reporters she had become known as the 'Hoodoo Girl' because of the number of men who died around her. She didn't like the title and thought instead it was just 'unfortunate that I should have been associated with these particular men who have died'. When reporters asked what had happened between Dulcie and her husband Frank Bowen, she replied: 'Frank and I are still friends, but we don't live together any more.'

Declaring her love for Fred Anderson – whom she purportedly had wanted to marry – Dulcie said they had known each other 'as long as I can remember'. They 'knocked about for a while and then fell for each other good and proper'. They had supposedly moved to Melbourne 'to get away from it all' – in other words from crime – and had plans to get a cottage in the suburbs: 'Everything went well until the other day, when he was arrested. When this is over, I'm going to divorce my husband and marry "Paddles".'

The trial went ahead in September, and the evidence made reporters reflect on their city now being 'more like Chicago than Melbourne'. Fred Anderson's defence case rested on his alibi: he claimed he was having supper with a taxi driver in a café on Bourke Street in the city, which the taxi driver confirmed. The Crown case seemed to rest on Abrahams and Anderson having had an argument in a car after their evening of cards. Witnesses said it was more of a 'tiff' than a fight, and the jury was not persuaded it was a motive for the killing. Those with inside knowledge of Melbourne's underworld, and the police, who knew how deadly simple arguments could become, were less convinced. Abrahams and Anderson had been arguing about continuing on to gamble at another house, Anderson having refused. There was also some speculation that the argument had been over the 'mysterious and intriguing blonde' – as the newspapers called her in reporting Anderson's trial – who left with Fred Anderson while the others moved on to continue gambling.

Had Dulcie been the cause of another deadly underworld argument? Was jealousy, combined with criminal rivalry, to blame?

Fred Anderson was found not guilty of the murder of John Abrahams. He stepped jubilantly out of the courtroom and straight into the orbit of *Truth* Melbourne reporters. He told them: 'God; that's better than winning all the lotteries in the world at the same time,' adding, 'Toward the last, I thought I was gone … It was terrible.' Turning to his lawyer, Maurice Goldberg, he thanked him and promised 'while I live you'll receive a present on the anniversary of this day'. There's a story that Paddles took a revolver into the courtroom and was going to try to shoot his way out if he was found guilty.

Chow Hayes, one of Paddles Anderson's Sydney mates, knew him from their teenage shoplifting years. They reconnected when Paddles was serving a two-year sentence for assault at Bathurst Gaol. According to Hayes, everyone knew Paddles shot Abrahams: 'he freely admitted it to his mates'.

Dulcie didn't need to apply for a divorce from Frank Bowen. He was apparently gunned down during a brawl in Kings Cross in 1940. There is no existing death certificate to support this (he is often confused with another Frank Bowen who died in Sydney that year) or newspaper stories about it, which is strange given the space in newspapers usually devoted to crime stories. This is, however, the story that was later mentioned in newspaper reports about Dulcie: that her ex-husband, Frank Bowen, had died in Kings Cross in 1940. What is clear is that Dulcie had already moved on from Frank before then.

'Paddles' Anderson and Dulcie didn't last either. There was no marriage, despite Dulcie's proclamation of love outside the courtroom. Dulcie went back 'into smoke' as she had done after Guido's death, and travelled north to Brisbane, via a brief stay in Sydney.

Fred Anderson also went back to Sydney, and became a big name in the drug and casino criminal underworlds. He was close friends with Sydney crime bosses Lenny McPherson and George Freeman, and mixed with politicians and police officers. One story has Anderson holding a jockey out of a city building window, many storeys up, and threatening to drop him because he won the race when Anderson hadn't put any money on it. Paddles Anderson died in 1985, aged eighty.

Much as she would dispute being called a 'Hoodoo Girl' or the 'Angel of Death' by the press, Dulcie had by 1940 lost three lovers and a husband to underworld violence, along with associates and close friends. She kept bad company and the standover violence was never far away. How long would it be before a bullet missed a lover and hit her? Or would she end up being the intended victim after her years of being embroiled in the Australian underworlds?

*

As Dulcie 'went into smoke' once again to Brisbane, World War II took a dramatic turn. After attacking Pearl Harbor in December 1941, Japan advanced aggressively across the Pacific and though Malaya. Australia was suddenly right in the thick of it. The federal government and Department of War worried that the threat of bombing was imminent.

It was. Darwin was bombed in a Japanese air raid on 19 February 1942. The following month, Broome was attacked by Japanese Zero fighters, as were Wyndham and Derby. The north and north-west of Australia were now under attack. More than 300 civilians and military personnel were killed and up to 400 injured.

Suddenly the war really felt like Australia's war. Unlike World War I, where the fighting took place on distant shores, World War II was now being fought very close to Australia, and even if the bombings in the north and north-west still felt remote from ordinary citizens in the major cities further south, the presence of Allied servicemen from the United States would soon change this.

In December 1941, a week after the bombing of Pearl Harbor, Brigadier General Dwight D. Eisenhower advised the US Army Chief of Staff that a base needed to be set up in Australia to win the fight against Japanese aggression in China, the Philippines and the Dutch East Indies (now Indonesia). The United States was now intent on winning the war in the Pacific, but it needed a base closer to the conflicts for its troops.

US headquarters were quickly established in Brisbane with the arrival of 4600 servicemen. By March 1942, new headquarters were set up in Melbourne, coinciding with the arrival of General Douglas MacArthur, appointed

Supreme Commander of the South West Pacific Area. MacArthur would coordinate land and sea operations. From late 1941 to the middle of 1942, some 100,000 US servicemen arrived in Australia, with the greatest numbers in Brisbane, Melbourne and Sydney, but also represented in Fremantle, an important base on the west coast. At its peak in September 1943, there were close to 120,000 Americans in Australia.

The newspapers delighted in the support being given to Australia, and were buoyed by a certain enthusiasm for American efforts in the war in the Pacific. The US government was not simply helping its Allied 'friends in Australia'; the Australian bases were part of a strategic decision to meet military objectives in the Pacific theatre of the war. Japanese invasion of Australia would thwart America's efforts to reassert control over the South Pacific.

A terrible psychological blow had been struck in February 1942 with the Fall of Singapore. In a speech to Dominion prime ministers in 1939, Churchill had reassured Australia that if it faced serious attack from the Japanese, this would take precedence over 'British interests in the Mediterranean' – a hollow promise, as it turned out. Australia looked to Britain to provide naval support in the Asia-Pacific region, should it come under threat.

It took the Japanese just seventy days to invade and take over Malaya and Singapore from January 1942.

In Singapore, the British Army severely miscalculated. Convinced the Japanese would invade from the south, it secured the coastal defences, but Japan came via the north-west region of the island. The Allies tried to regroup and prepare for the Japanese, but efforts and supplies were starting to fail. The British commander surrendered. Winston Churchill would later write in his memoirs: 'In all the war, I never received a more direct shock.'

Most of the Australian 8th Division, posted in Singapore, were taken as prisoners of war, something few had expected. Around 130,000 Allies were taken prisoner, including 15,000 Australians. More than 30,000 Australians would be taken prisoner over the course of the war, most of them by the Japanese.

It was with some relief, then, that thousands of American servicemen arrived in Australia throughout 1942. At the same time, the Australian prime minister, John Curtin, broadcast a speech on radio to the American people in which he argued that Australia was crucial to the defence of the West Coast of America. By the war's end, close to 1 million US servicemen had passed through Australia.

The Americans stationed in Australia during World War II were commonly referred to as 'overpaid, over-sexed and over here'. Some young Australian women were attracted to the Americans by the mere fact that they were different from regular Australian blokes. Some young women, interested in the Hollywood movies of the time, thought the troops were more like movie stars with their crisp uniforms, American accents and debonair demeanour. The pay difference was also stark: an American private was paid about seventeen pounds a month, while an Australian private received about nine pounds. At the end of the war, some 15,000 Australian war brides travelled to the United States to reunite with their wartime beaus.

The sex business also experienced wartime prosperity. As one historian of prostitution in Australia outlines, 'Professional prostitutes and amateurs arrived in droves wherever troops were stationed, cashing in on the inevitable soaring demand.' There were twenty major brothels in Brisbane during the war, in Albert and Margaret streets on the south side of the city, and in Spring Hill. They had existed there before, but their numbers now increased with the huge demand resulting from the arrival of the Americans. Business boomed, as James Morton and Susanna Lobez have written: 'During World War II, vice did an unprecedented trade in Brisbane. It is said that, with the volume of custom, the prostitutes were literally red hot and more recruits were needed.'

There's a story that a gambling house in Sydney heard about the money to be made in Brisbane and sent up a trainload of prostitutes. We don't know if Dulcie was on this train, but given she flitted back and forth between

Brisbane and Sydney in the early 1940s, it's possible. Some of the officers were known to look after their favourites, and ensured they were housed in paid accommodation. These women were usually the 'higher class of call girls', such as Dulcie Bowen.

*

Despite having cried on the shoulder of a friend and declared her love for Paddles Anderson outside the courtroom in 1940, as we have seen, Dulcie was less interested in him as a free man. She moved on quickly to another one of her boyfriends, James Arthur Williams, who had been living with her on and off in St Kilda since 1938. Williams, who was married, went to Brisbane with Dulcie in the early 1940s, but not before Dulcie had left behind another scandal in Melbourne.

Dulcie was charged with accosting a police officer for sex, causing a media sensation. Around midnight on 25 July 1941, Dulcie, using her Mary Eugene alias, propositioned a plain-clothes officer. The charge was thrown out of court when the magistrate suspected the officer had made the first advance and that Dulcie was therefore not the one making the proposition. Dulcie claimed she asked if he was an officer, to which he responded he was just a 'Gippsland boy'. Only a fortnight before, Dulcie had been less cautious when she, according to the newspaper, tried to get 'pally' with the chief of the Vice Squad. Her luck soon ran out. Later that year Dulcie was properly caught out and convicted for loitering, soliciting and using indecent language. She paid the fine.

Calling herself Dulcie Williams, she headed to Brisbane with Williams and moved into a house in Terrace Street, New Farm. Now a densely populated riverside inner-city hub, New Farm is one of the oldest suburbs in Brisbane. A worksite for convicts in the nineteenth century, the area was also used for farming and large colonial houses by the 1880s. As Brisbane's population increased into the twentieth century, the area became more urbanised, and low rents led to an increase in underworld types making it their home, alongside the regular working-class families of the neighbourhood. During World War II the area was also used as a marine base, and this is when Dulcie moved in and used it to full effect.

Terrace Street's reputation in the 1940s was similar to Dulcie's own. Kids growing up nearby at the time were told not to walk along Terrace Street on their way to school. Florence O'Brien lived next door to Dulcie in the early 1940s. Her family had lived on the street since 1928 and in 2011 – still living on Terrace Street – Florence recalled what it was like having Dulcie and James Williams as neighbours: 'My mother was petrified. There were lots of unsavoury characters. People would come from miles around to view the house.'

Dulcie set up her own brothel in the Terrace Street house and cashed in on the wartime demand for sex from visiting US troops. But it wasn't just prostitution that brought in the 'unsavoury characters' Florence's mother worried so much about. Dulcie also set up a sly-grog shop in her house and combined sex with booze – and most likely drugs. Even in the 1980s, until the renovations and gentrification of the early twenty-first century, New Farm as a wider area was renowned for its low rents and drug-addicted inhabitants. Back in the 1940s, it was the perfect place for Dulcie Williams to cash in on the demand for sly grog.

Dulcie had been in Sydney during the heyday of the sly-grog wars against restrictive government legislation from the late 1920s. She knew the fortune that could be made from it, and went on to establish her own list of standover men who would offer protection for the business. James Williams became her standover man in Brisbane in the early 1940s. He listed his work as taxi driver, and it was a fair bet he was delivering booze to the house as well as giving Dulcie lifts when she went out onto the streets to earn extra money.

Sometime in 1942, Dulcie gave birth to a daughter. Mention is made in a court case in 1944 of Dulcie being the 'mother of a child'. A few years later, Dulcie described to reporters in Sydney how hard things were on her daughter, having to move around regularly. Without a name publicly available, Dulcie's daughter remains a mystery, though she may still be alive today.

Living off the proceeds of Dulcie's wartime business in prostitution and sly grog, and his own line in theft, James Williams became known to the local police in Brisbane. He was charged and found guilty of stealing a huge quantity of alcohol from the storeroom of the Stock Exchange Hotel on the corner of Charlotte and Edward streets in 1943. When he was arrested by local detectives, Williams told them he was a mug and should have known the whisky was 'hot'.

Dulcie didn't fare much better. She was charged with having insufficient means of support in January 1944 but was acquitted. Having a small child to look after may have helped her case, though it certainly didn't stop her from continuing in the sex trade. Her own brothel would have made it easier for her to maintain business with a small child in the house rather than having to look after her on the streets or getting friends to care for her.

Outside of her own business, Dulcie also worked on and off for Nancy Ricardo (aka Nancy Wylie). Nancy ran a number of brothels in South Brisbane, including one of the city's most popular ones, the San Toy, on Montague Road.

But Dulcie's relationship with Nancy ended suddenly when Nancy accused Dulcie of theft. Dulcie appeared in Brisbane Police Court on 1 February 1944, and laughed off the stealing charge. Identifying her by her many aliases, including the 'Queen of the Underworld in Brisbane', police alleged Dulcie had stolen one of Nancy's diamond rings from Nancy's house in Highgate Hill. Nancy told police that her husband, Rex Ricardo, had bought the ring for her and that Dulcie had taken it. There was also the issue of the missing safe in which it had allegedly been kept in the front bedroom of the house.

When questioned by the police prosecution, Dulcie said it was 'ridiculous' to call her by all the underworld nicknames. She claimed that Maurice Dias, whom she had met in Sydney and known for twelve years, had given her the ring the previous December to mind for him. Dias also gave similar evidence, stating that he had given the ring to Dulcie to mind and that he had bought it in Sydney three years before. Maurice told the court: 'The whole thing boils down to this. The ring belongs to me and Dulcie is innocent.'

Dias was a questionable witness. He had a long record for gambling, theft and sly-grogging. In 1929, aged twenty-one, he had pleaded with a magistrate in Forbes, New South Wales, not to send him to prison, claiming hardship since he had been orphaned at twelve and 'experienced a hard life throughout'. He had criminal records in Sydney, wider New South Wales, and Melbourne. The month after appearing in Brisbane in February 1944 to support his old mate, Dulcie, he was charged and fined in Perth on an old idle and disorderly charge.

Dulcie was committed to stand trial and later in February was needed in court to face another consorting charge. In the meantime, she and Williams had 'shot through', according to police. Detective Senior Sergeant Buggy was glad to see the back of Dulcie, happy to 'keep her away'. In Dulcie's absence in court on the consorting charge Buggy said: 'She is not the type of woman we want here. She has ability, intelligence and appearance and was a lure and bait for the sly-grog trade.' It is interesting that rather than being referred to as a known prostitute, sly-grogger or associated with many in the underworld – as she had previously been – Buggy said Dulcie was 'one of the leaders of the underworld'.

Dulcie was sentenced to one month in prison and Williams six months for consorting. If they came back to Queensland, the police would be waiting to put both of them away. They had left for Sydney together to dodge prison time, but Dulcie and Williams wouldn't last much longer as a couple. Their relationship seems to have been all but over the following year. Facing a variety of stealing charges in July 1945, James Williams allowed his lawyer to blame Dulcie for his client's downfall.

Charged with breaking, entering and stealing in Mosman, Sydney, Williams was also up on a consorting charge. Police alleged he had stolen more than 3000 food ration books and close to 2000 clothing ration books from a Commonwealth distributing centre. It was a tale, according to the lawyer, of the 'Decline and fall of a married man from the path of fidelity and honesty' because of his association with Dulcie, a 'gun moll' and 'notorious member of the underworld'. Dulcie had also been charged with consorting, but she was absent from the courtroom. Newspapers alleged she was back in Brisbane, probably hoping to avoid time for her previous consorting charge there. Nothing seems to have come of the earlier theft charge against her.

James Williams was found guilty and sentenced to eighteen months in prison. The magistrate cautioned him that while he might try to blame Dulcie for his downfall, he should have ended his association with her years earlier. And yet, Dulcie was still held responsible for the decisions her lover made. She was again portrayed as the 'fallen' woman bringing about the downfall of a married man.

This branding of Dulcie as a bad influence and the root cause of many a man's downfall created her public reputation as a femme fatale. Here, in her relationship with James Williams, she was accused of having lured her lover away from his wife and into a life of crime. His downfall, according to his legal team, was caused by his attraction to the beautiful but bad Dulcie.

As we will see, by the middle of the 1940s, Dulcie's notoriety was also well established way out in the 'Wild West' of Western Australia. In January 1944, she was identified in *The Mirror* newspaper there as a the 'Widow of a murdered gunman, girlfriend of two other men who were murdered, and of a fourth who met a violent death'. With her 'innocent face and baby-blue eyes', she was already 'well known in Perth'. She would become better known there later in 1946. Before she appeared in Perth, Dulcie lost yet another lover to underworld violence.

There was growing speculation that a curse followed Dulcie around the world of Australian crime. We could explain this away as Dulcie simply living and working in criminal circles that brought with them their fair share of violence. What sets Dulcie apart, however, is that she was directly connected to a number of violent deaths and seemed to have become the pin-up girl for Australian crime. Crime reporters like Bondi's Bill Jenkings were always surprised that Dulcie was a central part of crime across three cities. She was far too pretty for what he expected of women involved in crime, and her public persona was almost Hollywood-like.

But all of this hid Dulcie's tough, no-nonsense side. While the newspapers might speculate about a curse following her, she was more in control of what was going on in the underworlds of Australian crime than they perhaps thought. Dulcie could get her revenge when she wanted to.

ABOVE LEFT Florence, Dulcie's sister, was eight years old when Dulcie ran away.

ABOVE RIGHT A prostitute by the time she was 15, and a gangster's girlfriend at 17. With her dyed blonde hair and deep blue eyes, young flapper Dulcie made her mark on Sydney.

BELOW Runaway girls like Dulcie made their way to the 'Loo, where they found work on the streets or in one of the many terrace-house brothels. Harmer and Palmer streets, Woolloomooloo, mid-1930s.

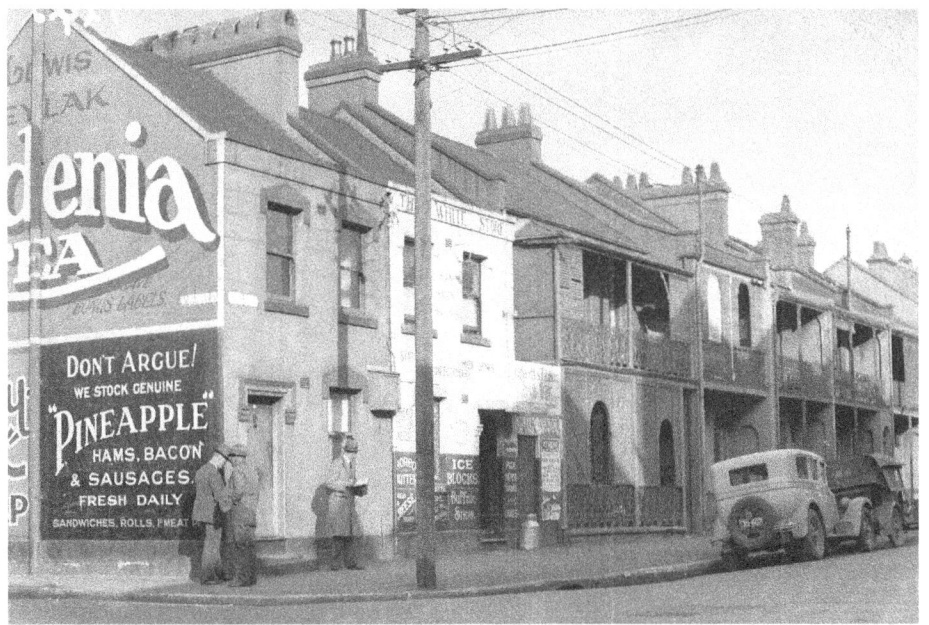

THIS PAGE Lillian Armfield, head of the Women's Police, Sydney. Her 'dawn patrol' scoured the streets of Surry Hills, Darlinghurst, Woolloomooloo and Kings Cross, in the hope of diverting runaway girls from a life of prostitution, crime and violence. Dulcie Markham (aka Marie or Mary Eugene, among other names) first came to Armfield's attention in 1929.

DEATH WALKS
with the
"BLACK WIDOW"

This is the story of a beautiful woman known to the Australian police as Marie Eugene.

Although the vicissitudes of her underworld life read like a "crime thriller," Smith's doesn't print the story for that reason.

One of the most heart-breaking tasks of social workers is to persuade their "problem children"—for that's what most delinquent adolescents are—that the glamor and excitement of underworld life conceal degradation and misery.

Annual police reports now being tabled show that female crime figures are rising, that juvenile delinquency is still a serious problem.

Marie Eugene's history should convince some of these foolish rather than abandoned adolescents that crime doesn't pay.

Marie Eugene, now only 33, is known by many names and titles. Some are commonplace, like Dulcie Williams. Some are colorful, like Yvea de Marquis. Others are sinister — The Black Widow" and "The Angel of Death".

The commonplace and colorful names she devised herself. The titles were coined by the underworld because so many of the men she has associated with have died, violent and dreadful deaths.

Like the men she has loved, Marie is a product of a violent, delinquent girlhood environment.

Her parents were decent folk so decent that police have protected their good name by never charging Marie Eugene under her correct name.

At 15 she made her debut in Sydney's underworld. She was tall, slim, with blonde curls, a perfect complexion and "baby blue eyes." Ace gunmen and petty thieves were attracted to her.

That year Cecil "Scotty" McCormack, 21-year-old thug and gunman, who had graduated from an apprenticeship of juvenile delinquency, was discharged from prison.

Marie threw in her lot with him. They planned to marry.

But McCormack had an argument with a man in a shop door-

way one night and was stabbed through the heart with a stiletto-like instrument.

Marie Eugene was sitting in a picture theatre and a girl friend rushed in to break the news to her.

She went to the Morgue, identified the gunman's body, and then disappeared.

Police arrested Alfred John Dillon at whose home Marie had been living before she joined McCormack. Their theory was that Dillon had been in love with Marie Eugene.

Marie was finally traced according to detectives disguised with a black wig.

Her beauty and bearing in court proved a sensation. She had really "arrived" as an underworld personality.

Alfred Dillon was found guilty of manslaughter and sentenced to 13 years' imprisonment.

McCormack was given an expensive gangster funeral with all the trimmings of elaborate coffin and pyramids of flowers.

Marie went to Melbourne and associated with Arthur Kingsley Taplin and Taplin was shot down in the Cosmopolitan Hotel, Swanston Street, Melbourne, in December, 1937. He died seven days later.

Returning to Sydney, Marie caught the eye of Guido Calletti, one-time pickpocket, box delinquent, reform school graduate, petty larcenist and gunman.

Calletti was shrewd. Although the police knew plenty about him, they could never shoot home a serious charge.

Longest sentence he ever served was five years. Following his regular technique, he hired a man who came to trial and and rob him. The intended victim thrashed Calletti, then frog marched him to the nearest police station, where he laid the charge that resulted in a two-year sentence.

"John proposed to me last night— that's the sign of an early Spring!"

Calletti became uncrowned "King" of Sydney's underworld. Marie became his "queen."

In 1939 a party was held in a Darlinghurst boarding house. Calletti and Marie were there. A fight started. Bottles and furniture were smashed. Then guns were drawn. Calletti fell dead.

Two men stood trial for the murder and were acquitted.

Calletti was given the most spectacular gangster funeral in Australian history. More than 5000 people filed past his coffin in the mortuary. More than 200 wreaths were sent.

While Calletti's body was lying in a Sydney funeral parlor Marie Eugene made a dramatic entrance to weep over the dead gunman.

Then she watched and police looking for her in a rumor could not find her until the murder trial was almost ended.

Grim Saga of Australia's Underworld

(CONTINUED ON PAGE 2)

ABOVE Harry Pigeon, 1925. He became a figure in Sydney's underworld, teaming up with fellow crim Scotty McCormack.

ABOVE Scotty McCormack's charge sheet from 1925, when he was just 16. By 1929, he and teenager Dulcie were lovers. Two years later the gangster was stabbed to death on William Street, Darlinghurst.

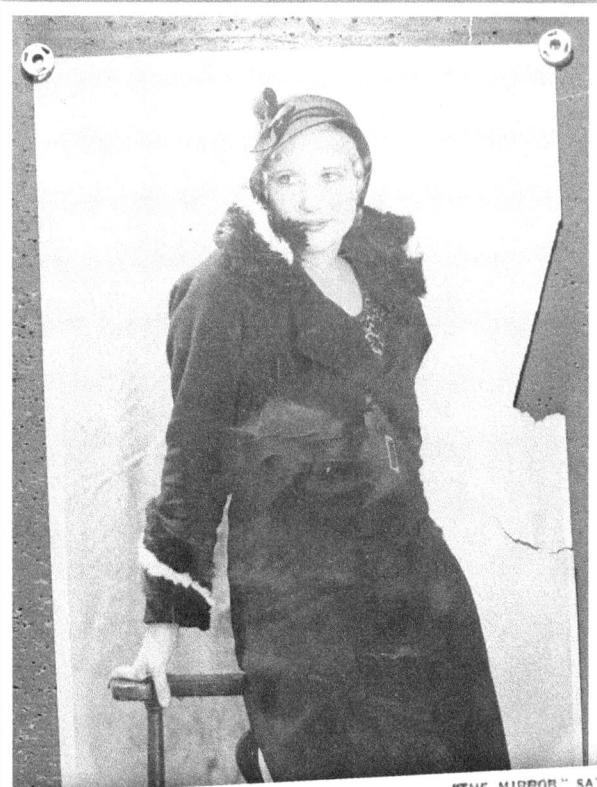

LEFT Pretty Dulcie: 'I was pert, more than ordinarily pretty, and fellows took a lot of notice of me.'

BELOW Guido Calletti: violent con man, pimp, extortionist and Dulcie's lover. He was fatally shot at a party in Brougham Street, Kings Cross, in August 1939.

For The Men Who Love "Pretty Dulcie"—
DEATH TAKES NO HOLIDAY

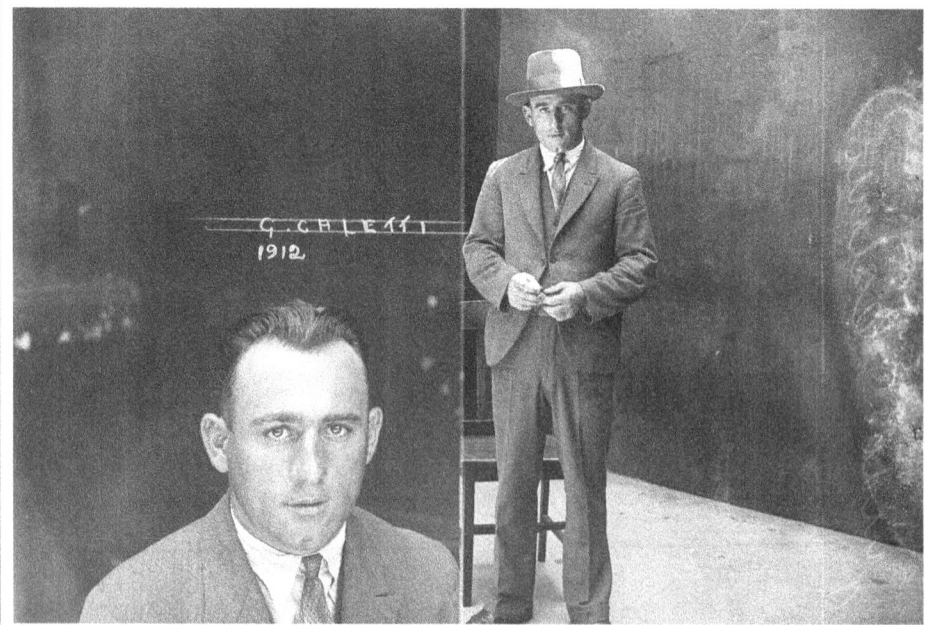

POLICE SEEK MYSTERY BLONDE

May Be Able To Throw Light On Killing

WELL KNOWN IN BRISBANE

TANGLED in the tragic threads of the latest "silent" crime of gangland—the sensational daylight shooting and killing of a well-known Sydney underworld character, Arthur Kingsley Taplin, in the bar of a Melbourne hotel—is the name of a girl familiar to the police of Brisbane, who never seems to be able to avoid having the questing finger of notoriety placed on her movements. Southern investigators consider that beautiful Dulcie Eugene might be able to throw some light on the crime that has cost Taplin his life, for according to them the girl was one of his closest associates, although, at the moment, her whereabouts is proving one of the greatest problems they have encountered in connection with this latest gangster outbreak. Thus, as has not been infrequent throughout her remarkable young life, does the spotlight swing again in the direction of the girl, who, not inaptly, has been termed, "Australia's most beautiful bad woman."

LEFT Notorious madam Tilly Devine operated brothels at the height of the 'Razorhurst' gang wars and was always on the lookout for new talent. This is her mugshot from 1934, when she was charged with being 'idle and disorderly' while working in Perth.

BELOW LEFT Pretty Dulcie followed in the footsteps of beautiful Nellie Cameron, pictured, who ran away from home in 1926 to work for Tilly Devine in Darlinghurst.

BELOW RIGHT A grieving Tilly was among the 700 mourners at Nellie Cameron's funeral in 1953.

ABOVE Kate Leigh (centre): sly grogger and cocaine dealer. At the height of her operations she had over 30 sly grog hotels in Surry Hills, and her terrace house was frequently raided by police. Both feared and respected, Kate threw annual Christmas parties for the kids in the neighbourhood, like this one outside her Devonshire Street terrace in 1953.

BELOW Josie's Bungalow, a prominent brothel on Roe Street in Perth, 1929–30. Dulcie was already well known in Perth when she sought work in Roe Street in 1946.

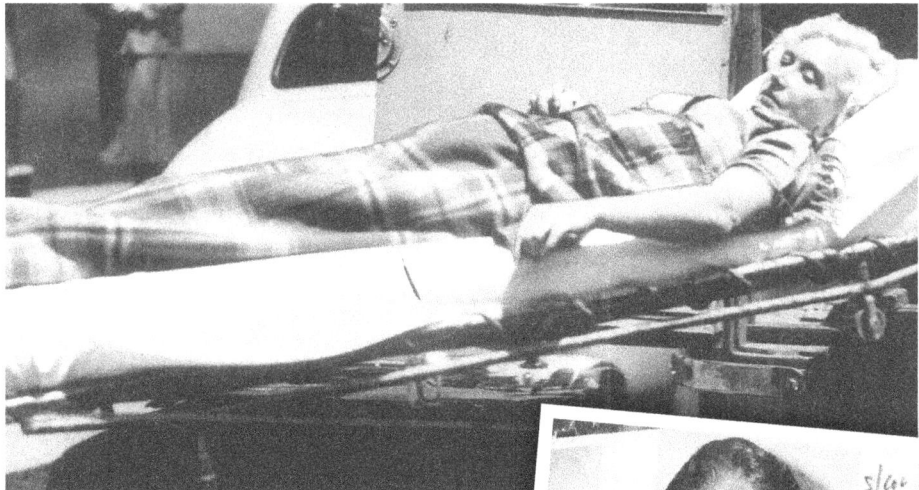

ABOVE A close shave for the Angel of Death, August 1951. While in bed in her house in Melbourne, Dulcie was shot by an intruder. Her lover was killed, his brother wounded and Dulcie's hip was shattered by the bullet – but in keeping with the underworld code of silence, she refused to give up the attacker's name in court.

RIGHT Leonard 'Redda' Lewis and Dulcie on their wedding day, in St Kilda, December 1951. Dulcie is sitting in the bed that she was shot in just months earlier.

Dramatic story of bedroom shooting; Two men to stand trial

After identifying Ernest James Martin (30), and Charles Henry Mills (29), in a police line-up as the two armed men concerned in the fatal shooting of his younger brother, Gavan Thomas Walsh, 23-years-old former boxer, in the St Kilda home of Dulcie Markham on September 25, Desmond Bernard Walsh visited a Melbourne newspaper office two days later and submitted a written statement denying that Martin and Mills were the men who shot his brother.

Desmond Walsh, also a former boxer, told the Melbourne coroner, Mr. Burke, S.M., during the inquest this week that, in making the statement, he wanted it that time, to make it known that Martin and Mills were not the men concerned.

He told associates what he had done, and claimed there was need for it to become known that his identification was wrong.

"Cop It Sweet"

He wanted it well circulated, and was told it circulated even to the police.

To Det.-Insp. H. R. Donelly, Walsh said that after he identified Martin and Mills, all he heard from others was, "You had better do the right thing. Cop it sweet. Don't squeal. If you squeal and don't cop it sweet, the same thing will happen to you."

Walsh continued: "So the next night I made the statement about Martin and Mills not being the men. But then I thought of Gavan again.

"And I thought to myself: Why should they get away with it? That's why I'm saying here that the written statement I made

in the newspaper office was wrong, and my evidence here is the true story."

Martin — dark, rugged and well groomed — and Mills—lithe, a head taller than Martin, and sallow—were sent for trial on a charge of having murdered Gavan Walsh.

And the true story, as alleged by Desmond Walsh, was:

Since returning from Brisbane in August, he had been living with Dulcie Markham at her home in Faulkner St, St Kilda. He took Dulcie to the nearby Court House Hotel for a few drinks on September 25, and they returned home about 5 p.m.

Dulcie was lying on the bed in the front bedroom, and he was clad only in a pair of trousers, when his brother Gavan arrived at 6.30 p.m. with a bottle of brandy. They were having a drink, when Mills knocked, entered, and joined them in a drink.

Mills said there was a man looking for the Walsh brothers, as there was £50 up to have them done over.

Mills asked whether they would "front" the other and both used it.

There was another man named Nut but Smith through together," he said.

Mills. Within a few minutes, there was another knock on the front door, and Gavan Walsh answered it.

"There were three shots and Gavan staggered back into the bedroom and fell on the floor by a wardrobe. Martin came in, pointed the gun straight at him, and put another one into him while he was on the floor," said Desmond Walsh.

"Shot In Hand"

"There were two more shots and Dulcie fell from the bed to the floor, just near the window. I was standing near the foot of the bed and reached out my left hand for Martin's gun. I went to grab it and was shot in the hand.

"I got under the bed and started to yell out, 'I've been shot in the guts.' One car left from outside, but when I heard another come along I went out the back and stayed near the next door fence until police arrived."

Mills, also carrying a gun, entered the room with Martin, but Walsh said he did not know whether he

do you take "done over" to mean?

Desmond Walsh: In my language, it could mean a bashing or a shooting.

To Mr M. Goldberg (for Martin), Walsh said he had five or six drinks before meeting Dulcie, and about a dozen altogether by the time he left the hotel.

Mr. Goldberg: You were

WOUNDED

DESMOND WALSH

DEAD

GAVAN WALSH

WOUNDED

DULCIE MARKHAM

when Mills was interviewed at Russell St. at 1 a.m. on September 26, he said he had not been at Pretty Dulcie's for at least a week.

"Mills admitted he had lived with Dulcie Markham at 55 Fawkner St., but when I asked whether he had been annoyed at the Walshes moving in with Dulcie Markham, he replied: 'No, I'm not annoyed. Redda Lewis moved in before them," said Oakes.

When told that Desmond Walsh had stated he and Martin were the two men concerned in the shooting, Mills said: "I was there, but I had nothing to do with any shooting. I shot through. I didn't want to be in it," added

on good terms with Martin when you last saw him, two months before this accident?—Yes.

Well what reason would he have to go looking for you and your brother with a gun?—No reason at all.

You might be mistaken over Martin?—When you see your brother shot dead on the floor you know who did it. Those two faces will stay in my mind for life!

Walsh added that Mills would not disclose who put up the £50 to have them done over.

Dulcie Markham was still in Alfred Hospital, with three bullet wounds in a shattered thigh.

Dr. Ross Anderson, of Alfred Hospital, said Gavan Walsh was admitted at 8.20 p.m. on September 25. He had two bullets in his left side.

Dulcie Markham was still in Alfred Hospital, with three bullet wounds in a shattered thigh.

Martin and Mills were placed in a line-up, Desmond Walsh walked straight up to Martin, grabbed him, and said: "You! Shoot the kid, eh?" Walsh named Martin as the man who had fired the shots.

Det. Oakes said that

FEED HUNGRY GLANDS QUICKLY

NEW SOUTH WALES POLICE

Name   MARY EUGENE.

Aliases   @ Tasca DE MARCA. @ Tosca DEMARENE.
       @ Dulcie WILLIAMS. @ Mary WILLIAMS.
       @ Dian Lee BOWEN. @ Dulcie LEWIS.
       @ Dulcie MARKHAM. @ Dulcie MARKHAM.
   @ Dulcie BOWEN. etc.

Photo No.   208 172.
Gaol No.   1506. L.B.
Date taken   6.5.52.

Date of Birth 28.2.16 Age 36-45.
(Day, Month and Year.)

Birthplace (Town and Country)   Sydney.

Arrival in Australia { Date / Ship

Height   5 feet   — inches

Weight   130 lbs. Build   Medium.

Complexion   Fair.

Colour of Hair   Fair.

Colour of Eyes   Hazel.

Occupation   D.D.

Religion   R.C.

Descriptive marks, including scars, tattoo marks, physical deformities, and other peculiarities, etc.:   Bullet wound left hip. Right forefinger injured. Small scar under left eye.

Finger Print Classification   1   U   MII   8   II
                         1   U   IMM   7   Hy   II

Previous and Subsequent Photos   Spl.Ph. 582/39, W.A. 31/293.

Docket

CRIMINAL HISTORY

Court.	Date.	Offence.	Result.
Central I.C.	28.11.45.	Assault.	1 mth. h.l. Pay comp. £5 or 10 days. APPEALED.
Central P.C.	28.11.45.	Consorting.	6 months.h.l. APPEALED.
Sydney Q.S.	15.4.46.	Appealed against conviction for Assault at Central P.C. on 28.11.45. The appellant not appearing, dismissed the appeal and confirmed conviction and sentence. No action on recogs. to prosecute appeal. No costs.	
Sydney Q.S.	15.4.46.	Appealed against conviction for consorting at Central P.C. on 28.11.45. The appellant not appearing, dismissed the appeal and confirmed the conviction and sentence with costs £3.3.0. to the Clerk of Peace within 28 days. No action on recogs. to prosecute appeal.	
(Warrants Executed 25.4.52.		to serve sentences imposed 28.11.45.)	

HAS PREVIOUS CONVICTIONS.

Dulcie's charge sheet in 1952, after she was arrested for consorting. In her obituary in the *Daily Mirror* in 1976, Bill Jenkins wrote that 'Dulcie Markham saw more violence and death than any other woman in Australia's history'.

CHAPTER 7

Shot in the face

Another lover dead

While Dulcie was trying to ward off vagrancy and theft charges in Brisbane, violence once again escalated in Sydney. This time another of her good friends, Donald 'The Duck' Day, was the victim. Donald ran brothels with his wife, Irene, in Kings Cross and on Elizabeth Street in the city centre. Dulcie had worked in the Day brothels, and was probably also sleeping with Donald.

Originally from South Australia, Donald also worked as a jockey for a while. By the 1940s, he was running two lucrative sly-grog shops and was involved in the business with a high-profile doctor, Reginald Stuart-Jones. According to fellow crook and Day's payroll and standover man, Chow Hayes, they also stocked the doctor's yacht full of booze. Stuart-Jones was shot in the chest in October 1944 by a small gang of crooks who wanted him out of the business. He survived, but his associate, Donald Day, was now on borrowed time. Dulcie was in Sydney that October, charged with driving a motor car under the influence of alcohol. Her mate, Donald, faced a far worse fate.

Donald Day's luck ran out on 28 January 1945. Darlinghurst Police Station officers were called out to a house on the corner of Crown and Foveaux streets, where they found Donald Day dead on a bed, blood splattered over his face and body. Two American servicemen who were found hiding with guns in a house next door were taken away and questioned by detectives. They were paying guests of the terrace house, and police initially thought they were more worried about being associated with a notorious group of people nearby rather than having actually been involved in the shooting. Police knew the victim well. His houses were regularly raided as places of 'ill fame', and they were aware that he was connected to the black markets in booze and rationing.

Donald's wife, Irene, and a woman called Daphne Kinney were arrested later on 28 January but discharged soon after. There was speculation that Irene was implicated after an argument with her husband, but the evidence was circumstantial. Police were then tipped off about the shooter and believed they had their man. During searches of houses in Haymarket, they arrested Keith Kitchener Hull on the corner of Castlereagh and Campbell streets.

Keith Hull, described in court as 'dark, sallow' in appearance, pleaded not guilty to the charge of murder after an inquest found there was a case to be heard on trial. Keith Hull claimed he shot Donald Day in self-defence, and also revealed that Day had beaten him up at a house on Crown Street. Day, Hull alleged, kicked in his bedroom door the next day and threatened to shoot him. When the gun didn't go off, Hull grabbed it and fired four times. Donald Day suffered horrific wounds in the face, heart and abdomen. Keith Hull lifted him onto the bed and felt for a pulse. He didn't find one. Someone in the house called the police but by the time the police arrived, Day's body had been moved to the attic. The Sydney newspapers commented on the appropriateness of Day dying in a brothel.

US sailor William Simponis gave evidence that the night before the shooting Day had an argument with him and another sailor. Day also allegedly said he was going to 'do over' Keith Hull.

It took the jury half an hour to acquit Hull. He was free, but was being closely watched by his enemies. Soon after, he was approached at the Mansions Hotel (now the Manor Hotel, not a pub) in Kings Cross by one of Donald Day's associates, George Barrett. Hull would later tell a court Barrett said to him: 'I don't want to talk to you. When I want to see you I will see you.'

Donald Day's funeral on 1 February 1945 was attended by 1500 people, with wreaths reportedly left by 'Bronze', 'La Belle', 'Violet' and 'His friends from Elizabeth Street'.

After Day's death, his links to Dulcie Bowen were revealed, and the newspapers jostled to add to her notoriety. In July 1945, the Perth *Mirror* ran a story on 'Pretty Dulcie' and the 'death curse' dogging her. Calling her an 'amazing virago', the newspaper claimed that death hovered around her like a shadow:

> *In the palm of her beautiful white hand, men dance to the tune she calls. And the tune she calls is DEATH! Year in, year out, it seems, this glamorous siren of the underworld dawdles on Death's door-step. And one after another the men who have loved her have met a tragic end.*

Dulcie herself was actually looking for revenge this time. Keith Hull and his wife Valma (aka Thelma and Judy) were reportedly living in Melbourne after the murder trial, on the run from the Sydney underworld's retribution. Dulcie headed to Melbourne and, soon enough, crossed paths with the Hulls. First, though, came the death of another man who was said to be her lover.

Dulcie's involvement in Melbourne crime escalated from the middle of the 1940s, as she became associated with the leaders of the city's illegal gambling scene. The police had targeted petty street betting throughout the 1920s, but the Great Depression hit the business hard and it was no longer a quick money-maker for the crooks. Bookmakers went further underground from the 1930s, operating out of private houses and hotels, and turning them into what they now called baccarat schools. These ruthless criminal operators combined gambling with sly grog, and benefited from Dulcie's business in sex.

Gambling in these private houses was a popular form of entertainment for many of Melbourne's gangsters, and was protected by one or two men keeping a lookout for police in the front bedroom while others were paid to drive clients to and from the establishments. Electrician by day, driver at night, Charles Kirby was employed 'by different persons directing people to Baccarat Schools'. His work usually started in the early evening, around 8 p.m., and could keep him out until the early hours of the morning. He was friends with a well-known gambler, gunman and underworld figure, Leslie Ernest Walkerden.

Leslie Walkerden was nicknamed 'Scotland Yard' because of his love of detective fiction, but he had form in the real world of crime too. In April 1935, when he was only nineteen, Leslie had been charged with unlawfully wounding twenty-three-year-old Maxwell Salter, intending to kill him. He was arrested in George Street, Sydney, on the run from police and using the alias Ernest Jackson. He was already such a hardened case at this young age that he told the police who arrested him: 'It's no use telling any more lies. I was there when the stink took place but I did not do the shooting. But if those coppers go to my home in Fitzroy and worry my people, I'll shoot the —, even if I get ten years for it.'

Back on 5 March 1935, Maxwell Salter had been walking with a mate along Russell Street in the Melbourne city centre a little after 11 p.m. when he crossed paths with Leslie Walkerden, who was leaning against a window and mouthing off at him. An altercation had taken place and Leslie and Maxwell fought it out in nearby Hayward Lane. Shots were fired and Maxwell fell to the ground, wounded in the thigh and abdomen. He was hospitalised for five days, undergoing three operations, and was then sent to a convalescent home. Detectives quickly caught up with Leslie Walkerden, but he was acquitted early in May 1935 when, unsurprisingly, Maxwell Salter refused to identify him as the shooter.

By the early 1940s, Leslie Walkerden's reputation as a gunman for hire was well established. He worked as a strong man for James Coates, who was known in the underworld as 'The Mark Foy'. Coates started out in crime as a pickpocket and cardsharp before becoming a trickster, posing as a grazier and surgeon during gambling games on ships travelling the Atlantic. When he returned to Melbourne in 1933, he bought a mansion in Toorak, and by the 1940s was a 'financier' of gambling. Coates was involved in racetrack swindles, and used blackmail to maintain baccarat schools. Some in the underworld thought he was also an informer. He was a poor choice of boss for Leslie Walkerden, because even in the swindling, standover circles of underworld Melbourne, Coates was one of the most loathed.

In the mid-1940s, Coates, wanting one of his rivals, Robert Walker, out of the way, allegedly paid Walkerden £150 pounds to kill him. Walkerden wasn't successful. (Lenny McPherson allegedly killed Walker in 1963.)

Walkerden was accumulating enemies in his work for Coates, and further upset gamblers when he was used to keep order at baccarat games. Leslie Walkerden was gunned down at close range with a shotgun in the early hours of 12 September 1945 while trying to put air back into his flat tyre, which had been punctured to render him vulnerable to attack. There were plenty of witnesses to the shooting, but those responsible escaped quickly, and no one could really say they knew who they were or what they looked like. It was dark, but it was certainly not quiet – the culprits ran off laughing.

Peppered by shots in the elbow and abdomen, Leslie Walkerden staggered along Goodwood Street, near Waltham Street in Richmond, where only a short while before he had been playing baccarat. After arriving around mid-evening, morose and out of sorts, he had sat in the corner and didn't leave when his wife came to tell him she'd had an accident in her car. She watched the betting for a couple of hours and left after midnight.

As he lurched along in agony, he called out to his mate George Newman. George and another friend, baccarat employee Charles Kirby, bundled Leslie into a car. In his statement, George recalled Leslie saying to him in the car: 'I'm done, hurry up.'

After two operations, Leslie Walkerden was returned to the ward in Melbourne's St Vincent's Hospital the following morning. His elbow was shattered but the wound to his abdomen was far worse. Doctors found many pellets inside, and the wall of his stomach was perforated. His torn spleen and kidney had been removed but doctors didn't expect him to make it through the morning. Detectives questioned him about the shooting, but he gave them no descriptions or names. Leslie Walkerden died at eight that morning.

(The family pain continued beyond Leslie's death. Five years later, Leslie's mother, Annie Walkerden, died in 'abject poverty' and was 'buried as a pauper'. Friends told the newspapers that she died of a broken heart. She had told *Truth* in 1945 she didn't care what people said about Leslie, 'he was a grand son'. Annie was buried beside her husband and her son.)

It didn't take long for the newspapers to connect Dulcie Bowen to Leslie Walkerden. His photograph featured in a newspaper story with the headline 'Why "Pretty Dulcie" is the "Angel of Death" '. Photographs of Scotty McCormack, Arthur Taplin, Guido Calletti and Donald Day were also included. While there is certainly a good deal of evidence linking Dulcie to the other men, her connection to Leslie Walkerden is more tenuous. On the night he was killed, he had spent some of the day with his lover, twenty-one-year-old Lorna Carol Maddox. She worked at the State Theatre (now the Forum Theatre), in Flinders Street, where she would often meet him. He showered her with gifts, including handbags, chocolates and flowers, but she didn't know he was married. Dulcie Bowen does not feature in the witness statements from the inquest, nor was she mentioned in the newspaper stories about Leslie's murder, as had happened with her other lovers. Dulcie moved in the same gambling circles and kept company with a few of the leading underworld identities at the time. She would have known Leslie Walkerden and she may have been his lover at one point, but by the time of his death, he was telling Lorna Maddox that he loved her. Walkerden was shot because of his thuggery in the gambling underworlds. It was his rivals who took him out rather than a curse following Dulcie.

A rumour also circulated among newspaper reporters during the inquest that Dulcie was not named in inquest statements for her own protection and may have in fact posed as the much younger Lorna Maddox, Leslie's twenty-one-year-old lover. This seems unlikely. Dulcie was well known across the Australian underworlds by 1945. It would have been very difficult for her to pose as someone else – someone would have found out she was at the inquest. The detectives also knew who Dulcie was and would have seen she was older than twenty-one if she had been playing Lorna. Or there is an outside chance they helped protect her by supporting this other identity.

*

The underworld violence continued in Melbourne unabated. John Gilligan was wounded four times in May 1947 when a barrage of bullets was fired at him on the corner of Elizabeth and Flinders streets in the city centre. The threat didn't work. Gilligan wanted his rival Frederick William 'Freddie the Frog' Harrison out of the city and away from competing with him in the gambling business. Gilligan continued his standover tactics and told Harrison that if he didn't leave Melbourne the same thing would happen to him as had befallen Walkerden – a telling admission.

Two months later, Leslie Walkerden's boss, James Coates, was also gunned down. He was moving further into gambling territory that wasn't his own, and was allegedly behind a number of attacks on baccarat schools aiming to intimidate gamblers into going to his schools instead. The violent nature of Coates' death worried the public, and made the police more intent on stamping out underworld violence. As *The Argus* reported: 'A sensational car chase along Punt rd, Windsor, is believed to have preceded the killing of international trickster James Coates, 46, of Walsh st, South Yarra, on Saturday night.'

Coates was brought down by the now well-established gangster method of a quick, surprise attack, giving him no opportunity to protect himself. His car was rammed on Saturday 17 July 1947 and pushed into the kerb in Gladstone Street, Southbank. Coates had skidded and tried to avoid the crash. He then fled the vehicle and ran to a nearby allotment, where he was cornered and shot as he tried to run through a gate. The post-mortem revealed the fatal shot hit Coates through the neck and the bullet came out through his face. He was also shot in the chest three times, and the angle of the bullets indicated they may have been fired as he fell to the ground. No arrest was made, and his murderer or murderers were never brought to justice.

There were also further attempts on John Gilligan's life. After one of them, in February 1950, newspapers described the scene of the shooting as like something out of Chicago, and provided photographs to prove it. Driving along Brunton Avenue near the Melbourne Cricket Ground, Gilligan and one of his associates were set upon at close range: 'One of the two men in the second car is alleged to have fired a fusillade of shots at Gilligan's car with a Thompson sub-machine-gun [i.e. Tommy gun].' Remarkably, Gilligan survived with only a gunshot wound to the arm. A few months later there was yet another attempt on Gilligan's life. This time, Freddie Harrison and Norman 'Norm' Bradshaw, two well-known underworld crooks, were charged with having fired the shots. These attempts were widely seen as payback for John Gilligan having been involved in the murder of Leslie Walkerden.

*

As the underworld violence continued to brew around her in Melbourne back in 1946, Dulcie moved on again. It was a smart decision. While she couldn't have known what lay ahead for James Coates or others associated with Leslie Walkerden, she knew that if their rivals were trying to get to them, they wouldn't stop short of intimidating and threatening her, or worse. For the first time, Dulcie went to Perth, to a road with a reputation befitting her own notoriety. Roe Street would have its own brush with Dulcie fame in 1946.

CHAPTER 8

Across the tracks at the 'Rue de la Roe'

A Perth sojourn

Dian Lee Bowen fixed her blonde curls and walked into the courtroom like a star in a theatre performance. Smiling over at the court reporters, who would later describe her as a 'pin-up girl' with a 'baby face', she was facing a charge of keeping a house of ill-fame and looking at six months in prison for vagrancy.

When police raided a house at 226 Roe Street, Perth, at three in the morning on 22 June 1946, on suspicion of it being run as a brothel, they found a number of young women living there. Dian's lawyer claimed the house was 'well-kept and orderly', but the police counterclaimed that there were complaints about the conduct of the place. They were also looking for two criminals from the eastern states said to be living there.

She might have changed her name, but the police and reporters knew who Dian Lee Bowen really was. The *Daily News* called her a 'notorious member of Sydney's underworld'. Dian was none other than Dulcie Markham, on her break from the eastern states and checking out business in the west. Her former boss from Sydney, Tilly Devine, had done the same and been charged with idle and disorderly in Perth in 1934. Now that Australia's 'most beautiful bad woman' was in Perth, the reporters were desperate to get a look at this real-life femme fatale. Dulcie was in Perth for the briefest of periods, but there was no escaping the notoriety that had followed her more than 2000 miles across the country.

She knew the business well, and in trying to escape the escalating violence in Melbourne and Sydney, went straight to Western Australia knowing there was demand for her work there. For an enterprising prostitute and brothel-owner, Perth's Roe Street brothel precinct was a perfect fit. Dulcie moved in and started business, adding to her already impressive portfolio.

The newspaper reporters had renamed the street the Rue de la Roe and followed its rise as the most scandalous street in Perth. Everyone knew where and what it was.

Kids used to hang out of the trains going past the street to catch a glimpse of the women on the porches of the brothels. The fence heights were increased in the 1940s so that the 'scandalous women' were out of view of children passing by. A short distance from Perth Railway Station, it was close to the city centre, but also only metres down the road from Perth Police Station and lock-up. Vice Squad detectives simply had to wander along the street to find idle and disorderly women working there. Once they learned Dulcie Markham was in town, the detectives were keen to keep her eastern states underworld associations away from Perth.

Timing was essential to Dulcie's swift arrest. Her arrival in Perth came after years of dramatic social and economic change, and her work was at the centre of increasing debates about the respectability of city life. The city was then much smaller than Sydney and Melbourne, and Perth locals quickly spotted a newcomer. In the Roe Street brothels it was only a matter of time before Dulcie was noticed. This was the same woman one Sydney detective described as having a 'magnificent figure' and walking 'better than any model'. This same detective, recalling Dulcie years later to crime writer Larry Writer, said: 'I'd rate her twelve out of ten.'

*

The years from 1900 to the onset of the World War II in 1939 marked a period of 'significant social change in Western Australia', during which the metropolitan area rapidly expanded around Perth and Fremantle. This came on the back of the most significant mining boom the state had then seen. Just as in Victoria in the 1850s the gold rush had led to the rapid expansion of urban Melbourne, the western gold rushes turned Perth into a boom town. By March 1901, Western Australia's population had increased dramatically from 29,708 in April 1881 to more than 184,000.

While it still harboured a country feel, the Perth of the early twentieth century was fast moving towards being a modern city with a growing CBD. Richer residents started to prefer the western areas to the previously favoured Esplanade and Adelaide Terrace. They moved further out to West Perth, Dalkeith and Claremont, most with riverside views. Subiaco, East Perth and Maylands housed more white-collar and skilled workers, while working-class people ended up in eastern suburbs like Bassendean and Midland, or the greater Fremantle area in the south.

With more and more people moving to the suburbs to live in small worker's cottages or family bungalows, living standards fell in the inner streets of Perth and Fremantle. King Street, for example, known today as an exclusive designer part of the CBD, was notorious in the early twentieth century for 'drunken orgies', and described as a 'disgrace to the town'. Western Australia's urban poor congregated in and around King Street, across the railway tracks in Roe Street, North Perth, parts of Leederville and East Perth. In Fremantle, the very poor lived in overcrowded housing around Market, High and Pakenham streets, these days cosmopolitan café precincts. While crime was not restricted to poor members of society, police often apprehended drunk, idle and disorderly women in these areas. They were labelled streets of vice and were well known to the general public.

As the metropolitan area increased in breadth, so too did criminal activities. Some streets were off limits from the late afternoon. Local residents wrote in to the papers about their evening mishaps and run-ins with local thugs. According to one resident of West Perth: 'Drunken men and women, with dress shamefully disheveled and using language that even devils would hesitate to use are the sights and scenes of which decent residents are compelled to see daily.' The inner-city slums around Murray and Hay streets in Perth were said to harbour all manner of criminal types, including thieving gangs and drunken standover men.

Most men and women in the Perth courts were charged with drunkenness or stealing. Only a minority faced charges for the more serious crimes of murder, manslaughter or assault. Historically, homicide accounts for only a fraction of all crimes, whereas petty offences feature largely in general crime statistics. It was no different in the Western Australian Magistrates' Courts, where charges for offences against good order vastly outnumbered other crimes, accounting for a little over seventy-four per cent of all crimes.

While it was still a small city, Perth's urban expansion into the 1920s brought with it increasing social problems, poverty and slum conditions. Slums and makeshift shelters dominated corners and laneways around George and Wellington streets, while 'hovels' were an eyesore in King Street and Melbourne Road (which later became part of Milligan Street). In these inner streets you could reportedly find 'houses of the worst slum type'. Another article in the *Sunday Times*, also in 1920, drew attention to slums in Pier Street, and around William and Roe streets, where you would see 'Ragged, half-clad children and women ... about these hideous dens and habitations'. It was 'one of the worst portions of our fast growing city'. From there the article descends into an almost Dickensian world of poor families 'glad to ave ad a pitch with yer'.

Prostitution was singled out in these years as emblematic of the further decay of the city. It coincided with the mining boom, the resulting dramatic increase in the population of people born interstate, and rapid urbanisation across the metropolitan area. Breadwinners leaving the eastern states to make a fortune in the gold rushes were responsible for some of the population increase. Desertion records in the various police gazettes show the other side of this phenomenon – the wives and children left behind. Western Australia experienced a boom in prostitution as rapid urbanisation and heightened immigration increased the demand for sexual services. It wasn't just men who contributed to an increase in prostitution. Like Dulcie, women looked for better business in the west, some wanting to escape police attention for their soliciting elsewhere in Australia.

Western Australia followed the pattern of other western societies in its efforts to deal with prostitution: suppression, regulation and abolitionism. The social purity movement, influenced by similar movements in Britain, focused on suppression of prostitution from the late nineteenth century. The Western Australian branch of the National Council of Women ran various campaigns throughout the first decades of the twentieth century to ensure prostitution was not legalised, and to offer educational assistance to prevent young people erring. The Social Purity section of the Women's Christian Temperance Union (WCTU) also played a key role in the push to suppress prostitution, as part of its focus on prioritising families rather than what it called 'fickle personal relationships'. While WCTU visits to Fremantle Prison focused on habitual female drinkers, temperance women trying to reform 'degraded' lifestyles also targeted prostitutes. Similar rescue organisations became popular across Australia from the middle of the nineteenth century, and were largely run by Christian denominations. Their work rested on the belief that some 'fallen' women could be rescued if given the opportunity to lead a 'respectable' life. The rescue home – such as the Home of the Good Shepherd in Leederville and Salvation Army homes – was thus used both to reform women and to regulate and suppress prostitution.

Suppression of brothels, in particular, was one of the main aims of purity movements, and was supported by community members. E. Harris, writing to the *West Australian* from Fremantle, argued:

How is it possible for parents rearing families and having the misfortune of living in close proximity to these places to keep their children deaf and blind to their immediate surroundings? Even the atmosphere of a pure home cannot wholly counteract the baneful influences of this steadily increasing evil.

The letter ends by demanding measures to rid the community of brothels that are 'retarding and threatening the progress of morality and purity in the coming generation'. Prostitution was likened to a pollutant in the community that would infect future generations should nothing be done to stem its flow. The *Sunday Times* called prostitution a 'cancerous growth' that was 'eating out both the moral and physical health and strength' of Perth.

From 1895, the Western Australian government had increasingly favoured a regulatory model. Police and authorities labelled the prostitute as an idle and disorderly person immorally affecting society, and a serious social problem. As a result, legal changes were enacted in Western Australia giving police the power to deal with 'unrespectable' women in public. As was the case across Australia at the time, women labelled as 'common prostitutes' were then subjected to charges of street offences such as loitering, vagrancy, disorderly conduct and idleness. Not all women charged with an idle and disorderly offence were prostitutes, but the 'Idle and Disorderly' section of the WA *Police Act 1892* allowed for prostitutes to be prosecuted as vagrants if unable to show lawful means of support. Common prostitutes could now be fined two pounds or imprisoned for at least a month. Brothel-keeping under the Criminal Code was a misdemeanour carrying a three-year gaol sentence with hard labour.

Just how many women the authorities were trying to regulate is interesting. The *Sunday Times* claimed in 1908:

'There is more prostitution amongst us, proportionately speaking, than in any of the other capital cities of the Commonwealth.' Was this true or rather a reflection of the supposed threat of prostitution? A decline in mining in the first years of the twentieth century saw more movement of people away from the goldfields to Perth and its outlying areas. At the same time, prostitution witnessed a decrease in business, with fewer men flowing through Fremantle port on their way to the goldfields. In 1901, prostitutes in Perth numbered about 140 out of a female population of over 17,000 – 0.8 per cent of the female population. In Fremantle, forty prostitutes were identified among a female population of 6342 – 0.6 per cent. According to some police evidence, in the years from 1900 to 1914, there were thirty to forty regular prostitutes listed as having 'no fixed address'. The infrequent nature of prosecutions for soliciting or loitering meant there were some 500 cases against women in the first four decades of the twentieth century in Western Australia, compared with more than 10,000 drunkenness cases. Thus the *Sunday Times*'s claim that Perth had proportionately the highest rate of prostitution in the Commonwealth is perhaps more reflective of its conservative stance than objective truth.

Perth was nevertheless a popular brothel site. Elaine McKewon has shown in her historical geography of sex work in the city that from the start of the twentieth century, the authorities and police were content to allow prostitution to operate in designated zones. A police report in August 1930 revealed:

> *A close watch is kept over these houses for anything in the nature of soliciting either in the street or from the houses and when found action is taken but so long as they behave themselves and conduct their calling in as quiet a manner as possible the long established custom is followed of not interfering with them.*

Brothels were easier to control. Their close proximity to Perth Police Station, for example, meant the sex trade could be closely monitored and prostitution contained. By the 1920s only a few scattered brothels remained in outlying suburbs. The regulation of the sex industry greatly benefited the madams, who were able to profit from the localisation of prostitution within a few brothels in Roe Street.

'Nera' was the first brothel of these, set up by Annie McKenzie in 1905. Police raids on brothels in the city centre led to a preference for opening brothels over the railway lines in the less residential Roe and James streets. By 1915, fifteen brothels operated on Roe Street, falling to around ten into the 1920s. Isolated houses were known in

East Perth, Victoria Park, West Perth and Leederville, but none rivalled the Roe Street businesses.

The notoriety of the street also meant it was a veritable hotspot for wives looking to catch out their husbands. Wives hired private detectives to stake out the brothels on Roe Street. The newspapers called the private detectives 'divorce sleuths', and were quick to report on their antics as they waited in the shadows on laneways near the brothels. The newspapers laid it on thick for their readers, and husbands were named and shamed. In the May 1944 divorce case before the courts, *The Mirror* reported: 'Caught in embarrassing situations, hubbies come out with some wide and varied excuses. Take, for example, Kenneth John Schryver. Caught by sleuth Alf Sleep coming out of a house in Rue de la Roe, he explained: "Oh, I was only getting a drink of water!" ' Edna Myrtle got her wish and the magistrate supported a divorce.

The brothels were run by some interesting characters through the years. Josie de Bray was similar in some ways to Dulcie. A beautiful Frenchwoman with peroxide-blonde hair, her real name was Marie-Louise Monnier. She was born in Saint-Nazaire in France before emigrating to Western Australia around 1903. Madame Monnier first worked in the brothels in Brookman Street (in a section later renamed Hay Street), Kalgoorlie. Newspaper reporters would claim in the 1940s that she could 'rattle many skeletons in cupboards' if she decided to speak out about some of the leading figures in mining in those days.

Josie moved to Perth before World War I and made a small fortune selling sex during the war in her establishments in Roe Street. Josie also worked up a business selling alcohol. While the temperance movement was looking to restrict after-hours drinking, Josie sold sly grog at exorbitant prices. By the 1930s, Josie had three successful brothels in Roe Street. Her rise in the sex industry was rarely without incident, however.

In September 1919 she appeared in court after shots were fired at one of her brothels, Josie's Villa. Describing herself to police as a woman who lived apart from her husband, she gave evidence about the shooting. Early in the morning of 13 August, four men – returned soldiers – came calling at the brothel. Josie, using a peephole, formerly a letterbox, refused the men entry. As she backed away from the door under a torrent of threats, a revolver was pushed through the peephole and two shots were fired. Josie was shot in the elbow.

Esther Miller, one of her workers, who had been with de Bray moments before in the kitchen, gave evidence implicating four men in the violent attack. They'd had a wild night of racing about in cars and hopping from one pub to another. Three of the men were sentenced to three and four months in prison, while the shooter, Frederick

Bridges, was found guilty of unlawful wounding and grievous bodily harm. He was bundled off to Fremantle Prison to serve a three-year sentence.

Madame Monnier later moved her 'villa' to 222 Roe Street, a large purpose-built space. She ran a garage on the adjoining street that had a back entrance into her brothel. While business was good, it drew too much attention from the newspapers. Josie headed back to France in 1937, and one story has it that after her hometown was bombed by the Nazis during World War II Josie was captured by the Germans and became a prisoner of war. She returned to Perth in 1949 but her hold on the sex business had been lost. She died aged seventy-two four years later.

*

Though she missed meeting the infamous Madame Monnier, Dulcie made Roe Street a short-term home in 1946. At the time of her arrest as Dian Lee Bowen in June, Dulcie was living and working with a number of the brothel madams and their workers, including Marie Richardson, who was arrested at the same time. Marie's mother, Mary, had also been a local brothel identity. Known as 'Roughie', she had featured in a riot in Murray Street in 1900. Kathleen Maureen O'Hara and Millicent Elizabeth Burrows were also arrested with Dulcie in June 1946.

The reporters claimed on seeing 'Dian' that it looked like 'butter wouldn't melt in her mouth'. She had changed her name not only to avoid a connection being made with her long criminal record but also, as former Roe Street madam Joan St Louis pointed out in an interview some years later, because it was common practice for professional prostitutes to use aliases both in their work and when appearing in court. Some of Joan's 'girls' later left her brothel and became 'farmer's wives' – in such cases, an alias in the public record could help them disassociate themselves from their former work. In Dulcie's case, the name change was more likely in order to dodge gaol time based on her long record.

Dulcie knew that unless she used an alias the Perth police would know exactly who she was. Once they found her out, which happened soon after her arrest, she assured Magistrate Moseley she would be no more trouble: 'I'm going back – to where I come from!' She was fined five pounds for assisting to keep a house of ill-fame and bonded ten pounds for six months on a vagrancy charge. She returned to Sydney and then moved on to Melbourne.

Remarkably, little remains in the historic record about Dulcie's brush with the law in Perth. There is no mug shot in the *Police Gazette*, and only minor notes in the police records. Police detectives were swift in their arrest, and even swifter in moving Dulcie back east before any of her associates could also make the trip west.

Dulcie's notoriety was Australia-wide. She could change her name and try to give local detectives the slip, but her infamy and good looks singled her out anywhere she appeared. Back in the eastern states, Dulcie returned to the unfinished business awaiting her in Melbourne. Keith and Valma Hull were now living in St Kilda. In usual underworld fashion, despite his probable guilt, he had been acquitted of the murder of Dulcie's friend, Donald Day, and his wife had been implicated in the attack. Dulcie now set off for St Kilda to settle old scores.

CHAPTER 9

Shots in St Kilda

Revenge cuts both ways

Dulcie was a key player in the post-World War II world of Melbourne crime. In 1946 she moved into a cottage at 55 Fawkner Street, St Kilda, and the house became synonymous with underworld crime. It was a regular meeting place for some of the city's most ruthless and violent standover men involved in the sly-grogging, prostitution and gambling underworlds. It was also well known as Dulcie's place. The last time the house was sold, in February 2015, it was advertised as a 'Charming 2 bedroom workers cottage oozing with character'. It's the kind of place that when you know the history associated with it, you wish the walls could talk. Back when it was a worker's cottage, with very little of what is now called

St Kilda's 'bohemian lifestyle', it was home to a whole cast of notorious underworld crooks.

Dulcie was well known as an eastern Sydney criminal identity, but St Kilda also suited her lifestyle and personality. Her place in Fawkner Street was, during her criminal career, a regular residence. This is important, given the irregularity of Dulcie's home life in her younger years. Tracking her movements from the 1930s to the 1940s involves a long list of shifts from Sydney to Brisbane to Melbourne and back again.

In the nineteenth century, St Kilda was a wealthy area favoured by rich Melburnians, who built mansions down on the water to enjoy a seaside lifestyle. From 1912, the opening of Luna Park rapidly turned a seaside attraction into a popular tourist area. After World War II, St Kilda became home to many postwar immigrants won over by the opportunity to live the Australian dream: affordable housing close to the beach. The rich moved further out, leaving behind large houses rented out at low cost. Many of these were fitted out as gambling houses and brothels, and the area became a haven for Melbourne criminals. St Kilda's bohemian identity came later, when the wider area became attractive to artists and musicians.

In the late 1940s, when St Kilda was a hotbed of Melbourne crime, Dulcie fitted right in. She featured in a local St Kilda story that's still shared today. Fearsome and unforgiving, she was arrested after police came across her outside a hotel dressed only in her underwear. This wasn't the reason the police nabbed her. She was chasing a man with an axe. When the police arrested her, she haughtily explained, 'the bastard insulted me about the price'. Which, in Dulcie's eyes, meant she was completely within her right to chase him with an axe. Having defended herself through her many years of living and working in organised crime, and having had lovers stabbed and gunned down, it made perfect sense to Dulcie to use whatever means were necessary to deal with this latest grievance.

Dulcie's 55 Fawkner Street residence was like a halfway house for hired drivers and gunmen paid to intimidate the competition at rival gaming houses. By 1947, regular visitors included Dulcie's new lover, Ernest Alfred Martin, who lived at Punt Road, South Yarra, while his twin brother, Charles, moved into her place. Another of the major crime figures living in Fawkner Street was Norm Bradshaw, a gunman and extortionist. He worked for Freddie Harrison, who controlled a number of gambling houses. Harrison was gunned down at the South Wharf on the Melbourne waterfront in 1958.

Australian actor, director and writer Frank Howson grew up in the house next to this mass of criminal characters. As Frank recalls:

*Growing up in St. Kilda taught you to be tough,
alert and street wise. Sometimes your life depended
on it. Fawkner Street St. Kilda was a notorious and
sometimes dangerous shortcut to Luna Park. It
was a street I was brought home to as a baby in my
proud mother's arms. At that time it was also home
to some dangerous criminals such as the Shannons,
Norm Bradshaw and Pretty Dulcie. Growing up
in that street gave you a few interesting options in
life. You could either learn to be a gangster yourself,
or else, if you were of a more sensitive nature, you
could observe the human condition in all its most
glorious and contradictory terms. As a budding actor
or writer you were truly blessed by the abundance
of original characters that performed every day in
the street theatre outside your window. They could
ignite the curious spark in the fertile creative brain
of a lonely child.*

It was also perhaps more than a child should see or hear,
as Frank would find out in 1951 when shots rang out from
Dulcie's place.

Dulcie used the Fawkner Street house as her main centre
of business. She ran a sly-grog shop out the back of it too,
and offered a safe house for local crooks. Dulcie could
also look after herself and fight back, but underworld

intimidation was a feature of life in Fawkner Street. Norm Bradshaw was rumoured to have been involved in the shooting death of Leslie Walkerden. Now he was living in a house with Leslie's reputed former lover, Dulcie Markham. Dulcie, aware of how volatile underworld relationships could be, carefully navigated them for herself.

Other non-criminal locals also knew to keep their distance. Frank Howson remembers his father being confronted by underworld crook Norm Bradshaw. Frank's parents were woken one evening by raised voices outside their window. They sneaked a look through the blinds and saw Norm punch another man to the ground. As Norm walked away with a third man, the person on the ground said something to him he didn't like. Norm Bradshaw walked back to him and shot him dead. Frank Howson's father, knowing he would be a key witness, took some drastic steps to avoid this, knowing Bradshaw would come looking for him if he talked. Frank says:

> *My dad, being a quick thinker, instructed my mum*
> *to help him move the bed to the back of the house.*
> *He then moved the living room furniture up to the*
> *front room. When the police knocked on our door*
> *and questioned my father as to whether he'd seen*
> *or heard anything during the night, he replied in*
> *the negative, stating that, as the bedroom was at*

the back of the house, he hadn't heard a thing. The
police checked this out for themselves and then went
on their way.

Norm Bradshaw came knocking as predicted. He asked 'Jacky' Howson how he had been sleeping lately, his subtle way of asking whether he would tell police he had witnessed the shooting. Howson told him he had been sleeping like a baby and Bradshaw was satisfied: 'That's all I wanted to know, Jacky. Have a good day.'

The twin brothers Charles and Ernest Martin became embroiled in two attempted murder cases in 1947, both linked to Dulcie. Charles was living at the Fawkner Street house when he was arrested and charged with shooting Dulcie's old adversary Keith Kitchener Hull on the afternoon of 27 July 1947. As we have seen, Keith and his wife, Valma, had fled Sydney after he was acquitted of Donald Day's murder in 1945.

Keith Hull was shot half a mile from his Fitzroy Street home in St Kilda. Witnesses would later tell the police he was held at gunpoint in the cabin of his truck on Neptune Lane, only a short walk from Fawkner Street. Hull was shot twice and two gunmen absconded while their victim yelled for help. He staggered around the corner onto Robe Street and was taken to hospital by a man who was driving by. Remarkably, Hull survived the attack; one of the bullets narrowly missed his heart, grazed his ribs and came out of his chest. The other bullet hit him in the wrist.

It was soon revealed that Charles Martin and his mate, George Barrett, were with Keith Hull in the truck. They had been drinking and, as Keith Hull would testify in court, talking about Donald Day's death. Hull claimed their friendship had fallen apart because they believed he shot Day. The defence case rested on self-defence. Barrett claimed Hull was angry and pulled out a gun, Barrett made a grab for it and turned it away from himself, when the gun went off, firing the two shots. Barrett's counsel claimed he had seen Hull many times since Day's murder and 'had had ample opportunities to shoot him, if he had wanted to'. After a three-hour deliberation by the jury on 3 September, Martin and Barrett were acquitted of the attempted murder.

Charles Barrett didn't enjoy freedom for long. He was shot and killed by Joseph 'Joey' Turner on 28 November 1947. The coroner ruled that Turner had shot Barrett in self-defence. On the day of the shooting, Barrett had told a female friend he was going to get even with two men he had argued with. According to his girlfriend, Mavis Helen Miller, of Fawkner Street, the men, Joey Turner and Leslie Day (no relation to Donald), owed Barrett money. Mavis accompanied Barrett to Day's house in Collingwood, where Barrett threatened to shoot Day and ordered him into a taxi to visit Turner, telling him: 'I'm going to take you out to Coburg and shoot you.' The three of them got out of the taxi in Fitzroy and were joined by Day and another man, who was shot when he ran away. Joey Turner, fearing for his life during a scuffle with Barrett, grabbed the revolver and shot him. Turner told the Coroner's Court he fired at Barrett out of fear he would be kicked to death.

Soon after Keith Hull was shot, his wife, Valma, was threatened on 31 July. This time it was Charles's twin brother, Ernest, who was in trouble with the police. He was arrested along with his girlfriend, Dulcie, on 9 August.

Dulcie arrived at the City Court on Monday 11 August 1947 smartly dressed in a light-blue jacket and looking beautiful, according to the crime reporters. The evidence against her was less flattering. She was at the centre of allegations she had threatened to kill Valma Hull as payback for the murder of her friend, Donald Day. Ernest Martin also faced a trial later that month, with bail set at £300. Dulcie was again dressed for the part when facing trial on 23 August: all black, finished off with a silver fox fur.

Dulcie had allegedly turned up drunk to Valma's house on Fitzroy Street, St Kilda, on 31 July 1947. Journalist Ron Testro, who wrote a number of pieces about Melbourne's seedy streets, said Fitzroy Street was one of his favourites for its share of 'characters' and 'identities'.

He met 'the ladies of the shadows' – the streetwalkers plying their trade – and knew of Dulcie Markham. Testro was captivated by the 'real life stories' of 'drama, pathos, comedy, and even sometimes tragedy'.

Dulcie certainly added to the drama and tragedy in the area. On that July evening in 1947, she arrived in Fitzroy with her lover Ernest Martin, looking for Valma Hull. When Estelle McGregor, another resident in the house, answered the front door, Dulcie said she was there to see 'Judy' (i.e. Valma). After telling Dulcie that Valma wasn't at the house, Estelle walked back into the lounge room, where her mother and a friend, Eddie McLean, were seated. Intoxicated, excited and unsteady, Dulcie told Eddie that he 'would do'. He went off with her and Ernest, returning an hour later pale and shaken. His face was swollen and he looked as if he had been crying. Estelle McGregor's mother told the magistrate that she had heard Dulcie muttering something about 'bumping Judith off'.

Eddie McLean had known Dulcie and Ernest for about two years. In court, with the defendants closely watching him, Eddie said he had gone with the pair to Dulcie's house in Fawkner Street, where he stayed for about an hour. He denied nearly collapsing on his return. This evidence was contrary to information he had given the detectives.

For the first time, Dulcie wasn't the victim but the perpetrator of underworld intimidation and violence. This wasn't the case of a lover or husband being killed. Police alleged that when they questioned Ernest, he said Dulcie was a cocaine user who 'went mad' when she drank or took drugs. He also told them: 'She is mad, and likely to do anything.' He claimed he had only gone with Dulcie to make sure she 'wouldn't do anything'. Dulcie's lover was landing her in hot water and trying to distance himself from her as much as he could.

Dulcie presented a different picture to the police. Detective Cyril Currer said that when she was questioned at police headquarters about her intention to murder Valma Hull, Dulcie said: 'I have been unlucky! Every man I have lived with either gets picked up for shooting or has been shot himself.'

With no hard evidence of them planning to murder Valma and the main witness refusing to admit much in court, Dulcie and Ernest were acquitted. They returned to the Fawkner Street house, but there wasn't a great deal for Dulcie to celebrate. Her life was becoming ever more erratic, and her safety was a concern to the police. If Ernest Martin was willing to turn on her, what else was he capable of?

In December 1947, Dulcie was a passenger in a taxi when it careered off the road not far from her place in Fawkner Street, mounted a footpath and came to a stop after hitting a fence. Rushed to the Alfred Hospital with a fractured pelvis, Dulcie refused treatment and signed off on that at her own risk. If Dulcie was injured as an innocent passenger in the crash, why had she refused treatment?

On cocaine and drinking to excess by now, Dulcie dodged serious charges in 1947, but was clearly linked to some of the most violent men in Melbourne crime. In order to stay alive, Dulcie had to negotiate her relationships with these underworld figures carefully. It didn't help matters that her lovers were often rivals, not only for her affection but for control of the mainstays of the criminal business at the time. It was a murky world of illicit booze, illegal betting houses, prostitution and drugs, and Fawkner Street was at the centre of it all.

By the end of the 1940s, Dulcie was no longer in a relationship with Ernest Martin, and Charles had moved out of Fawkner Street. Dulcie continued to feature in police raids on the street though. She was charged with various offences through 1950 and 1951, including 'accosting for prostitution', offensive behaviour and using insulting words.

*

In July 1951 Dulcie was charged with theft and appeared in court alongside two other people who were living with her at Fawkner Street – twenty-eight-year-old Millicent

Markham and forty-six-year-old George Collins (also referred to as George McKay). They identified as Dulcie's brother and sister. Dulcie's younger sister, Florence Ena, was thirty-one at the time. She could have been giving a different age and using her mother's name as an alias, but there's no definitive evidence to support this.

Millicent Markham popped up again in 1954, charged with keeping a house of ill-fame in Melbourne. She appealed the conviction and this was upheld. Millicent's photograph appeared in a *Truth* Sydney article on women who were the 'shame of Sydney' in 1954. They were predominantly sex workers and brothel-owners. Millicent was said to have made 130 court appearances. If Millicent was indeed another sister to Dulcie, she was giving her older sibling a run for her money with the number of charges placed against her.

Who was George Collins? He was nine years older than thirty-seven-year-old Dulcie, meaning Florence Parker, Dulcie's mother, would have to have been ten when he was born. Had Dulcie's mother remarried and was George a child from her new husband's previous relationship? Or was he Millicent's husband and thus Dulcie's brother-in-law? Or was Dulcie simply claiming that Millicent and George were family to try to convince the magistrate they were just family living together and the house wasn't a notorious spot for gambling, prostitution and sly grog?

In the end, the case was dismissed on the grounds of insufficient evidence of possession of stolen goods.

The sister we do know about, Florence Ena, married Albert George Pennington in Sydney in 1937 when she was sixteen years old, having already given birth to Albert's daughter the year before. At almost the same age her older sister ran away from home, Florence had fallen pregnant and married the father of her child. She may have been pressured into getting married by her mother, or herself feared the social implications of bringing up an 'illegitimate' child. Florence herself was 'illegitimate', as her birth certificate attests. When Florence later remarried, this time to Oliver Gale in 1946, she was said to be working as a waitress and living in Surry Hills. Oliver Gale died in 1950 in Warren near Dubbo, New South Wales, and in 1952, Florence married Percy Reeves in Warren. Florence could well have been in Melbourne with Dulcie in 1950 and 1951, but she was also the mother of five children ranging in ages from fourteen to eight. This would made it hard for her to move around and find her children a place with their aunt in St Kilda. Police would also have been likely to mention a number of children living at Dulcie's place, which was quite small. It seems unlikely, then, that Millicent Markham was Dulcie's younger sister, Florence.

*

The worst of the violence was not over for Dulcie in 1951. Brothers Desmond and Gavan Walsh started frequenting the Fawkner Street house, and twenty-two-year-old Gavan became Dulcie's new lover. The Walsh brothers, especially Gavan, were known about Melbourne's boxing scene, but they had become embroiled in standover work, and both crossed rivals in the business. Desmond's criminal record was mainly for what he called 'smash and grab' robbery jobs.

On 25 September 1951, Dulcie was shot while lying in her bed in the front room of her Fawkner Street house, where she and the Walsh brothers had allegedly been partying with booze and cocaine earlier on. Desmond Walsh, who was living with Dulcie at the time, finished work around three that afternoon and went to the Prince Charles Hotel (now the Hotel Barkly) on the corner of Fawkner Street for a drink. Dulcie was at the pub, and they had at least half a dozen drinks together over another hour or so before going back home.

Gavan appeared at Dulcie's place after six with a bottle of brandy, and the three of them continued drinking in the front bedroom. Dulcie was lying on the bed when there was a knock at the front door. A Charles Mills was let into the house, where he joined in drinking with the Walsh brothers. Charles started accusing the brothers of being up to something and said someone was looking for them. The brothers agreed to front the man, after which Charles went out then knocked again on the front door. Dulcie was still on the bed.

When Gavan Walsh answered the door, three shots rang out. Shot in the stomach, Gavan staggered back into the bedroom and fell down near the wardrobe, holding himself. Desmond Walsh would later testify that the man with the gun, Dulcie's former lover Ernest Martin, stood over Gavan and shot him again. Two more shots rang out and Dulcie was hit where she lay on the bed. Medical practitioners would later testify that she had three wounds in her left leg. She fell to the floor with a shattered femur and lay under the window, also near the wardrobe. Desmond confronted Martin and as he reached for the gun was shot in the hand. He scrambled under the bed and started yelling. Martin and Mills raced out of the house when a car pulled up outside.

Dulcie's neighbour Frank Howson, then a young lad, remembers the night these men burst into Dulcie's house and began shooting. Stray bullets came through the wall near where the Howson family were having dinner.

Badly wounded in the hip, Dulcie lay bloodied on the floor with her lover, Gavan, who was close to death. All three of the victims were rushed by ambulance to the Alfred Hospital, where Gavan Walsh died around 1.30 the next morning. Desmond received treatment and later that morning was taken to the City Watchhouse, where he identified Martin and Mills. Charles Mills had come to the hospital to give Desmond some cigarettes and check on Dulcie. Dulcie Markham's friend, Phyllis Rose Doran, also visited her in hospital. She had been drinking with Charles Mills and other men that day. In her deposition to the coroner, Phyllis repeatedly referred to Dulcie as 'Pretty Dulcie'.

Coroner James Burke ruled that Charles Mills and Ernest Martin (called Alfred Martin in court) had murdered Gavan Walsh, and directed that they stand trial in November. Sensationally, Dulcie was wheeled into the courtroom for the trial on a stretcher. Press photographers snapped her being taken out of the ambulance on the stretcher, covered in a tartan blanket, her eyes closed, holding what looks to be a packet of cigarettes. As the pained victim of a shooting, it was an even more dramatic entrance into a courtroom than her other appearances.

Dulcie testified from the stretcher, claiming not to have seen 'the man who shot me'. Yet while Dulcie was still unwilling to break the underworld code of silence, she told the magistrate: 'I am not going to forgive anybody, and I am not going to cover anybody.'

With no evidence to corroborate Desmond Walsh's claims that Alfred Martin had shot Gavan Walsh, and Dulcie failing to identify either Martin or Mills as having been at the house, the prosecution case fell apart. The magistrate was frustrated by the underworld code of silence and determination to simply 'cop it sweet', keep away from the police and get revenge when the time was right. The jury found Martin and Mills not guilty and they were acquitted.

One underworld figure told newspaper journalists that Dulcie had in fact been brought down from Brisbane to befriend the Walsh brothers in St Kilda so that Gavan Walsh could be dealt with. It's a stunning claim, with nothing in the archival records to support it, but it certainly added to Dulcie's notoriety at the time.

Still in pain and recovering from her shattered hip, Dulcie wed for the second time in December 1951. Leonard 'Redda' Lewis was a sly-grogger and gambler, known to police in Melbourne and Sydney. Sensationally, the pair posed for press photographers from Dulcie's bed where, due to her hip injuries, they had been married. Propped up by Redda and with her hip encased in plaster, Dulcie smiled for the photographers while the reporters later told the story of how police had raided the house of the newlyweds only hours after their nuptials. *Truth* Sydney reported:

The ceremony was held in the small weatherboard home where she was maimed, and where former boxer Gavan Walsh was slain by the gunman on the same occasion. There were about 25 guests, and more than 100 onlookers. The Rev. Perkins, a Church of England minister, officiated. During the wedding, detectives mingled with the crowd. 'Pretty Dulcie,' who has been referred to in court as 'The Angel of Death' – because many friends have met violent ends – told Truth: 'I am very happy.' Redda Lewis, who has nursed Dulcie since she was wounded, said: 'I have married her for life and love. 'I will keep her O.K. No police will touch her any longer.'

The newspaper also used the wedding as an opportunity to rake over Dulcie's history:

Dulcie was married to gunman Frank Bowen, who was shot dead at King's Cross in 1940. Dulcie, whose real name [sic] is Mary Eugene, made her debut in the Sydney underworld at 15. She was tall and slim, with baby blue eyes and a perfect figure. One of her friends, Guido Calleti [sic], gunman, was shot dead in a Darlinghurst boardinghouse in 1939. With a weeping Dulcie at the grave, it was the biggest underworld funeral in Australia. More than 5000 people filed past his body in the mortuary.

After this evening's ceremony, the guests began a party.

Crime reporter Bill Jenkings later recalled that the best man sang 'You Always Hurt the One You Love' at the wedding. Was this interesting choice of wedding song a reflection on Dulcie and Redda's relationship? Had Redda been a part of the Fawkner Street shooting out of jealousy? Perhaps it indicated an already volatile relationship.

Redda was no different from any of Dulcie's other lovers and husbands. Her type was always obvious: he was a man wanted by both the police and crooks of Melbourne. It's difficult to think of Dulcie having the opportunity to meet a man who was not associated with crime in Brisbane, Sydney or Melbourne. These were the circles she moved in, and her partners offered the protection she needed. They were violent standover gunmen.

The couple moved to Sydney after their wedding, where Dulcie was promptly arrested for vagrancy by NSW police officers and spent seven days in prison. Redda was also imprisoned, for consorting with a criminal – no matter that she was now his wife. It was a rough welcome-home present for Dulcie, and the couple were soon back in St Kilda.

CHAPTER 10

'I've had enough'

A slow change of heart

One day early in the 1950s, Dulcie Lewis was sitting outside one of St Kilda's roughest pubs, the Prince Charles. It was the kind of place where even the most dedicated, regular drinkers only went if they absolutely had to. Dulcie didn't have far to go to get to the pub from her house a few doors down on Fawkner Street. With her leg in a cast, propped up on a chair, she enjoyed being waited on with beer by her various male admirers. The cast on her leg was a tell-tale sign for the locals of her violent lifestyle.

A young Brian Matthews, local resident and future writer, stared at Dulcie with one of his childhood mates by his side. They knew who she was. Everyone did. According to Brian, she was the most famous resident of St Kilda's Fawkner

Street. Though she had been shot in the hip only a month before, the boys knew 'Pretty Dulcie Markham' was not someone to mess with. She had become a local identity with her blonde hair, good looks – though they were starting to show the wear and tear of her life – and no-nonsense attitude. Dulcie caught sight of the boys ogling her and engaged them in true Dulcie fashion. Years of living a rough, violent life had made her brutally honest and in need of her own space sometimes. She told Brian and his mate to fuck off.

In January 1952, Dulcie was apprehended by a detective for using indecent language at this very location. Detective Keith Stafford told the court the following month, in Dulcie's absence, that she had been abusing people from her wheelchair while being 'propelled around St Kilda' and outside the Prince Charles Hotel. When he told her to stop it, she used an expression that the detective wrote down on a piece of paper and passed to the bench, clearly believing it too offensive to be said aloud in the court. When Stafford told her not to use such language, she replied with another 'indecent expression'. Dulcie was fined (and would spend fourteen days in prison if she didn't pay).

Back in Sydney three months later, Dulcie spoke with newspaper reporters in her Surry Hills home: 'I've had enough, don't want to be involved in any more shootings.' After more than twenty years of living and working in prostitution and being associated with organised crime,

Dulcie was ready to give it all up. She finally wanted a quiet life away from the newspaper headlines – though she was effectively creating one with the interviews – and was looking to retire. She was only thirty-eight years old. It's hard to believe she wasn't much older, considering all she had experienced.

Though a part of her really did want to be free of underworld life, she found it difficult to disentangle herself entirely. She might not want to be involved in any more shootings, but that didn't mean she was giving up prostitution. She was still married to Redda Lewis, and he enjoyed the benefits of his wife's sex work. Dulcie did not attract husbands who were upstanding members of the community with a decent job and uncompromised by crime. Regardless of whether her lovers supported her work, they had always been associated with organised crime groups and gangs. Breaking this mould would be the test of Dulcie's life.

Her announcement to the press came after a violent row in Melbourne two months beforehand, a story that made the newspapers:

WOMAN HURT IN FIGHT

*Mrs. Dulcie Lewis, 32, of Fawkner st., St. Kilda –
formerly Dulcie Markham – was admitted to Alfred
Hospital after a brawl on Saturday night. Wireless*

patrol police, called to her home by neighbors,
found the front bedroom in disorder. Three men,
including Mr. Lewis, and two women were in the
house. Mrs. Lewis was in a neighbor's house. Both
her eyes had been blackened, and her face was
extensively bruised.

Mrs. Lewis, known throughout St. Kilda as
'Pretty Dulcie,' was crippled in a triple shooting on
September 25, when a young boxer was murdered.
She was married on December 8 to Leonard Lewis,
33, in the front bedroom of her home where the
shooting occurred.

The Fawkner Street brawl had been followed by a violent attack on Dulcie's husband, Redda, on 23 April. He was shot in the stomach outside his parents' home in Melbourne. By then, the couple were living back in Sydney, and he had come south alone, leaving behind Dulcie, who was still on crutches from the bullet wound to her hip. Police were sent to guard the house, and a young constable was wounded in a drive-by shooting only hours after Lewis was shot.

After that, the police were out in force, not for Redda's protection but because one of their own had been shot. Homicide and consorting detectives questioned close to a hundred people in their search for the gunman. They were continually frustrated by what the police described to the newspapers as a 'wall of silence and denial'.

Redda was admitted to the Alfred Hospital, and journalists in Sydney rushed to get a statement from Dulcie. She told the *Sun* reporters, who were among the first to talk to her, she couldn't understand why her husband had been targeted, and said she had 'no men friends who could be jealous of "Redda," and I don't know any woman who might be jealous of our marriage'. Craftily, she made no mention of any criminal business being the cause of the shooting. In an interesting side note, Dulcie adds that she is frustrated that 'every time something like this happens' she has to move her ten-year-old daughter to a new school.

In yet another perfectly staged scene, replete with Dulcie at her most dramatic, she soon became frustrated by the media attention. When more 'press-men' tried to interview her, she poured drinks for herself and the two female friends with her and said to the reporters: 'So you've found me, you mongrels.' Not wanting to tell them anything further, she yelled: 'I'm still here and not in Melbourne, so —— well blow through. Get to hell out of it.' Dulcie got up with the aid of her crutches and chased the men out of her house. She hit a reporter in the back but, still unsteady on her feet, promptly fell over.

Within half an hour of Redda Lewis's release from hospital in Melbourne on 2 May, he was arrested for warrants issued for unpaid fines. Redda Lewis had cockily told reporters on his wedding day the previous December that the police would no longer be able to bother Dulcie. He would look after her. He was wrong. While Redda was still hospitalised, the police swooped on Dulcie. She had blabbed to the press and they knew she was back in Sydney.

Detectives from the CIB Consorting Squad raided Dulcie's Surry Hills home the same day as her April interview appeared in the paper. She was taken to Central Police Station before being transferred to serve six months at Long Bay Prison for a previous consorting charge.

Dulcie's police mug shot from May 1952 is telling. It reveals the toll that her underworld life had taken. Dressed in a two-piece skirt suit and blouse, her hair softly brushed in a part to the right side, she looks tired, particularly in the eyes. She is using a crutch to prop herself up and be measured against the height chart. She was still in pain from the shooting only months before, and the crutch is an obvious sign of her crippled body.

When she was released from Long Bay Prison, Dulcie continued with her old associations and work in Sydney. She pleaded guilty to a consorting charge in November 1952 (relating to her 'consorting with reputed criminals between September 11 and October 12'). Detective Brooks from the CIB stated that he had seen Dulcie with known criminal Leonard Lewis. Dulcie's solicitor contested this, pointing out that they were married. Dulcie's arrest, however, also related to her associations with other reputed criminals, Stuart Davis and Elizabeth Lee. Dulcie claimed she was to be matron of honour at Stuart and Elizabeth's wedding and had been with them to arrange the ceremony. The magistrate was unimpressed and sentenced Dulcie to seven days in prison, telling her she had been warned about associating with the couple.

Her limp hadn't stopped Dulcie from looking for business on the streets and continuing in her usual line of work. She was arrested in June 1953 for consorting. The charge was recorded alongside a brief description of her as a 'known prostitute' who would 'solicit for immoral purpose'. Dulcie was sentenced to three hours in the police cells. Between September 1952 and August 1953, Dulcie was convicted on thirty-one occasions for offensive behaviour. She hadn't quite 'had enough' yet.

Redda was busy too. In June 1953, a year after he was first shot, he was shot again, this time in the spine while walking along Spencer Street in West Melbourne. The bullet was successfully removed, but when police asked Redda who had shot him, his memory failed him again and he couldn't identify the shooter.

The Lewis marriage had fallen apart by 1954, by which time Dulcie was calling herself Dulcie Johnson, after her lover, Neil Johnson, a low-level crook outside his legal work as a labourer. A wedding conducted with the bride in a plaster cast after a fatal underworld shooting was probably never destined for longevity. Dulcie had been looking for a quieter life when she settled back into her hometown. Sydney's organised crime scene was also changing by the 1950s, shifting towards new crime leaders. The great matriarchs of underworld crime, Kate Leigh and Tilly Devine, were headed towards bankruptcy and lonely lives tucked away from the public.

*

Kate Leigh had married unsuccessfully for the third and last time in 1950, flying all the way over to Fremantle to wed her old mate from her early days in Surry Hills, Ernest 'Shiner' Ryan. He was one of Australia's most notorious crooks, with a long list of convictions for theft, assault, robbery and shooting a police officer. He was also a gaolbreak and an expert lock-pick. After his last stint inside, this time in Fremantle Prison in the 1940s, he was determined to win over Kate Leigh and have her marry him. But their dramatic love affair, reported across all the leading newspapers in the country, was short-lived. Shiner ran away on their car trip back to Sydney and lived out his last years close to poverty in South Fremantle, a much-admired local. When Shiner died in 1957 at the age of seventy-one, the Mayor of Fremantle served as a pallbearer at his funeral. Though she was embittered by their marriage break-up only a few years before, Kate Leigh was sentimental about her 'Ernie'. She told the Perth *Mirror* editor Frank Davidson that Ryan's 'brain was in his fingertips'.

Pleading bankruptcy in the courts in the 1950s, Kate Leigh claimed the 'bloom' had gone off sly grog and she was relying on the charity of family and friends. The Taxation Office took anything that was left and Kate carried on, almost reclusively, living in her Devonshire Street house in Surry Hills, letting rooms out to renters to pay the bills. She died of a massive stroke in 1964, one month short of her eighty-third birthday.

Tilly Devine lived longer, though she was also brought down by the Taxation Office. Frail in her later years, she never felt completely accepted in eastern Sydney as Kate seemed to have been. When she died in November 1970, one patron at the Tradesman's Arms (now the East Village Hotel) in Surry Hills proposed a toast, remembering it as one of Tilly's favourite drinking spots. No one else lifted a glass. In direct contrast to police descriptions of Kate Leigh on her death, Police Commissioner Norman Allan described Tilly as a 'villain'. Ron Saw, writing for the *Daily Telegraph*, labelled her a 'vicious, grasping, high-priestess of savagery, venery, obscenity and whoredom'. For Saw, the former rascal Kate Leigh was 'a kindly and generous old trot with many friends', while Tilly Devine was a 'wretched woman' missed by no one. Leigh was eulogised as a woman who, despite her years of crime, did all she could for her community. Kate Leigh's Australian background aided her local appeal in a way London-born Tilly could never match.

Worn down by their rough lives, the former brothel and booze madams still outlived Dulcie's old rival, the beautiful Nellie Cameron. She once told policewoman Lillian Armfield, 'I've got so many bullets in me I rattle when I walk, and I'm satisfied no bullet will ever kill me.' Like Dulcie, she attracted violent, ruthless, and sometimes opportunistic crooks who enjoyed what Armfield described as Nellie's 'air of rather disdainful nonchalance, and she continued to queen it over men'.

A month before Dulcie was telling reporters she wanted nothing more to do with the underworld, Nellie Cameron was shot in the stomach by her lover of the time. She survived the attack but it launched her further into depression. The former runaway who had taken up prostitution aged sixteen and survived the most violent years of the Razor Wars was now a recluse and tired out. The following year, in November 1953, she placed her head inside the oven in her Taylor Square apartment in

Darlinghurst and turned on the gas. She was just forty-one years old. In one of the many obituaries and reports of her death in newspapers across the country, Nellie was described as 'one of the Sydney underworld's "fabulous characters" '.

With all the 'pomp and ceremony of a national celebrity', Cameron was taken into the chapel in Darlinghurst in a rose-covered coffin. Her former boss, Tilly Devine, wept for one of her favourites, but Lillian Armfield thought the service too dignified: 'Nellie would have been happy if there had been a brawl at her funeral, a real ding-dong affair in which a few would have been wiped out. That's the sort of funeral Nellie would have liked for herself.'

*

The crime scene in the early 1950s, was very different from the one Dulcie had entered at the end of the Roaring Twenties. The Australian criminal underworlds were now dominated by clubs and drugs. Prostitution was still a part of this outfit, but the brothel madams of old were ageing and frail. They couldn't command the same power they had done back at the height of the Razor Wars.

In this postwar world – a reconstruction period as the governments were calling it – Dulcie was at a crossroads. She could stay in the criminal scene she had occupied since she was a teenager, or she could start to move into an early retirement. One thing was clear: she wasn't taking Redda with her.

After Redda was shot and survived in 1953, they started living apart. By 1954, Redda was living in Hobart, away from his standard criminal associations in Melbourne and Sydney, and spent time in prison early that year. In July 1954, he was arrested again after he struck a man over the head with a bottle in a Hobart pub. He was described in the local press as a 'notorious inter-state criminal', and an 'associate' of 'Sydney underworld woman "Pretty" Dulcie Markham'. Despite pleading not guilty and launching an appeal against the sentence, Redda Lewis was imprisoned for three months.

Dulcie also faced police pressure, with criminal charges early in 1954. In January she pleaded guilty to possessing a pistol. She was now living with Neil Johnson in a flat in Lang Road, Centennial Park. Detectives from the Vice Squad had followed Dulcie and Neil back there a little after midnight on 20 November 1953. When questioning the pair, they found an unloaded pistol. Both were charged with possession of the pistol, but Dulcie later provided the police with a written statement:

About three months ago I heard that 'Redda'
Lewis, my husband, was coming to Sydney from

Melbourne to cause me trouble. I heard that he
would be in possession of a revolver so I decided to
get a revolver myself as I was frightened of him. I
bought the revolver off someone I know and I took
it to my flat in Centennial Park. The revolver was
not loaded and I did not have any bullets for it. I put
the revolver in an old pair of pants belonging to Neil
Johnson which were hanging behind a door in the
flat. He knew nothing about the revolver.

The charges against Neil Johnson were dropped but Dulcie was convicted and fined. Had Dulcie said the pistol was hers to protect Neil? It's possible, or he could have threatened her so she would say the gun was hers. Intimidation from a whole host of underworld figures had been a normalised part of Dulcie's life for many years now. It is telling, however, that Dulcie mentioned her ex-husband, Redda. Dulcie could well have been scared and arming herself as protection. She and Redda hadn't divorced and now she was seeing another man. His jealousy might have led him to seek revenge.

The following month, February 1954, Dulcie was charged with providing false information on an application for a driver's licence. She didn't turn up at the Traffic Court to hear the evidence and decision. The newspaper reporters claimed the police 'threw the book at her' for giving false details. She had used a new alias, calling herself Dulcie Johnson, and on the application for the licence 'forgot' about her previous convictions for drunkenness and driving without a licence. She had already lost her licence twice, once for a year. Constable Smith of Darlinghurst Police Station gave evidence that she was a woman of many aliases and had used the name Dulcie Johnson to throw police off the search for her real identity. Her police record covered three foolscap pages. When questioned about the false information she gave – not admitting the previous licensing suspensions – Dulcie told the constable, 'I thought that meant if your licence was suspended at the present time.' She was fined and disqualified from holding a licence for more than two years.

Dulcie's relationship with Neil Johnson didn't last either, and the underworld threats continued. She moved to a flat in Bondi, but the intimidation followed her there. She faced death once more in January 1955.

CHAPTER 11

A 'model housewife'

A quiet life and a dramatic end

There were many moments in Dulcie's life when she felt directly threatened by the underworld violence that reigned over so much of the crime business in Brisbane, Sydney and Melbourne. She had already suffered the loss of lovers and husbands, and survived the Fawkner Street shooting that crippled her for the rest of her life, but in 1955 an even more serious incident occurred. The underworld code of silence, to which she had adhered for many years, had always been maintained by violence that could be fatal, as Dulcie well knew. Her own intimidation now reached a crisis point.

Dulcie was found in excruciating pain inside the Bondi flats on 11 January 1955. Neighbours called the police after hearing an altercation and Dulcie screaming soon after. Speculation was rife that Dulcie had been thrown from the window of her top-floor flat. Reporters scrambled to talk to neighbours and verify the rumours, but they, like Dulcie, kept quiet. Dulcie told the police she had fallen down the stairs. She was rushed to St Vincent's Hospital and treated for broken ribs, a pierced lung and other injuries.

From an oxygen tent in hospital, Dulcie told reporters she hadn't been thrown out of the window and that the story was 'rubbish'. She said, turning to one reporter, 'There's nothing to it, dear. I simply rolled down a flight of stairs. I'm a very sick girl, but don't worry about me, honey, I'll come good.'

But the police and newspaper reporters were having none of it. Perth's *Mirror* reported Dulcie's dramatic catalogue of underworld experiences, alongside the question: 'Did she fall – or was she pushed?' Frank Davidson, the *Mirror* editor, was in regular contact with leading underworld figures in order to obtain the best possible story for his readers. These included Kate Leigh, who, like so many others in the underworld, would have heard various details about what actually happened.

According to *The Mirror*, doctors and detectives at the hospital with Dulcie were not buying her story. Her injuries were clearly far worse than could be sustained from falling down the stairs: 'They think that she was overpowered, thrown more than 20 feet over a balcony to the concrete below.' It's remarkable Dulcie survived.

Detectives speculated that Dulcie's 'accident' might have been the result of an underworld feud or the handiwork of a jilted lover, as had happened in the past, though the violence had usually been inflicted on the male competitors for her attention. Dulcie had heard and seen a lot of things in her many years of associating with and providing business for Sydney's criminal identities. Had she threatened to go the police? Did she see something she shouldn't have? Was it an underworld job?

In a 2011 interview for an oral history project, Joe Shaw, a former child migrant and Melbourne local, talked about growing up in a Melbourne orphanage, and the many boxing and criminal identities he came to know there. Many of them ran with the local gangs and knew Dulcie Markham when she was in Melbourne. Of 'Pretty Dulcie' he said, 'the gangs got her and threw her off a two-storey building at one stage and she still didn't squeal'. Dulcie's fall in Bondi may well have involved the Melbourne underworld catching up with her in Sydney.

Sydney's sex workers feared underworld violence but they also faced retribution from corrupt police officers. Dulcie's perilous position brings to mind the tragic death of thirty-one-year-old Sydney prostitute Sallie-Anne Huckstepp. The mother of a teenage daughter, she was found dead in Busbys Pond in 1986 by a morning walker in Centennial Park. She had been strangled and then drowned. She was known heroin addict who associated with leading crime figures and had links to a number of corrupt police officers, and her whistleblowing was instrumental in the launching of the 1981 Wood Royal Commission into corruption in the NSW Police Force. The inquest into Sallie-Anne Huckstepp's death lasted nineteen days but these were spread over a long period, from 1987 to 1991. At the time of her death, she was having an affair with federal police officer Peter Parker Smith. He told the inquest that Sallie-Anne was afraid she would be murdered by criminals Neddy Smith or David Kelleher, or by notorious NSW detective Roger Rogerson, who is now serving a life sentence for the 2014 murder of Sydney student Jamie Gao. The inquest found Sallie-Anne Huckstepp was killed by a person or persons unknown.

Despite Dulcie's public show of calm and control, the 1955 Bondi incident affected her deeply. She appeared in court for the last time in 1957, on a charge of soliciting and having no lawful means of support. Crime reporter Bill Jenkings wrote that although her once 'glamorous looks had faded', she could still create a sensation. She told the magistrate she had sold 'the last of her jewels and furs to survive'. When that same magistrate asked Vice Squad detective Frank 'Bumper' Farrell, a legend of the

NSW Police Force and long-standing member of the Vice Squad, if Dulcie would 'mend her ways', Bumper said she was 'past redemption'.

Left to sit in a cell below the court – to think over her situation, according to the magistrate – Dulcie concluded that she had finally had enough, for real this time. The old scene wasn't the same any more. Dulcie was still young enough for sex work, but she wasn't the favourite she had been in those early years. By the middle of the 1950s, her youthful beauty was fading and she was hindered in her work by her limp – and her fall two years earlier hadn't helped.

And so in 1957, Dulcie ended her years spent moving from city to city, sometimes on the run from the police or other crooks in the business. The Australian underworld's prettiest prostitute and deadliest underworld lover retired from the sex business. Dulcie stayed in Bondi, not far from where she had lived as a child, spending her free time on Sydney's beaches. The female police officers had tried to encourage a change of lifestyle back in the 1930s, but Dulcie hadn't been ready for it then. Nearly thirty years later, it really looked like she was finally going to settle down.

Dulcie's reputation followed her into Bondi, and the fall from the flats had only added to her infamy – fellow local Bill Jenkings now called her 'Bondi's Angel of Death'. Jenkings had come to know Dulcie well over the years in his work as a crime reporter. Looking back on his career, he recalled her as a 'tall, slim, striking blonde, a true *femme fatale*'. In a court appearance in 1955, waving to him as she went in, the forty-one-year-old Dulcie still caught Bill's eye. She was, in Bill's words, 'stylishly dressed in a mauve frock' and made an entrance 'like the return of a celebrity'.

Bill and Dulcie would chat outside courtrooms, but he knew to keep his distance too. She had a fearsome reputation, for very good reason, as all crime reporters knew. One of these chats, at Sydney's Central Court, stood out for Bill. Dulcie watched two fair-haired schoolgirls as they walked past, and said to Bill: 'Look at them, ain't they angels?' Bill, intrigued that this 'Angel of Death' would say such a thing, looked a little more kindly at Dulcie. He told her: 'Perhaps you looked like them when you were their age. Maybe you looked like a little angel.' More than once, Dulcie revealed this softer side to Bill in her more candid moments: 'I watched her deteriorate over the years, but every once in a while you'd see a flash of softness shine through her hardened countenance. "You know, Bill," she once said to me, "I love kids. You've got a family haven't you? You're lucky." '

This reflective moment also brings Dulcie's daughter to mind. Had she put her into care? Given her to family? There are only two mentions of a child in court proceedings, the last when that child was ten.

Dulcie's early retirement was also born out of fear. She had weathered more violence than any other woman in the underworld, but now she feared it might actually take her life. The brothel business and streetwalking were changing around her, and the escalation in police crackdowns had made it harder for her to live well off the business. Brisbane's city brothels were finally closed down in 1959, pushing sex workers onto the streets and into setting up 'massage parlours'. These were still open to police extortion. Sex workers in Melbourne faced harsher conditions, with gaol time now preferred over fines. Police raids on brothels in St Kilda also brought down some in the business, and streetwalkers were increasingly being reported on by residents who'd had enough. In Sydney, prostitutes were still being regularly fined for soliciting, but it was said they could get out of it by bribing certain police officers.

She might have retired from prostitution, but Dulcie's illegal activities were not yet through. She appeared in a special Federal Court hearing in January 1959, charged with not having filed a tax return in 1957. Like Kate Leigh and Tilly Devine before her, Dulcie was found guilty and fined.

Dulcie's father, John Markham, died on 2 January 1963 in Dunwich, Queensland, aged seventy. He might have been one of the reasons Dulcie made a number of trips to

Brisbane around this time, perhaps hoping to reunite with her father. Maybe she did.

Sometime around the early 1970s, Dulcie fell in love with Sydney sailor Martin Rooney. The match surprised Bill Jenkings, but he was pleased to see Dulcie finally marry a 'law-abiding man' in 1972. According to Bill, they were a 'loving couple', and Dulcie enjoyed being a 'model housewife'. Dulcie's life had come full circle. Now living at 12 Moore Street, Bondi, she was only a few streets away from being a Waverley girl once more, and a mere six-minute walk from her childhood home.

Death had one more important roll of the dice. On the evening of 20 April 1976, Dulcie went to bed, leaving Martin to clean up and feed the dog. A little after ten, he smelled smoke and rushed up to find the front bedroom 'ablaze', as he later described it. Dulcie did not make it out of the room alive. Her death certificate records the cause of death as: 'Burns suffered there and then when a fire accidentally broke out in the front bedroom of that residence when she was smoking in bed.' In a tragic twist of fate, the beautiful woman of three underworlds across Brisbane, Sydney and Melbourne, was left unrecognisable.

The teenager who ran away to the streets of eastern Sydney and survived when so many of her lovers and husbands did not, some of them dying right next to her, was finally taken down not by underworld violence, but a fire in her bedroom. She had outlived crime bosses Kate Leigh and Tilly Devine, and Lillian Armfield, the policewoman who had watched her grow into the sensationalised 'Angel of Death'. But Dulcie was younger than all three of them. She was sixty-two.

The funeral was held on 27 April at St Patrick's Catholic Church, Bondi. Dulcie was cremated and a memorial placed in the Round Rose Garden at Eastern Suburbs Memorial Park, Matraville. Bumper Farrell, who gave the eulogy, was quoted in the *Sydney Morning Herald* as saying: 'There will never be another like her. She ran with a hard bunch and she was a hard woman.'

Bumper Farrell had developed an interesting relationship with Dulcie in her younger years. He often used her notoriety to full effect in his police work, and to show at least one new recruit what it was like to police prostitutes. The constable, who had grown up in the bush and was unfamiliar with eastern Sydney, though he knew of its notoriety, was taking part in a clean-up of the brothels along Palmer Street, Darlinghurst. Bumper Farrell raided one of the brothels and told a number of prostitutes to go outside and get in the police truck, an old Ford ute with the top cut off. As the constable jumped in first so he could help the women in, Bumper had a word with one of the women and asked her to go to the young constable. She promptly did so and, as he helped her into the truck, grabbed his penis through his trousers and squeezed hard. Wracked with pain and hearing the laughs from locals who had gathered nearby, the police officer realised Dulcie Markham had been put up to it by Bumper.

In her final years, Mrs Dulcie Rooney was a different woman. Distraught and speaking to reporters after her death, her husband Martin said: 'I loved the woman. She was marvellous … For four years we lived happily married.' He asked for her to be remembered as Dulcie Rooney, because both of them wanted to 'forget the past'.

It was true, as Bumper Farrell said, that 'she lived a violent life', and her own death was violent in its ferocity, if not its intent. Given the company she kept and that she lived and worked through some of the most dangerous years of Australian crime, it's remarkable that Dulcie had survived so long. Her lovers and all but one of her husbands didn't make it past their thirties. Had Sergeant Lillian Armfield still been alive, she would no doubt have been surprised. The once 'incorrigible' Dulcie Markham left behind a quiet, domestic life and a grieving husband. She died as Dulcie Rooney, but her infamy as Dulcie Markham lived on.

'What does it matter so long as you get the money?'

Dulcie May Markham had a remarkable criminal career. With close to 100 convictions across four cities (including her brief appearance in Perth's Roe Street brothels) in a career spanning almost thirty years, Dulcie was one of the most famous criminals to walk through Australia's courtrooms. She was charged and convicted many times over with idle and disorderly, consorting and vagrancy. This was to be expected given her choice of profession as a streetwalker and then professional prostitute. Her greatest profits – and more serious convictions – came from combining prostitution with sly-grog selling and illegal gambling. She was also accused of intent to murder, and police wondered about just how much involvement she had in some of the arranged underworld shootings that killed a number of Sydney and Melbourne crime figures.

As we have seen, Dulcie wasn't alone in capturing the public's interest from the 1920s on. Kate Leigh and Tilly Devine successfully combined sex, drink and drugs to create unique criminal empires in Sydney until they were forced into retirement by the taxman in the 1950s. What made Dulcie remarkable, according to crime reporter Bill Jenkings, was her underworld reputation as a 'true *femme fatale*'. From her sensational entry into the public realm, appearing in a blood-red dress at Scotty McCormack's inquest, Dulcie was consistently portrayed in the courts and newspapers as using beauty and sex appeal to seduce male gangsters and criminal bosses. Gangsters offered her protection, she lavished her attention on them, and she made as much from the association as she could, profiting from businesses in booze, drugs and sex. Dulcie kept lovers across the main cities of her criminal operations and was a coveted mistress in the Australian underworlds.

An important point here, however, is that despite newspaper stories to the contrary, Dulcie was not luring upstanding members of society away from their wives and families. It is impossible to depict her lovers as righteous men led into downfall by the wrong woman. They were already on the wrong side of the law.

The sensationalised depiction of Dulcie as a femme fatale was good for newspaper sales, but even the most experienced police detectives knew her powers of seduction. Greg Brown, who worked closely with Detective Ray Blissett, knew Dulcie well and recalled how good-looking she was: 'She could look and act beautifully and you'd never pick her as a prostitute and gangster.' One can't help but wonder just how much of a coincidence it was that she was far from the scene or in another city when some of her lovers were gunned down. Dulcie was no pawn. This shrewd survivor very carefully maintained her position in the underworlds of Brisbane, Sydney and Melbourne. Although she abided by the underworld code of silence while answering police questions and testifying in court, Dulcie wasn't afraid to take matters into her own hands, as evidenced by her revenge on Keith and Valma Hull for the murder of her friend and lover Donald Day.

Those who knew or met Dulcie understood she was not to be messed with. Brian Matthews, writer and one-time neighbour of Dulcie's on Fawkner Street, St Kilda, captured her essence in his memoirs. One day Brian's aunt walked out behind Dulcie from the ladies toilets in the Middle Park Hotel, a few blocks closer to the ocean from where Dulcie lived. When Brian's aunt noticed that Dulcie's dress was 'accidentally hooked up at the back', she leaned down to fix it. Dulcie stopped and turned, telling her: 'You lay a finger on me again, and I'll have the boys break your fuckin' arms.'

Dulcie's infamy endures. In 2009, she featured in an exhibition at Sydney's Justice and Police Museum, titled *Femme Fatale*. The curator, Nerida Campbell, brought together some striking female stories, but Dulcie featured a little differently. Among the mug shots of the other woman criminals on display, Dulcie's photograph is striking. She is posing for the camera, her tight blonde ringlets and signature red lipstick reminiscent of a postwar movie starlet. Nerida Campbell believed this was because the photograph was taken in a studio or by a press photographer. The girl with the movie-star looks left behind a number of striking shots, most of them taken by press photographers. Dulcie managed her image carefully, and was frequently captured in flattering poses. Even when she was being wheeled into a courtroom on a hospital gurney, recovering from bullet wounds to her leg and hip, Dulcie's photograph is peaceful and serene.

Dulcie's good looks assisted in the sensationalist portrayals of her in the 1950s as a femme fatale, but so did her remarkable tally of dead lovers – at least half a dozen – and one dead husband in violent circumstances over the course of twenty-five years. The nation's most famous prostitute of the early twentieth century has left a startling and unmatched record of what those around her believed was a 'death curse'. Under headlines like ' "Angel of Death" weds' and ' "Angel of death" got a fright', the newspapers ran photographs of Dulcie's husbands and lovers – alongside one of her looking beautiful and manicured.

The femme fatale image is a captivating one but Dulcie also requires consideration as a modern woman. This unconventional and controversial female entered the Sydney crime scene as a teenager and discovered she had much in common with the flappers of the time. As writer Linda Simon tells us, in the 1920s the flapper, both product and symbol of that decade's social and cultural anxiousness about adolescent girls, went from problem girl to temptation and aspiration. Dulcie used her sexuality and unrespectability to create a formidable reputation in the Australian underworld.

In the old usage of the term, she was a larrikin girl. Back in the late nineteenth and early twentieth centuries, a larrikin was a rowdy young person usually associated with a gang and juvenile criminality. This is quite different from the more positive and endearing image of today's larrikins. Female larrikins of Dulcie's era found that the gangs offered them a place and sense of identity to match their unconventional aspirations. As historian Melissa Bellanta discovered, some young women told the authorities in reformatories they had 'no desire to be respectable'. Dulcie was no different.

Dulcie Markham shows us what it was like to live and work on the inside of organised crime without having to run the show. Crime leaders like Kate Leigh and Tilly Devine are only one part of the overall story. The criminal economy functions and makes gains when the criminal players lower in the chain engage in illicit activities to create the profits that benefit the leaders. As a middle person in organised crime, Dulcie illustrates some of the realities of what this meant, outside the exceptionalism of the crime leaders. Her story reflects the experience of most people working for the criminal bosses of the time.

Part of Dulcie's allure has to do with the questions that remain about her life. Unlike Lillian Armfield, the woman who policed her for so many years, and who was keen to ensure that her own work was understood and respected, Dulcie Markham never told journalists her full story. Even Kate Leigh gave *People* unprecedented access when she sat down with them in 1950 to explain her life's achievements, trying to create an image of a neighbourhood matriarch who had only ever dabbled in a bit of sly grog. Kate *was* a matriarch to the kids, but she downplayed the other side of her life as a criminal matriarch. Dulcie Markham did what most criminals and organised crime figures do: she let the questions remain and gave very little away.

This was largely to protect herself from prosecution – and retribution. She would have been a valuable police informant and the detectives knew this, so she kept tight-lipped. She also made no excuses for the work she did and the illegal life she led, telling police in December 1944: 'There are ways of getting money without working for it, and what does it matter so long as you get the money?'

Dulcie Markham achieved fame in Australia's underworld such as we have never seen, then or since. The reporters turned her into a criminal celebrity, and although that still happens – consider the Melbourne gangland identities of recent years – it was her glamour they focused on rather than her crimes. Their highly charged sexual portrayals of Dulcie would not wash with readers today. A more critical public would also question the glamorisation and sensationalisation of her violent life and criminal associations. In today's world of reality television, however, perhaps Dulcie would have become a TV star.

Dulcie's story is also important in the ongoing project of writing of women in all their varied forms back into history. In the 1970s, Anne Summers wrote the ground-breaking book *Damned Whores and God's Police*, placing women at the centre of history while showing how their roles had been dictated by a patriarchal gender order that categorised them as either moral upholders of society or transgressive, fallen women. While Lillian Armfield was 'god's police', Dulcie Markham was the 'damned whore'. As Michelle Arrow has written recently, despite some problems with Summers' analysis – such as the exclusion of Indigenous women and lack of attention to class differences – it 'lay the groundwork for women's history in Australia'.

Dulcie was cast as the 'damned whore' from a young age. As a runaway on the streets, she hid from the female police officers who were given the job of reforming wayward girls and making them mend their ways. Even if she had got out of prostitution much earlier, perhaps in her twenties, she would either have carried the stigma or had to repudiate it and separate herself from her previous life, denying that part of herself. Dulcie didn't do either. She continued on in sex work, and the police, courts, welfare officials and religious groups stigmatised her as a prostitute, a 'fallen woman'. She combined her 'fall' with criminal transgressions too, working and associating with some of Australia's most hardened and ruthless gangsters. She lived in 'unrespectable' neighbourhoods, the places where polite society would not dare tread. She was a prostitute and a criminal, and beyond redemption.

Dulcie was cast out of society for her transgressions. Her involvement in crime was considered unnatural. She endangered the social order, first through her involvement in prostitution and then with drugs, sly grog and the criminal underworlds. She was both a criminal and a deviant woman. When men engage in crime, their presence is largely understood in criminal terms. They have committed an offence and face punishment for it. When women commit crimes, they are singled out, or at least were until recently, as *females* who have failed in their moral obligations to society. Women are punished for criminal activities as well as a supposed 'fall' from femininity. Men don't suffer a 'fall' from masculinity; they enter into crime. Whereas male offenders come under extreme social control only if they are 'less than adult, psychopaths, [or] have inadequate personalities', crime researchers argue that in the case of female offenders, 'it is sufficient justification that they are women'.

Dulcie's life is a study in what it was like to be a leading criminal woman in the early Australian underworlds. Equality for women was difficult throughout society, but especially in the world of crime. Dulcie was often relegated to the role of mere gangster's 'moll', and suffered abuse at the hands of the men who profited from her work, but she made a name for herself despite the inequalities.

We need to account for all women in history as best we can. This means examining the lives not only of those who seem to have been what some would regard as a good example of womanhood. The 'good woman' tells an empowering story, but it is still only one part of the whole story about women in Australian history. Women lead complex, diverse and varied lives. Dulcie Markham epitomises the girl who refuses to fit in, the young woman with a drug problem who seeks solace in people she thinks can protect her, the sex worker who sees herself as a representation of femininity and not a fall from it, and the resilient woman who after all her years of living a life on the 'wrong side of the tracks' decides to get out and lead a quieter existence.

What makes Dulcie Markham's life so deeply fascinating is that she chose to own the space she was cast into. From a young age she refused to conform to societal expectations, using her looks as a way show the contradictions within society. Outwardly beautiful – with attractive, fair, soft looks – she dressed well and made sure she was immaculate for court appearances, challenging the stereotypes of 'fallen' criminal women and sex workers.

One question that remains, too, is just how scared *was* Dulcie? Her public face of youth, beauty and confidence may well have been bravado to deny the reality of what her life was like. While she could hold her own – with anything from bad language aimed at gawking kids to chasing after a customer with an axe – Dulcie suffered underworld intimidation and violence. Even after being reportedly thrown from a block of flats, she still didn't name names. Dulcie's 1952 mug shot in Sydney is telling, especially bearing in mind that she was only thirty-eight at the time. She has lost some of the old spark and she looks tired. Leaning on the crutch she needs to walk after the bullets to her hip, she has seen too much of Australia's violent underworlds.

This richly complex, tough and resilient woman was also one of her place and time. Australia's organised crime scene from the 1920s to the 1950s was a violent place to live and work, and if you wanted to survive, you needed to know who was next on the hit list. Dulcie excelled at this. She flitted between victim and villain as the circumstances suited, and negotiated a place for herself in Australia's underworlds. The moralists of her time would never have agreed with it, but she established a favourable and formidable reputation in her line of work, and she was good at it.

I started out researching and writing this book because I wanted to figure out who Dulcie Markham was. I thought, after years of pressmen ogling her and commenting on her as a woman, that she deserved to have her story told by another woman. I had no particular lens through which I sought to understand her life; I simply pieced its many parts together in order to create a fuller picture of what it was like to be Dulcie.

In my search for Dulcie May Markham I found a beautiful and intelligent, foul-mouthed and funny, violent and vengeful woman. She was part femme fatale, part outlaw crook. Her striking looks and physique went with a quick temper and a desire for revenge. She also had something of the antihero about her in defying conventions and embracing her 'bad girl' identity. Perhaps in this way she continues to resonate for women today who defy social expectations and take their own path. Through it all, she left behind a captivating criminal story.

Maybe Dulcie *was* simply close to the deaths of men who were involved in crime and organised crime rather than having had any hand in those deaths herself. As she told reporters: 'Because men who have loved me have died, I've been called the "Hoodoo Girl".' She was lucky to have cheated death on at least two occasions herself. It is more likely, however, that Dulcie was far more involved in violent underworld vendettas than she would ever admit, as was hinted at in the manner of Gavan Walsh's death. Regardless, some mystery remains about Dulcie's inside knowledge. I've tried not to sensationalise her story too much, but it remains captivating, complex and deeply fascinating.

What we do know is Dulcie May Markham was one of the toughest crime figures in Australia from the 1930s to the 1950s. In the violent neighbourhoods of crime across three cities, she proved herself by utilising the avenues then open to women involved in crime – prostitution, sly-grogging and gambling houses. Dulcie showed great intelligence, resilience and a staggering ability to live through intimidation and violence. She was a survivor in a world that saw few live to retire as she did to a quieter life.

Let's imagine here, for a final moment, a fifteen-year-old Dulcie May Markham of 1929 standing alongside her sixty-two-year-old self in 1976. Fifteen-year-old Dulcie is on the cusp of a womanhood. Young and beautiful, she perhaps sees running away to eastern Sydney as an opportunity for a new life. Sixty-two-year-old Dulcie has seen it all. She has lived at the centre of organised crime across three cities for close to three decades. Apart from the ageing to be expected from the passage of the years, the emotional and physical impacts of her life had left significant and patent scars.

Dulcie Markham's was an intriguing, lasting performance. She continues to captivate and intrigue us, just as she did the newspaper reporters who scrambled to talk to her outside courtrooms. Femme fatale, notorious crook, unconventional woman: Dulcie's movie-star looks gave her a different kind of success, one that sustained her lifestyle and work in the Australian underworlds. She really was, as the papers described her at the time, 'Australia's most beautiful bad woman'. Bill Jenkings believed 'her story would make a terrific movie'. The remarkable thing is there would be little need to invent anything. Her true story is already dramatic enough.

Writing Dulcie's story

This book has given me the opportunity to travel and experience places where Dulcie lived and worked. I also often work in the bush out at West Toodyay, 85 kilometres north-east of Perth. I feel like a Heidelberg School artist of the late nineteenth century, out in a bushland area with easel and paints, writing *en plein air*.

Place is central to my writing. I couldn't have enjoyed writing this book as much as I have without being connected to the neighbourhoods featured in Dulcie's story. I often sat with a notebook and jotted down details about buildings, people and places, but there were times when I had to write my thoughts into my laptop immediately. It's probably best if you imagine me sitting in a pub in Brisbane, Darlinghurst, Woolloomooloo or

St Kilda. I've also been known to sit and write in Bar Orient in Fremantle.

You can't write Dulcie's story without walking the streets of three cities as she did, and also, for a short time, Roe Street in Perth. The brothels no longer line Roe Street, after campaigns against them in the 1950s and their closure in 1958, but the main geography of the place remains. You can see where they once stood in close proximity to the railway line, and imagine what it would have been like to tout for business outside a brothel while also keeping a close eye out for patrolling officers coming down from the station at the other end of the street. Perth plays a brief role in Dulcie's story, but she was, as we know, Sydney born and bred.

Like Louis Nowra watching the locals around Kings Cross and Woolloomooloo for his books, I found myself writing large chunks of this book in places that inspired my creativity. In fact, I wrote this part of the book in several locations in Sydney, Brisbane and Melbourne.

Right now, I'm in Trinity Bar (in the 1920s the Hotel Victoria) on Crown Street, Surry Hills. I'm having a schooner of Carlton Draught – recommended by the staff here – and wondering at the oddness of writing up more of the Sydney side to this story while drinking a Melbourne brew. It's still research, though. After all, Dulcie Markham lived in Melbourne too.

I was in Trinity Bar, writing up some research on Dulcie's early life in Sydney, when I felt compelled to write about 'place' in my work – as I'm doing here. I always find that Sydney does that to you – its grandeur grabs you full pelt and fills you with awe. Or maybe I'm just being sentimental because we used to rent a terrace on Esther Street, just around the corner from the Trinity.

Next up, I'm in the East Village (which used to be the Tradesman's Arms) on Palmer Street. The refit has more of a 1960s–70s retro feel, with the old floorboards sanded back. That's perhaps better than the sand and bits of straw they had in here in Dulcie's day to mop up the blood and vomit that mixed together on the floor. It wasn't always as crazy as that, but it did help not to have nice carpet over the floorboards.

As I sit here in the refurbished pub, professional workers pass by on the street outside and tourists pop in to have a look. It's a little more eclectic here than over in Surry Hills, and that doesn't surprise me, having lived in Darlinghurst. One woman, waiting on her friend, is wearing a floral dress with what makes me think of a Frank Sinatra Rat Pack hat. She carries it off well and I admire her confidence. She looks like an actress I've seen on television but I might be wrong. I want to say she used to star on *All Saints*, but don't believe me on that. I once saw Barry Manilow walking along a street in Melbourne.

It wasn't Barry, but if you squinted at the sun and looked back at the man, perhaps.

There are those who are a little choosier about the places they go to drink. One gentleman wanders in and asks about a draught beer. They don't have it so he exits quickly. It's a long way from the six o'clock swill, when the bartenders used a hose to quickly fill the punters' glasses with beer before the pubs closed. They weren't so fussy back then.

I wander past Tilly's old brothel on Palmer Street too. The street layout is very similar to what it used to be, but the housing exteriors have been what we call 'gentrified'. Tilly would probably have approved; she liked fancy things and wanted the wealth she had been deprived of when growing up in East End London.

I've walked the streets where Dulcie worked and lived as a way to understand her more fully. Time and a heck of a lot of redevelopment separate it from being exactly as it was, but visiting the places that tell Dulcie's story helps me better connect to her life. This is what biographers do – imagine what life was like for our subjects and recreate that as best we can. And historians enjoy living in the past because that's where they take their imagination and let it run riot. I'm in my element.

In Melbourne I visit Fawkner Street in St Kilda, which has also changed a great deal since Dulcie was there.

St Kilda has certainly gone through its fair share of gentrification, but there is still the remaining feeling of a bygone era. Like the updated areas of eastern Sydney, it carries the scars of its former life and of the scrapes it has come through over the decades.

Writing this book has also taken me to Brisbane. Over the last few days now I have toured Brisbane trying to imagine Dulcie here and the life she led.

Brisbane has a vibrant, busy city centre with grid-like Victorian streets from its nineteenth-century town planners, like the majority of Australian cities. The newer buildings reach high into the sky – most of them apartment blocks – but if you keep your eyes lower and close to the street, the early twentieth century is still there. Dulcie walked along the main thoroughfares George, Albert and Edward streets. She also conducted some casual business on Charlotte Street, and some over on the South Bank, where she also lived. In the war years she wandered close to the servicemen at Town Hall.

This is a city Dulcie kept coming back to. Perhaps she was drawn by the warmer climate, though the rains can be drowning, or the fact that it was a mix of both Melbourne and Sydney. Whatever the reason, I experience it from my modern perspective. I enjoy sitting in the Croft House on Charlotte Street and watching people pass by while I imagine Dulcie watching busy street scenes decades before.

I visit 271 Grey Street, South Brisbane, where Dulcie lived with her husband, Frank Bowen, in the mid-1930s. South Brisbane was also an area where she conducted some of her business. It would have been a far cry from today's up-market cultural precinct with luxury apartments. As I look back over to the main city and some of the original buildings that remain, I imagine Dulcie standing there taking in the scenery too. For a writer, this connection to place and character is an essential part of being immersed in another life.

At the end of the day, this is Dulcie's story. I'm pretty sure she would swear if she read it, and tell me I've given the coppers and reporters too much credit, but I think she would also be pleased that her wider story has been told. While I've used Dulcie's married names where relevant, along with her aliases based on her lovers' names, in my mind she remains Dulcie Markham. She died, as we know, as Dulcie Rooney, but there is a lot to be said for imagining her throughout as Dulcie Markham, the tough teenager who took off for a new life and somehow managed to survive the most violent streets in Australian crime history from the 1920s to the 1950s. Something of that fiery, beautiful, determined, unconventional young Dulcie always remained. She made her name as Dulcie Markham and she has certainly left her mark on my life.

Having researched and written Dulcie's story, I'm not the same as I was. She has shown me that there is more to Australian history, and has made me appreciate the diverse women's histories that make up our nation's story. It's easy to condemn people; much harder to take the time to really understand them and their circumstances. I've been living with the ghost of Dulcie for a long time now, and I don't believe I'm quite ready to let her go. She will remain with me for a long time, I think.

Timeline

27 February 1914 Born Dulcie May Markham at Crown Street Women's Hospital, Surry Hills.

13 July 1920 Sister, Florence Ena Markham, born.

1924 or earlier Parents divorce.

1929 Runs away from home and takes up prostitution, soon becoming one of Tilly Devine's girls.

1930 While her lover Cecil 'Scotty' McCormack is in gaol, takes up with small-time crook Alfred Dillon.

13 May 1931 Scotty McCormack fatally stabbed in Darlinghurst by Alfred Dillon.

15 June 1931 Makes her first public appearance as a member of Sydney's underworld, giving evidence at Scotty McCormack's inquest.

September 1931 Spends her first seven days in prison, for vagrancy (i.e. streetwalking).

1933 First stint living in Melbourne.

January 1935 Back in Sydney.

July 1935 Spends twenty-one days in Long Bay Prison for soliciting and breach of a good behaviour bond.

August 1935 First stint living in Brisbane.

1936–37 Dividing her time between Sydney, Melbourne and Brisbane.

September 1936 Suspended soliciting conviction if she keeps away from Kings Cross and Woolloomooloo.

4 March 1936 Marries Francis 'Frank' Bowen in Brisbane, becoming Dulcie Bowen.

1937 Living with Arthur Taplin when in Melbourne and calling herself Dulcie Taplin. Also uses the name Tosca De Marca.

15 December 1937 Arthur Taplin shot by Harcourt Lee, dying in hospital six days later.

6 August 1939 Her lover Guido Calletti shot dead in Woolloomooloo by rival gang members.

September 1940 Her lover Frederick James 'Paddles' Anderson acquitted of murdering Charles Abrahams in Melbourne.

1942 Gives birth to a daughter, about whom nothing else is known.

28 January 1945 Her friend and possibly lover Donald 'The Duck' Day shot in Sydney by Keith Kitchener Hull.

June 1946 Turns up in Perth's red light district, Roe Street. Swiftly arrested by police and told to go back to the eastern states.

August 1947 Arrested with her lover Ernest Martin for intent to murder Valma Hull.

25 September 1951 Shot three times in the leg and hip in the front room of her St Kilda house. Her lover Gavan Walsh is shot dead and his brother injured.

8 December 1951 Marries Leonard 'Redda' Lewis in Melbourne.

April 1952 Tells reporters she has had enough of her life of crime, but she still has a few convictions to come.

20 May 1953 Last recorded conviction. Held in a cell for 24 hours for consorting under the orders of a magistrate who told her to spend the time thinking about changing her ways.

11 January 1955 She retires from her life of crime after being thrown off top floor of block of flats in Bondi.

1972 Marries Sydney sailor (and non-criminal) Martin Rooney. They live quietly in Bondi.

20 April 1976 Dies in a bedroom fire after smoking in bed.

27 April 1976 Funeral at St Patrick's Catholic Church, Bondi.

Notes

Prologue: Alias Mary Eugene, 6 August 1939

'Pretty Dulcie'

One of Dulcie's friends and associates, Phyllis Rose Doran, while testifying at the 1951 inquest into the murder of Gavan Walsh, repeatedly referred to Dulcie as 'Pretty Dulcie'. See: State Coroner's Office, Inquest Deposition Files, 'G.T. Walsh', 1951, series VPRS 24, P0000, unit number 2054, p. 26–30.

Guido Calletti

State Archives and Records New South Wales (hereafter SRNSW), State Penitentiary, 'Long Bay Gaol Photographic Description Books, 1914–1960,' 'Guido Calletti', NRS 2497, No. 29332, 17/1515.

Brougham Street

Louis Nowra, *Kings Cross: A Biography*, NewSouth Books, Sydney, 2013, p. 68–74.

16 Brougham Street

I have referred to police photographs of the interior of the terrace, along with a floor plan of the first level of the house. See: Papers and depositions, Supreme Court, Sydney and on Circuit, November 1939, [9/7384] or [9/7385], R v Allan/Allen or Branch, Murder, NRS 880.

Murder of Calletti

SRNSW, Papers and depositions, Supreme Court, Sydney and on Circuit, November 1939, [9/7384] or [9/7385], R v Allan/Allen or Branch, Murder, NRS 880; SRNSW, Transcripts of evidence of the various courts, 1939, Criminal, [6/2031], A-B, NRS 2713; 'Death of Guido Calletti. Women's Evidence', *Sydney Morning Herald*, 14 September 1939, p. 7; 'Pistol shots in dark', *Argus* (Melbourne), 22 September 1939, p. 5; 'Shooting in house. Two versions', *Sydney Morning Herald*, 23 September 1939, p. 20; 'Sudden death of Detective Sgt. Milton Dimmock', *Sun-Herald* (Sydney), 4 July 1954, p. 2; '5000 file past body of Guido Calletti', *Tweed Daily*, 9 August 1939, p. 2; 'Halo-factories for gangsters. Why 5000 people swarmed to Calletti's funeral', *Smith's Weekly* (Sydney), 19 August 1939, p. 1; 'Calletti killing; 2 charged', *Daily News* (Sydney), 10 August 1939, p. 5; 'Death of Guido Calletti. Two men in dock', *Singleton Argus*, 20 November 1939, p. 2; '"A conspiracy of silence" Caletti case, Judge's view', *Sun* (Sydney), 27 November 1939, p. 3.

Dulcie Markham

Mary Baker, interviewed by her granddaughter Jeannine Baker, 18 April 1998, transcript copy given to the author; 'Police seek mystery blonde, *Truth* (Brisbane), 26 December 1937, p. 7; 'Glamorous young underworld girl's amazing life story', *Truth* (Brisbane), 9 January 1944, p. 10; 'No witness for Markham case', *Argus* (Melbourne), 22 February 1952, p. 5; Vince Kelly, *Rugged Angel: The Amazing Career of Policewoman Lillian Armfield*, Angus & Robertson, Sydney, 1961, p. 167–68; Frank Howson Blog, 'Fawkner Street, St Kilda', frankhowsonblog.wordpress.com/2014/04/03/fawkner-street-st-kilda, accessed 16 November 2017; Bill Jenkings, *As Crime Goes by … The Life and Times of 'Bondi' Bill Jenkings*, Ironbark Press, Sydney, 1992; Bill Jenkings, 'Dulcie Markham obituary', *Daily Mirror*, 21 April 1976; 'The mysterious Mr Lewis. Fake wire signed by Under Secretary wasn't official', *Truth* (Brisbane), 24 May 1936, p. 23.

Notes

Chapter 1: Waverley runaway

Dulcie's birth and her parents' marriage

NSW Government, Registry of Births, Deaths and Marriages (hereafter NSWBDM), 'Markham, Dulcie May', 516/1914, reproduced birth certificate in possession of the author; NSWBDM, 'Markham, John and Parker, Florence Millicent', 2988/1913, reproduced marriage certificate in possession of the author; 'Reeves family tree', ancestry.com.au, access to information and family records by permission of Liz Reeves (this family tree includes family archival records). Liz Reeves has set up the family records with the assistance of her husband, who is Dulcie's nephew.

Florence Parker

'First offenders discharged under Crimes Act 1900', *New South Wales Police Gazette* (hereafter *NSW Police Gazette*), 27 September 1911, p. 357, digitised volume, Archive CD Books Australasia; 'First offenders discharged under Crimes Act 1900', *NSW Police Gazette*, 15 November 1911, p. 427; 'Ran away twice', *Sun* (Sydney), 19 September 1911, p. 8; 'An escaped "nun"', *Truth* (Sydney), 10 September 1911, p. 8; 'A servant's lapse', *Sun* (Sydney), 8 November 1911, p. 8; 'St. Magdalen's new refuge', *Sydney Morning Herald*, 21 March 1904, p. 8; 'Laundry captives', *Watchman* (Sydney), 10 February 1910, p. 12.

Waverley

'Waverley', Dictionary of Sydney, dictionaryofsydney.org/place/waverley, accessed 2 February 2018; 'Suburban Sydney', Dictionary of Sydney, dictionaryofsydney.org/entry/suburban_sydney - ref-uuid=ee57534b-6283-d20f-8e08-9075ae8d976b, accessed 4 February 2018; 'Bronte', Dictionary of Sydney, dictionaryofsydney.org/entry/bronte - ref-uuid=ee57534b-6283-d20f-8e08-9075ae8d976b, accessed 4 February 2018; 'Waverley's progress' *Sun* (Sydney), 12 January 1914, p. 5; 'Bondi-Waverley School of Arts. Opened by the Premier',

Sunday Times (Sydney), 22 March 1914, p. 14; 'Young man's death', *Star* (Sydney), 29 April 1909, p. 6; 'The Waverley street fight', *Evening News* (Sydney), 4 March 1909, p. 5; 'Waverley shooting case', *Maitland Daily Mercury*, 30 January 1913, p. 4; 'Waverley shooting case', *Daily Telegraph* (Sydney), 25 February 1913, p. 4; 'Death sentences commuted', *Leader* (Orange), 16 April 1913, p. 3.

Dulcie in her own words
'Hoodoo Girl's 3 lovers killed', *Daily Telegraph* (Sydney), 21 July 1940, p. 6.

John Henry Markham
'Warrants', *NSW Police Gazette*, 21 September 1927, p. 541; 'Apprehensions', *NSW Police Gazette*, 1 April 1931, p. 278.

Lillian Armfield
Kelly, *Rugged Angel*, p. 40, 175.

Missing girls
Kelly, *Rugged Angel*, p. 176; 'Now we know what policewomen do', *Sun* (Sydney), 18 August 1938, p. 30; 'Where are those missing persons?', *Sydney Morning Herald*, 1 May 1948, p. 7; 'Missing girls. Police searches', *Canberra Times*, 25 August 1934, p. 1; 'Parents believe missing girl is still alive', *Newcastle Sun*, 29 May 1941, p. 11; 'Handkerchief no clue', *Newcastle Morning Herald and Miners' Advocate*, 22 July 1943, p. 1.

Dulcie reported as 'uncontrollable child'
'Offences not otherwise described', *NSW Police Gazette*, 3 April 1929, p. 256.

Descriptions of eastern Sydney
Ruth Park, *The Harp in the South*, Michael Joseph, London, 1948. For her fictional account of life in eastern Sydney, particularly Surry Hills, Ruth Park toured the streets and talked to locals when writing the book.

Notes

Anne Ramsay's Redfern childhood

Anne Ramsay, interviewed by Sue Rosen, 21 September 1994, 'City of Sydney Oral History Collections', s3.amazonaws.com/media. cityofsydney/OralHistories/Our+City/AnneRamsay/Ramsey,+Anne. pdf, audio and transcript accessed 5 February 2018.

Factory work and women's work

Joy Damousi, 'Female factory inspectors and leadership in early twentieth-century Australia', in Joy Damousi, Kim Rubenstein & Mary Tomsic (eds), *Diversity in Leadership: Australian Women, Past and Present*, ANU Press, Canberra, 2014, p. 169–88, press-files.anu. edu.au/downloads/press/p292111/pdf/9.-Female-factory-inspectors-and-leadership-in-early-twentieth-century-Australia.pdf.

Chapter 2: 'I went out for a good time'

Poverty, morality and prostitution

'Poverty's prostitution', *Labor Daily* (Sydney), 24 May 1929, p. 4; 'Prostitution cause', *Labor Daily* (Sydney), 8 July 1929, p. 4; Judith Walkowitz, *Prostitution and Victorian Society: Women, Class and the State*, Cambridge University Press, Cambridge, 2001 (published 1980), p. 8; Sharyn L. Anleu, *Deviance, Conformity and Control*, Pearson, Sydney, 2006, p. 197–98.

Prostitution

Raelene Frances, *Selling Sex: A Hidden History of Prostitution*, UNSW Press, Sydney, 2007, p. 134–35, 155, 244–47; Peter N. Grabosky, *Sydney in Ferment: Crime, Dissent and Official Reaction 1788–1973*, ANU Press, Canberra, 1977, p. 126; Alfred W. McCoy, *Drug Traffic: Narcotics and Organised Crime in Australia*, Harper & Row, Sydney, 1980, p. 138; Judith A. Allen, *Sex and Secrets: Crimes Involving Australian Women since 1880*, Oxford University Press, Melbourne, 1990, p. 73, 93–94, 174, 177; Kelly, *Rugged Angel*, p. 65, 67; 'Plea for chastity', *Sunday Times* (Sydney), 6 November 1927, p. 5.

Ray Blissett

Ray Blissett, interviewed by Stephen Rapley, 2 March 1988, NSW Bicentennial oral history collection, 3 sound cassettes (c. 140 minutes), National Library of Australia, ORAL TRC 2301/197, nla. gov.au/nla.obj-216363690/listen, accessed 1 February 2018; Larry Writer, *Razor: Tilly Devine, Kate Leigh and the Razor Gangs*, Macmillan, Sydney, 2009 (published 2001), p. 138, 139, 141.

Chow Hayes on Ray Blissett

David Hickie, *Chow Hayes Gunman: Australia's Most Notorious Gangster*, Angus & Robertson, Sydney, 1990, p. 112–13.

Brothels and prostitution in Woolloomooloo

'Alleged disorderly house', *Newcastle Morning Herald and Miner's Advocate*, 16 November 1893, p. 5; 'Porter's Palace. A den of depravity', *Truth* (Brisbane), 30 October 1921, p. 10; 'Frenchman must go', *Truth* (Sydney), 28 April 1929, p. 15.

J.E. St Louis on prostitution

J.E. St Louis, interviewed by Chris Jeffery, 1988, Oral History Records Rescue Group, OH1978, State Library of Western Australia, catalogue.slwa.wa.gov.au/search~S2?/Xinterview+j+e+st+louis&searchscope=2&SORT=D/Xinterview+j+e+st+louis&searchscope=2&SORT=D&SUBKEY=interview+j+e+st+louis/1,2,2,B/frameset&FF=Xinterview+j+e+st+louis&searchscope=2&SORT=D&1,1, accessed 22 January 2018.

Real estate

For an example see the BresicWhitney advertisement at: realestate. com.au/sold/property-house-nsw-darlinghurst-127460634, accessed 1 August 2018.

Tilly Devine

SRNSW, State Penitentiary for Women, Long Bay, 'Photograph Description Book 1910–1930', 'Matilda Devine', NRS 2496, No.

Notes

659, 3/6007; SRNSW, State Penitentiary for Women, Long Bay, 'Photograph Description Book 1930–1970', 'Kate Leigh', NRS 2497, No. 155/92; Catie Gilchrist, 'Tilly Devine', Dictionary of Sydney, dictionaryofsydney.org/entry/tilly_devine, accessed 27 January 2017; Kay Saunders, *Notorious Australian Women*, HarperCollins, Sydney, 2011, chapter 14; Judith Allen & Baiba Irving, 'Devine, Matilda Mary (Tilly)', *Australian Dictionary of Biography*, National Centre of Biography, Australian National University, adb.anu.edu.au/biography/devine-matilda-mary-tilly-5970, accessed 29 January 2017; 'Tilly Devine', *National Advocate* (Bathurst), 27 May 1925, p. 2; 'Tilly Devine's shoe hits constable', *Evening News* (Sydney), 22 April 1925, p. 7; 'Says Tilly to Kate. Underworld hymn of hate', *Truth* (Sydney), 29 June 1930, p. 15; 'Husband charged', *Sydney Morning Herald*, 10 January 1931, p. 8; *Daily Mirror* (Sydney), 24 November 1970, p 9; Kelly, *Rugged Angel*, p. 191–92; Writer, *Razor*, chapters 3, 12 and 18; Original police and court records are included in: Lucy Mae Beers, 'Chilling mugshots of the razor gang queens who ruled Sydney in the 1920s as they battled to control the criminal underworld – and their dirty deeds revealed in detail for the first time', *Daily Mail* Australia, 25 May 2016, dailymail.co.uk/news/article-3607042/Photos-emerge-Tilly-Devine-Kate-Leigh-controlled-1920s-Razor-gangs-Sydney.html, accessed 27 January 2017; Zoe Nauman, 'Making up for my evil gran, Tilly Devine', *Sunday Telegraph* (Sydney), 16 July 2011, dailytelegraph.com.au/making-up-for-my-evil-gran-tilly-devine/news-story/e03456111ecf415a3fa5ba5219ceef3f?sv=fec80effb189c9cc78a7d33e1547934e, accessed 4 April 2018.

Tilly's brothels
Writer, *Razor*, p. 95; Darcy Dugan with Michael Tatlow, *Bloodhouse*, HarperCollins, Sydney, 2012, p. 26.

Nellie Cameron
For more information on Nellie Cameron, see: Colin Kelly's AIF record; Kelly marriage record; 'In Divorce', *Sydney Morning Herald*,

24 February 1922, p. 6; 'Nellie's emotions', *Arrow* (Sydney), 4
December 1931, p. 1; 'Death of notorious underworld blonde',
Examiner (Launceston), 10 November 1953, p. 4; 'Underworld
mourns Sydney "queen"', *Advertiser* (Adelaide), 11 November
1953, p. 1; Writer, *Razor*, p. 58–60; George Blaikie, *Wild Women
of Sydney*, Rigby, Adelaide, 1980, p. 181–82; 'Gangster's girl of the
city's "Lead Age"', *Sun-Herald* (Sydney), 15 November 1953, p. 88;
Kelly, *Rugged Angel*, p. 40, 42–43, 168–69, 191, 192, 211; Writer,
Razor, p. 102–108.

Tilly and Dulcie
While I was living in Darlinghurst, locals often talked about 'Pretty
Dulcie' and how she was one of the girls 'plucked off the streets'
when she walked past Tilly's brothel.

Maria Tinschert's childhood
Maria Tinschert, *Daughter of the Razor: An Australian True Crime
Story*, Publicious, Currumbin, 2016.

Tilly 'not really bad'
Zoe Nauman, 'Making up for my evil gran, Tilly Devine', *Sunday
Telegraph* (Sydney), 16 July 2011, dailytelegraph.com.au/making-up-
for-my-evil-gran-tilly-devine/news-story/e03456111ecf415a3fa5ba5
219ceef3f?sv=fec80effb189c9cc78a7d33e1547934e, accessed 4 April
2018; '"K-K-K Katey … You're the only 'Girl' that I abhor!"', *Truth*
(Sydney), 7 February 1932, p. 21; 'Tilly Devine "broke" at death',
Canberra Times, 25 November 1970, p. 3.

Louis Nowra on Woolloomooloo
Louis Nowra, *Woolloomooloo: A Biography*, NewSouth Books,
Sydney, 2017 (quoting directly too from p. 35); 'Louis Nowra's
new books surveys the history and people of Sydney's mean streets',
Sydney Morning Herald, 6 March 2017, smh.com.au/entertainment/
books/louis-nowras-new-book-surveys-the-history-and-people-of-
sydneys-mean-streets-20170301-guo602.html, accessed 25 April

2018; Louis Nowra's book on Kings Cross is also interesting for the stories it reveals about areas close to the 'Loo.

Sex worker on living conditions

Author's conversation with an anonymous sex worker, Palmer Street, Sydney, 2004.

Judy Chambers

'Our place – Judy Chambers – Woolloomooloo', Judy Chambers, interviewed by Sue Rosen, Sue Rosen Associates, see text under video still, suerosenassociates.com/videos/our_place_woolloomooloo_judy_chambers, accessed 7 February 2018.

Chapter 3: Little Chicago's 'hold-up man'

'hold-up man'

'Lurid romance crime stiletto behind', *Truth* (Sydney), 17 May 1931, p. 15.

'the foot soldiers of organised crime'

Robin Hammond, 'Young men with guns: crooks, cops and consorting law, Sydney 1920s–1930s', Master of Arts thesis, University of New England, Armidale, NSW, 2009, e-publications. une.edu.au/vital/access/manager/Repository/une:3467?source=Advanced&field1=text&query1=young+men+with+guns, accessed 21 July 2018.

Background history for Scotty McCormack

NSWBDM, 'McCormack, Cecil William Bethel', 17435/1909, reproduced birth certificate in possession of the author; SRNSW, State Penitentiary, 'Long Bay Gaol Photographic Description Books, 1914–1960', 'Cecil William McCormack', NRS 2467, No. 20967, 3/6114; 'Apprehensions', *NSW Police Gazette*, 30 April 1930, p. 359; Writer, *Razor*, p. 105.

Gosford Farm Home

'Gosford Boys Home', *Gosford Times and Wyong District Advocate*, 17 May 1923, p. 12; 'Escapees from Gosford Boys' Home', *Newcastle Sun*, 17 June 1939, p. 1; 'Gosford Boys' Home', *Scone Advocate*, 23 January 1945, p. 1.

Chow Hayes

Hickie, *Chow Hayes Gunman*, p. 23, 32–33.

Harry Pidgeon

SRNSW, State Penitentiary, 'Long Bay Gaol Photographic Description Books, 1914–1960', 'Harry Pidgeon', NRS 2467, No. 20963, 3/6114; 'Arrested development', *Sun* (Sydney), 20 June 1925, p. 2.

McCormack and Pidgeon charged and sentenced

'Quarter Sessions', *Sydney Morning Herald*, 20 June 1925, p. 12.

Push gangs and decoys

'Lust & larrikinism', *Truth* (Sydney), 12 October 1913, p. 2; Melissa Bellanta, *Larrikins: A History*, University of Queensland Press, Brisbane, 2012, chapter 3; Vince Kelly, *The Shadow: The Amazing Exploits of Frank Fahy*, Angus & Robertson, London, 1955, chapter 12; 'Sydney bludgers', *Farmer and Settler* (Sydney), 1 June 1915, p. 4; Alan Wright, *Organised Crime*, Routledge, London and New York, 2011 (published 2006), p. 29, 31, 41–42; Jacob Riis, *The Battle with the Slum*, Patterson Smith, Montclair, New Jersey, 1902; James Morton & Susanna Lobez, *Gangland Australia: Colonial Criminals to the Carlton Crew*, Melbourne University Press, Melbourne, 2007, p. 15; Kelly, *Rugged Angel*, p. 137–41; '"Push" gangs. Police offensive', *Sydney Morning Herald*, 11 March. 1925, p. 15.

Fruit business deal between Calletti and McCormack

Writer, *Razor,* p. 105.

Notes

Dulcie and Scotty

'Lurid romance crime stiletto behind', *Truth* (Sydney), 17 May 1931, p. 15; 'Vagrancy charge', *Telegraph* (Brisbane), 7 February 1930, p. 7; 'Quarter Sessions', *Sydney Morning Herald*, 7 November 1930, p. 8.

Organised crime

Wright, *Organised Crime*, chapters 1 and 2.

Sydney's criminal reputation

'Little Chicago', *Western Champion* (Parkes), 28 February 1929, p. 17; 'Ousting thugdom from Razorhurst', *Truth* (Sydney), 30 June 1929, p. 18; 'Sydney's noisome out they go', *Truth* (Sydney), 13 January 1929, p. 1.

Women and crime

Satyanshu K. Mukherjee, *Crime Trends in Twentieth Century Australia*, Allen & Unwin, Sydney, 1981, p. 80–83; Pike quoted in Clive Emsley, *Crime and Society in England, 1750–1900*, Pearson Longman, London, 1987, p. 32, 92–93; Gregory Durstan, *Victims and Viragos: Metropolitan Women, Crime and the Eighteenth-Century Justice System*, Arima Publishing, Bury St Edmunds, 2007; Antonia Fraser, *The Weaker Vessel: Woman's Lot in Seventeenth-century England*, Random House, London, 1994 (first published 1984); Leigh S.L. Straw, *Drunks, Pests and Harlots: Criminal Women in Western Australia, 1900–1939*, Humming Earth, Kilkerran, Scotland, 2015; 'As our own see us', *West Australian*, 27 March 1916, p. 3.

Kate Leigh

Leigh Straw, *The Worst Woman in Sydney: The Life and Crimes of Kate Leigh*, NewSouth Books, Sydney, 2016.

Sly grog

Ross Fitzgerald & Trevor L. Jordan, *Under the Influence: A History of Alcohol in Australia*, ABC Books, Sydney, 2009, p. 31–35, 62–65, 214; Quentin Beresford, 'Drinkers and the anti-drink movement in

Sydney, 1870–1930', PhD Thesis, Australian National University, Canberra, July 1984, p. xiii–xiv, 1–2, 234; 'Youthful criminals', *Sydney Morning Herald*, 6 September 1889, p. 8; New South Wales Parliament, Legislative Council, Standing Committee on Social Issues, 'Report on the *Inebriates Act 1912*', Sydney, Report 33, August 2004, p. 15–21; Walter Phillips, '"Six o'clock swill": the introduction of early closing of hotel bars in Australia', *Historical Studies*, vol. 19, no. 75, 1980, p. 261, 263, 264; Writer, *Razor*, p. 39; Diane Kirkby, '"Beer, glorious beer": gender politics and Australian popular culture', *Journal of Popular Culture*, vol. 37, no. 2, 2003, p. 245, 246; Tanja Luckins, '"Satan finds some mischief"? Drinkers' responses to the six o'clock closing of pubs in Australia, 1910s–1930s', *Journal of Australian Studies*, vol. 32, no. 3, 2008, p. 302.

Kate Leigh and sly grog

'Study in scarlet: an uncrowned queen of slumland drips with diamonds and charity', *People* (Sydney), 15 March 1950, p. 15; Hal Baker, interviewed by the author, 16 August 2013; 'Fined for selling sly grog that was water', *Mirror* (Perth), 6 February 1954, p. 4; 'Warns witness of language in Kate Leigh "sly grog" case', *Courier-Mail* (Brisbane), 30 January 1954, p. 3; 'Kate Leigh gets 6 month's gaol term on sly-grog charge', *Truth* (Sydney), 21 March 1943, p. 11; '"Not British justice," says counsel to S.M. in sly grog case', *Truth* (Sydney), 7 February 1943, p. 19; Blaikie, *Wild Women of Sydney*, p. 149; Grabosky, *Sydney in Ferment*, p. 119; '"Hills" hotels', *Evening News* (Sydney), 5 October 1922, p. 7.

Mary Baker

Mary Baker, interviewed by her granddaughter Jeannine Baker, 18 April 1998, transcript copy given to the author.

Gang members and violence

SRNSW, 'Tilly Devine & the Razor Gang Wars, 1927–1931', records.nsw.gov.au/archives/magazine/galleries/tilly-devine-and-the-razor-gang-wars, accessed 2 June 2018; 'Gunman Gaffney fined', *Daily Advertiser* (Wagga Wagga), 27 March 1928, p. 2; 'Acquitted', *Maitland Daily Mercury*, 13 June 1930, p. 6; '"Fight with fists" advises judge', *Truth* (Sydney), 15 June 1930, p. 17; 'Gang war', *Sydney Morning Herald*, 19 July 1929, p. 13; 'Gang feud', *Argus* (Melbourne), 10 August 1929, p. 25; 'Gang war. Women involved', *Sydney Morning Herald*, 12 November 1929, p. 11; 'Man shot dead in city last night', *Truth* (Sydney), 10 November 1929, p. 20; 'Man shot dead', *Sydney Morning Herald*, 11 November 1929, p. 11; Writer, *Razor,* chapters 13–15.

Henry 'Jack' Baker

Hal Baker, interviewed by the author, 16 August 2013; Mary Baker, interviewed by her granddaughter Jeannine Baker, 18 April 1998, transcript copy given to the author; Chow Hayes, interviewed by Margaret Throsby, 1990, ABC Radio, mpegmedia.abc.net.au/ innovation/sidetracks/sydney_content/mp3/ChowHayes/ChowHayes. mp3, 1 November 2017; 'Guns blazed in Sydney's underworld', *Argus* (Melbourne), 8 July 1950, p. 26–27.

Consorting Squad

'Consorting', *Truth* (Sydney), 19 January 1930, p. 12.

William 'Big Bill' Mackay

Frank Cain, 'MacKay, William John (1885–1948)', *Australian Dictionary of Biography*, National Centre of Biography, Australian National University, adb.anu.edu.au/biography/mackay-william-john-7381/text12829, accessed 22 March 2018; 'House of thieves? C.I.B. Chief Mackay in a swirl of fists and boots at "party"', *Truth* (Sydney), 29 January 1928, p. 8; 'Gang war', *Sydney Morning Herald*, 19 July 1929, p. 13; 'Gang feud', *Argus* (Melbourne), 10 August 1929, p. 25; 'Gang war. Women involved', *Sydney Morning Herald*, 12 November 1929, p. 11; 'Man shot dead in city last night', *Truth* (Sydney), 10 November 1929, p. 20; 'Man shot dead', *Sydney*

Morning Herald, 11 November 1929, p. 11; Ray Blissett, interviewed by Stephen Rapley, 2 March 1988, NSW Bicentennial oral history collection, 3 sound cassettes (c. 140 minutes), National Library of Australia, nla.gov.au/nla.obj-216363690/listen, accessed 1 February 2018.

Chapter 4: 'Man stabbed in heart'

Stairway to brothel

Hickie, *Chow Hayes Gunman*, p. 76.

Kathleen Scurrie giving evidence in Wulf case

'Quarter Sessions', *Sydney Morning Herald*, 4 July 1929, p. 8.

Murder of Scotty McCormack

Register of Coroners' Inquests and Magisterial Inquiries, 1834–1942, Inquest Deposition Files, 'McCormack, Cecil', NRS345, 2/10513-15; 'Shocking crime. Man stabbed in heart', *Northern Star*, 14 May 1931, p. 5; 'Lurid romance crime stiletto behind', *Truth* (Sydney), 17 May 1931, p. 15; 'Dramatic evidence in Sydney's stiletto mystery', *Labor Daily*, 16 June 1931, p. 5; 'Darlinghurst murder. Man stabbed to death', *Sydney Morning Herald*, 16 June 1931, p. 6; 'Stiletto pierced both lungs', *Daily* Examiner (Grafton), 16 June 1931, p. 5; *Newcastle Sun*, 17 June 1931, p. 5; 'Murder charge. Death of Cecil McCormack', *Sydney Morning Herald*, 18 June 1931, p. 6; 'Dumb tragedy. No shriek or cry. Law probes mystery of sinister stiletto murder', *Truth* (Sydney), 21 June 1931, p. 22; Hickie, *Chow Hayes Gunman*, p. 76.

Dulcie at the Coroner's Court

'Dumb tragedy. No shriek or cry. Law probes mystery of sinister stiletto Murder', *Truth* (Sydney), 21 June 1931, p. 22; 'Perth knew lovely blonde whose husband & lovers were murdered', *Mirror* (Perth), 22 January 1944, p. 1.

Detective Sergeant Kennedy

'Policemen run in family life', *Sun* (Sydney), 29 October 1933, p. 9; 'Work rewarded. Inspector Kennedy', *Sun* (Sydney), 24 September 1936, p. 32.

Alfred Dillon's trial

'Hoodoo of No.13', *Arrow* (Sydney), 4 December 1931, p 7; 'Manslaughter. William Street stabbing', *Sydney Morning Herald*, 2 December 1931, p. 12; 'Stiletto murder: dramatic trial', *Truth* (Sydney), 6 September 1931, p. 11; 'Darlinghurst murder. Man stabbed to death', *Sydney Morning Herald*, 16 June 1931, p. 6.

Alfred Dillon released

'Final chapter of past underworld sensations: two prisoners freed', *Truth*, 24 October 1937, p. 12.

Flappers

Judith Mackrell, *Flappers: Six Women of a Dangerous Generation*, Pan Macmillan, London, 2014, p. 5–11; 'Decadent times', *Northern Star* (Lismore), 7 September 1921, p. 2; Linda Simon, *Lost Girls: The Invention of the Flapper*, Reaktion Books, London, 2017, p. 8–11; Arthur Mizener, *The Far Side of Paradise: A Biography of F. Scott Fitzgerald*, Houghton Mifflin, Boston, 1951 (first published 1949), p. xii; F. Scott Fitzgerald, *The Great Gatsby*, Scrivener, New York, 1925; F. Scott Fitzgerald, *The Crack-Up*, Scrivener, New York, 1945; Thomas Keneally, *Australians: Flappers to Vietnam*, Allen & Unwin, Sydney, 2015 (published 2014), p. 13–15; 'Flappers everywhere', *Grenfell Record and Lachlan District Advertiser*, 22 July 1926, p. 2; 'Flapper manners', *Sunday Times* (Sydney), 16 June 1929, p. 3; 'Do they liked being called flappers?', *Sun* (Sydney), 19 August 1928, p. 21.

Charges against Dulcie in 1931 and 1933

State Penitentiary, Long Bay, 'Description card', 'Mary Eugene', NRS, 2494, 11/3127.

Chapter 5: 'Police seek mystery blonde'

Crime in Melbourne

'Where crime and vice abide', *Weekly Times* (Melbourne), 4 March 1922, p. 32; 'Schools of crime', *Weekly Times* (Melbourne), 26 April 1924, p. 10; Morton & Lobez, *Gangland Australia*, p. 24–33, 79; 'Gang of footpads', *Age* (Melbourne), 1 August 1927, p. 10: Chris McConville, 'Melbourne crime: from war to Depression, 1919–1929', *Australian Dictionary of Biography*, National Centre of Biography, Australian National University 23 May 2013, adb.anu.edu.au/essay/6, accessed 3 April 2018; Richard Evans, 'The police are rottenly corrupt': policing, scandal, and the regulation of illegal betting in Depression-era Sydney', *Australian and New Zealand Journal of Criminology*, vol. 48, no. 4, 2015, p. 572–87.

Marriage of Cameron and Calletti

Registry of Births, Deaths and Marriages, Victoria, 'Guido Caletti and Ellen Kelly', Marriage Certificate, online.justice.vic.gov.au/bdm/indexsearch.doj?viewSequence=200&language=en&trxId=IDX&commandAction_displayDetailsAction=F64D2DCD2215E931FB49EAD972D11361, digital copy obtained 11 June 2018.

Defunct bank book

'Two perjury charges', *Argus* (Melbourne), 14 November 1933, p. 11; '"Straw bail" cases. Trading on defunct bank book', *Age* (Melbourne), 5 December 1933, p. 13.

Dulcie's Sydney convictions in 1935

SRNSW, State Penitentiary, Long Bay, 'Description card', 'Mary Eugene', NRS, 2494, 11/3127.

Prostitution in Brisbane

James Morton & Susanna Lobez, *Gangland Queensland*, Melbourne University Press, Melbourne, 2012, p. 29–38; Christopher Dawson, *Intemperance and the Train of Evil: A Life on the Wrong Side of the*

Notes

Tracks in Colonial Brisbane, Boggo Road Gaol Historical Society, Brisbane, 2008; Raymond Evans, '"Soiled doves": prostitution in colonial Queensland', in Kay Daniels (ed.), *So Much Hard Work: Women and Prostitution in Australian History*, Fontana Collins, Sydney, 1984; Police Department, Police Service Commissioner's Office, Police Correspondence, VD Suspects and Prostitution, 1 January 1899 to 31 December 1932, item no. 318632, Queensland State Archives.

Newspaper description of Dulcie's looks

'Police seek mystery blonde, *Truth* (Brisbane), 26 December 1937, p. 7.

Marriage to Frank Bowen

Copy of Marriage Certificate made available to author by permission of Liz Reeves, access to information and family records made available on ancestry.com.au.

Dulcie violent in cells

'SRNSW, State Penitentiary, Long Bay, 'Description card', 'Mary Eugene', NRS, 2494, 11/3127; Woman breaks bucket in watchhouse', *Sunday Mail* (Brisbane), 29 March 1936, p. 4; 'Woman destroys bucket in cell at watchhouse', *Telegraph* (Brisbane), 28 March 1936, p. 7.

Bogus telegram

'The mysterious Mr Lewis. Fake wire signed by Under Secretary wasn't official', *Truth* (Brisbane), 24 May 1936, p. 23.

Soliciting in Sydney, 1936

SRNSW, State Penitentiary, Long Bay, 'Description card', 'Mary Eugene', NRS, 2494, 11/3127.

Arthur Taplin's prior convictions

'Assault by police alleged', *Labor Daily* (Sydney), 13 June 1933, p 5; 'Murder intent charge made against youth', *Labor Daily* (Sydney),

4 August 1933, p. 7; 'New science. Ballistics in crime cases', *Sydney Morning Herald*, 4 August 1933, p. 9; 'Ran, heard shots', *Truth* (Sydney), 6 August 1933, p. 24.

Dulcie as Tosca De Marca

SRNSW, State Penitentiary, Long Bay, 'Description card', 'Mary Eugene', NRS, 2494, 11/3127.

Taplin murder

'Police seek mystery blonde', *Truth* (Brisbane), 26 December 1937, p. 7.

Murder of Guido Calletti

I have referred to police photographs of the interior of the terrace, along with a floor plan of the first level of the house. See: SRNSW, Papers and depositions, Supreme Court, Sydney and on Circuit, November 1939, [9/7384] or [9/7385], R v Allan/Allen or Branch, Murder, NRS 880; SRNSW, Transcripts of evidence of the various Courts, 1939, Criminal, [6/2031], A-B, NRS 2713; 'Hoodoo Girl's 3 lovers killed', *Daily Telegraph* (Sydney), 21 July 1940, p. 6; 'Halo-factories for gangsters. Why 5000 people swarmed to Calletti's funeral', *Smith's Weekly* (Sydney), 19 August 1939, p. 1.

Dulcie in Lithgow

'Woman sentenced', *Sydney Morning Herald*, 31 October 1939, p. 11.

Chapter 6: 'Good-bye, sweetheart!'

Declaration of war

Beau Gamble, 'On this day: Australia at war', *Australian Geographic*, 2 September 2011, australiangeographic.com.au/blogs/on-this-day/2011/09/on-this-day-australia-at-war, accessed 15 March 2018; Leigh Straw, *After the War: Returned Soldiers and the Mental and Physical Scars of War*, UWA Publishing, Perth, 2017; Robert

Menzies, *Afternoon Light: Some Memories of Men and Events*,
Penguin, Melbourne, 1969, p. 16–17; My colleague at the University
of Notre Dame Australia, Professor Deborah Gare, has used this in
lectures and I share it here from also listening to the original source:
Joan Stingemore (née Brophy), interviewed by Larraine Stevens,
22 June 1999, oral history project, LHC OH/STI, Fremantle City
Library.

Murder of John Abrahams

'Fatal shooting. Detectives raid a house', *West Australian*, 17 June
1940, p. 4; '"Good-bye, sweetheart!" Brunette's cry to lover on charge
of murder', *Truth* (Sydney), 21 July 1940, p. 23; '"Paddles," or "The
Big Doll", not guilty', *Truth* (Sydney), 22 September 1940, p. 24.

Dulcie living with Fred 'Paddles' Anderson

'Murder case mentioned', *Argus* (Melbourne), 15 August 1940, p. 12.

Gambling in Melbourne

McConville, 'Melbourne crime: from war to depression, 1919–1929'.

'Red' Maloney

'"Red" Maloney must serve gaol sentence', *Herald* (Melbourne),
9 July 1935, p. 22; '"Red" Maloney to go to gaol', *Herald*
(Melbourne), 22 February 1939, p. 10; 'Two acquittals on theft
charges', *Herald* (Melbourne), 19 June 1939, p. 3; 'Violent robbery
charge', *Herald* (Melbourne), 29 April 1939, p. 8; A decade after
John Abrahams was killed, Maloney was still facing gambling house
charges. See: '"Red" Maloney fined £30', *Herald* (Melbourne),
27 November 1950, p. 3.

'Paddles' Anderson and Sydney crime

Michael Duffy & Bob Bottom, 'Paddles Anderson: boss of bosses',
Sydney Morning Herald, 3 June 2011, smh.com.au/entertainment/
paddles-anderson-boss-of-bosses-20110602-1fiqg.html, accessed
9 August 2018.

Dulcie in her own words

'Hoodoo Girl's 3 lovers killed', *Daily Telegraph* (Sydney), 21 July 1940, p. 6.

'he freely admitted it to his mates'

Hickie, *Chow Hayes Gunman*, p. 133.

US servicemen and the Second World War

Steven Lomazow & Eric Fettman, *FDR's Deadly Secret*, Public Affairs, New York, 2009, p. 78; Kate Darian-Smith, *On the Homefront: Melbourne in Wartime, 1939–45*, 2nd edn, Melbourne University Press, Melbourne, 2009; John Hammond Moore, *Over-Sexed, Over-Paid and Over Here: Americans in Australia 1941–1945*, University of Queensland Press, Brisbane, 1981; Kelly, *Rugged Angel*, chapter 32; A.C. Welburn, 'The Singapore Strategy', *Australian Defence Force Journal*, no. 100, June 1993, p. 45.

War and prostitution

Morton & Lobez, *Gangland Queensland*, chapter 5; Frances, *Selling Sex*, p. 251.

Dulcie accosting police officer

'Cop's charge against pretty blonde fails', *Mirror* (Perth), 26 July 1941, p. 13.

Dulcie loitering St Kilda

'Glamorous young underworld girl's amazing life story', *Truth* (Brisbane), 9 January 1944, p. 10.

Terrace Street, New Farm

Gerard Benjamin, 'Florence and Les still telling the Village history', *Village News*, September 2011, p. 13, issuu.com/newfarmvillagenews/docs/villagenewsseptember2011, accessed 10 August 2018.

Florence O'Brien living next door to Dulcie

Gerard Benjamin, 'Florence and Les still telling the Village history', *Village News*, September 2011, p. 13, issuu.com/newfarmvillagenews/docs/villagenewsseptember2011, accessed 10 August 2018.

Dulcie's daughter

Dulcie is called 'mother of a child' in '"Angel of Death?" – blonde's denial', *Truth* (Brisbane), 6 February 1944, p. 14. Ten years later, in 1952, she mentioned her ten-year-old daughter to reporters in Sydney. See: 'Had enough, says Dulcie. Dogged by curse of violent death', *Mail* (Adelaide), 26 April 1952, p. 2.

Stealing and consorting charges

'"Angel of Death?" – blonde's denial', *Truth*, p. 14; 'The blonde's gone, too!', *Truth* (Brisbane), 27 February 1944, p. 19.

Maurice Dias

'Racecourse arrest', *Forbes Advocate*, 23 June 1929, p. 1.

James Williams in court

'Charged with stealing £140 worth of liquor', *Telegraph* (Brisbane), 14 September 1943, p. 2; 'Brisbane's "Pretty Dulcie" bobs up again!', *Truth* (Brisbane), 22 July 1945, p. 13.

Chapter 7: Shot in the face

Donald Day brothels and grog

Ray Blissett, interviewed by Stephen Rapley, 2 March 1988, NSW Bicentennial oral history collection, nla.gov.au/nla.obj-216363690/listen, accessed 1 February 2018; Hickie, *Chow Hayes Gunman*, p. 153, 156–57.

Murder of Donald Day

'Murder in Underworld, "Donald the Duck" shot, *Sun* (Sydney), 29 January 1945, p. 5; 'Killing of "Donald the Duck"', *Townsville Daily Bulletin*, 16 June 1945, p. 2.

'the tune she calls is DEATH'

'For the men who love "Pretty Dulcie" – death takes no holiday', *Mirror* (Perth), 28 July 1945, p. 16.

Gambling in Melbourne

McConville, 'Melbourne Crime: From War to Depression, 1919–1929', adb.anu.edu.au/essay/6, accessed 24 August 2018.

Charles Kirby and baccarat schools

State Coroner's Office, Inquest Deposition Files, 'Leslie Ernest Walkerden', 1946/1982, series VPRS 24, P0000, unit number 1534, Public Record Office Victoria.

Shooting of Maxwell Salter

'Shooting in lane', *Herald* (Melbourne), 18 April 1935, p. 5; 'Shots fired in lane', *Age* (Melbourne), 20 April 1935, p. 12; 'Acquittal on charge of wounding', *Shepparton Advertiser*, 8 May 1935, p. 5.

Leslie Walkerden's murder

State Coroner's Office, 'Leslie Ernest Walkerden', 1946/1982, series VPRS 24, P0000, unit number 1534; 'Shooting at Richmond', *Age* (Melbourne), 13 September 1945, p. 6; 'Knuckleman "bumped off"', *Truth* (Sydney), 16 September 1945, p. 18; 'Gunman's mother pined to death', *Truth* (Sydney), 22 January 1950, p. 2.

Dulcie linked to Walkerden

'Why "Pretty Dulcie" is the "Angel of Death"', *Truth* (Brisbane), 4 May 1952, p. 8; James Morton & Susanna Lobez, *Gangland Melbourne*, Victory Books, Melbourne, 2011, p. 82.

Underworld feud continues

'Tommygun shooting of car driver in Melbourne', *Morning Bulletin* (Rockhampton), 7 February 1950, p. 1.

James Coates and his murder

John Lack, 'Coates, James (1901–1947), *Australian Dictionary of Biography*, National Centre of Biography, Australian National University, adb.anu.edu.au/biography/coates-james-5694, accessed 9 September 2018; 'Coates was killed as he ran from car', *Argus* (Melbourne), 22 July 1947, p. 1; 'Why they murdered James Coates', *Argus* (Melbourne), 25 July 1947, p. 1.

Police stamping our crime

'Police move to curb gunmen', *Argus* (Melbourne), 30 July 1947, p. 1.

Chapter 8: Across the tracks at the 'Rue de la Roe'

Dulcie charged in Perth

'Curly blonde "had" Perth', *Mirror* (Perth), 22 June 1946, p. 7; 'In the Rue de la Roe', *Mirror* (Perth), 20 May 1944, p. 7; SRNSW, State Penitentiary, Long Bay, 'Description card', 'Mary Eugene', NRS, 2494, 11/3127.

Detective describing Dulcie

Writer, *Razor*, p. 185. Used with permission from Larry Writer to include sections from interviews conducted for his book.

Perth's crime background

Straw, *Drunks, Pests and Harlots*; Raelene Davidson, 'Prostitution in Perth and Fremantle and on the Eastern Goldfields, 1895 – September 1939', MA thesis, University of Western Australia, 1980, p. 51; 'High life in King Street: a pestilent spot', *West Australian*, 4 July 1900, p. 2; Statistics compiled from annual registers covering the years 1900–1939. See: Government Statistician's Office, *Statistical Register of Western Australia*, Perth, 1903–1939; Adam

Graycar & Peter Grabosky, 'Trends in Australian crime and criminal justice', in Graycar & Grabosky (eds), *The Cambridge Handbook of Australian Criminology*, Cambridge University Press, Cambridge, 2009, p. 15.

Slums

'Glimpses of the city', *Sunday Times*, 3 October 1920, second section, p. 1; 'The slums of the city', *Sunday Times*, 5 December 1920, p. 5.

Prostitution in Perth

Melissa Hope Ditmore, *Prostitution and Sex Work*, Greenwood, Oxford, 2011, p. 43; Frances, *Selling Sex*, p. 129, 162; *Statistical Register of Western Australia for the Year 1916*, 'Part 1, Population and Vital Statistics', p. 3; *West Australian*, 29 May 1925, p. 8; 'An unpleasant subject', *Sunday Times* (Perth), 12 January 1908, p. 6; Rita Farrell, 'Dangerous women: constructions of female criminality in Western Australia 1915–1945', PhD Thesis, Murdoch University, 1997, p. 387; *West Australian*, 29 September 1900, p. 2; Chris McConville, 'The location of Melbourne's prostitutes', *Historical Studies*, vol. 19, no. 74, 1980, p. 90.

Roe Street brothels

Frances, *Selling Sex*, p. 205, 208; Elaine McKewon, 'The historical geography of prostitution in Perth, Western Australia', *Australian Geographer*, vol. 34, no. 3, 2003, p. 300–302; Davidson, 'Prostitution in Perth and Fremantle and on the Eastern Goldfields, 1895 – September 1939', p. 95.

'Nera' and Josie de Bray

Jill Julius Matthews, *Good and Mad Women: The Historical Construction of Femininity in Twentieth-Century Australia*, Allen & Unwin, Sydney, 1992 (published 1984), p. 127; Frances, *Selling Sex*, p. 211; 'Women's Christian Temperance Union', *West Australian*, 3 September 1919, p. 8; 'Roe-Street shooting outrage', *West Australian*, 12 September 1919, p. 8; 'De Bray's evidence', *Daily News* (Perth), 2

September 1919, p. 6; 'Rue de Roe ructions', 25 October 1919, p. 5.; 'Josie a prisoner of war', *Mirror* (Perth), 12 October 1940; 'Madame Josie is back in Perth again, 12 years in France', *Mirror* (Perth), 9 April 1949, p. 1–3; 'Perth estate left to Frenchwoman', *West Australian*, 27 October 1953, p. 4.

Husband caught out

'Only wanted a drink in Rue de la Roe', *Mirror* (Perth), 22 July 1944, p. 5.

Dodging time in Sydney

'"Pretty Dulcie" Lewis taken to jail after raid', *Sun* (Sydney), 26 April 1952, p. 2.

Chapter 9: Shots in St Kilda

55 Fawkner Street, real estate

'55 Fawkner Street', realestate.com.au, realestate.com.au/sold/property-house-vic-st+kilda-118983767.

Fawkner Street

Frank Howson Blog, 'Fawkner Street, St Kilda', frankhowsonblog.wordpress.com/2014/04/03/fawkner-street-st-kilda, accessed 16 November 2017.

Attempted murder of Keith Hull

'He said a woman got "Donald the Duck"', *Mirror* (Perth), 30 August 1947, p. 17; 'Gunmen try to murder man in truck', *Argus* (Melbourne), 28 July 1947, p. 1; 'Accused says Hull "pulled" gun. St Kilda shooting evidence', *Argus* (Melbourne), 16 September 1947, p. 6; 'Two acquitted in St Kilda shooting case', *Argus* (Melbourne), 17 September 1947, p. 7; 'Acquittal in Hull shooting charge', *Townsville Daily Bulletin*, 17 September 1947, p. 1.

Death of George Barrett

'Shot in self-defence, says coroner', *Argus* (Melbourne), 20 December 1947, p. 11.

Fitzroy Street

Ron Testro, 'Fitzroy St. Streets of adventure', *Argus* (Melbourne), 12 February 1955, p. 39.

Conspiracy to murder case

'Murder plot charge against woman', *Daily Telegraph* (Sydney), 10 August 1947, p. 16; 'Woman on murder conspiracy charge', *Argus* (Melbourne), 11 August 1947, p. 3; 'Conspiracy to murder charge', *Truth* (Brisbane), 24 August 1947, p. 26'; 'Two cleared of conspiracy to murder charge', *Sunday Mail* (Brisbane), 24 August 1947, p. 4.

Taxi accident

'Taxi runs amok and crashes', *Age* (Melbourne), 3 December 1947, p. 3.

Dulcie's brother and sister

'Police finds goods in floor cache', *Argus* (Melbourne), 13 July 1951, p. 3; 'Woman wins appeal', *Herald* (Melbourne), 18 March 1952, p. 2, 'The shame of Sydney', *Truth* (Sydney), 2 May 1954, p. 4.

Gavan Walsh murder and shooting of Dulcie

State Coroner's Office, Inquest Deposition Files, 'G.T. Walsh', 1951, series VPRS 24, P0000, unit number 2054; 'Alibi in St Kilda shooting', *Argus* (Melbourne), 21 November 1951, p. 7; '"Pretty Dulcie" gives evidence for defence. Jury acquits Martin in Walsh murder case', *Argus* (Melbourne), 22 November 1951, p. 7; '"Pretty Dulcie's" code is silence', *Argus* (Melbourne), 23 November 1951, p. 1; 'Conflicting stories on fatal Vic. shooting', *Truth* (Sydney), 25 November 1951, p. 9; Frank Howson Blog, 'Fawkner Street, St Kilda', frankhowsonblog.wordpress.com/2014/04/03/fawkner-street-st-kilda, accessed 16 November 2017.

Dulcie's marriage to Redda Lewis

'Maimed, 'Pretty Dulcie' weds at murder scene', *Truth* (Sydney),
9 December 1951, p. 3; '"Pretty Dulcie" is married', *Argus*
(Melbourne), 10 December 1951, p. 3; Jenkings, *As Crime Goes By*,
p. 137.

Chapter 10: 'I've had enough'

Dulcie shouting at kids

Brian Matthews, *A Fine and Private Place: A Memoir*, Picador,
Sydney, 2001 (published 2000), p. 13.

Offensive language at the Prince Charles Hotel

'Dulcie fined on language charge', *Herald* (Melbourne), 12 February
1952, p. 10.

Dulcie had enough

'Had enough, says Dulcie. Dogged by curse of violent death', *Mail*
(Adelaide), 26 April 1952, p. 2.

Brawl, Redda Lewis shot and Dulcie arrested

'Woman hurt in fight', *Argus* (Melbourne), 25 February 1952, p. 7;
'"Redda" Lewis released', *West Australian*, 3 May 1952, p. 9; '100
armed police hunt gunmen', *Argus* (Melbourne), 24 April 1952,
p. 1; '"Pretty Dulcie" Lewis taken to jail after raid', *Sun* (Sydney),
26 April 1952, p. 2; 'Wedding story; jail as sequel', *Sun* (Sydney), 25
November 1952, p. 3.

Dulcie's mug shot

State Penitentiary, Long Bay, 'Photographic Description Sheet', 'Mary
Eugene', NRS 2497, 14/3142, photo no. 208/172.

Dulcie convictions 1952–1953

SRNSW, State Penitentiary, Long Bay, 'Description card', 'Mary
Eugene', NRS, 2494, 11/3127.

Kate Leigh in later life

'Kate in no mood to talk after tiring air trip', *Mirror* (Perth), 26
November 1949, p. 8; 'Kate was married without her rings', *Mirror*
(Perth), 21 January 1950, p. 9, 11; 'Shiner Ryan may marry', *Daily
News* (Perth), 29 July 1942, p. 4; 'Newlyweds book posh Sydney
club', *Mirror* (Perth), 21 January 1950, p. 11; 'Kate's the girl for him,
says W.A. beau', *Truth* (Sydney), 6 November 1949, p. 3; 'Shiner
Ryan weds NSW woman here', *Mirror* (Perth), 17 January 1950, p. 2;
Ron Davidson, *High Jinks at the Hot Pool*, Fremantle Arts Centre
Press, Fremantle, 1994, p. 223; 'Former underworld queens are in the
limelight again', *Truth* (Sydney), 7 January 1951, p. 9; 'The bloom
has gone off sly grog, Kate says', *Truth* (Sydney), 8 August 1954,
p. 12; 'Kate Leigh in form from witness box', *Cootamundra Herald*,
15 October 1954, p. 1; Tanja Luckins, 'Pigs, hogs and Aussie blokes:
the emergence of the term "six o'clock swill" ', *History Australia*,
vol. 4, no. 1, 2007, p. 12; 'Time gents! ... For a word on beer',
Truth (Sydney), 7 November 1954, p. 7; *Sydney Morning Herald*,
6 February 1964, p. 5; Jenkings, *As Crime Goes by ...*, p. 132;
Wendy Wilson, interviewed by the author, 10 September 2015; 'Kate
and "Shiner" at war again', *Truth* (Sydney), 7 June 1953, p. 48;
Metropolitan Cemeteries Board, 'Summary of Record Information –
Ernest Alexander Ryan', www2.mcb.wa.gov.au/NameSearch/details.
php?id=FB00020099; Davidson, *High Jinks at the Hot Pool*, p. 223–
24; Straw, *The Worst Woman in Sydney*, chapter 9.

Tilly Devine death

Tilly Devine obituary, *Sydney Morning Herald*, 25 November 1970,
p. 18; Ron Saw, Tilly Devine obituary, *Daily Telegraph* (Sydney), 25
November 1970, p. 6.

Nellie Cameron

Kelly, *Rugged Angel*, p. 169; 'Lonely death for lady of the
underworld', *Mercury* (Hobart), 10 November 1953, p. 6. 'Nellie's
emotions', *Arrow* (Sydney), 4 December 1931, p. 1; 'Death of

notorious underworld blonde', *Examiner* (Launceston), 10 November 1953, p. 4; Underworld mourns Sydney "queen"', *Advertiser* (Adelaide), 11 November 1953, p. 1; Blaikie, *Wild Women of Sydney*, p. 181–82.

Redda Lewis in Hobart

'Criminal in trouble again', *Advocate* (Burnie), 5 July 1954, p. 3.

Licensing and weapon charges

SRNSW, State Penitentiary, Long Bay, 'Description card', 'Mary Eugene', NRS, 2494, 11/3127; 'A limping blonde who lied for her license', *Truth* (Sydney), 7 February 1954, p. 13; 'Why "Pretty Dulcie" is the "Angel of Death', *Truth* (Brisbane), 4 May 1952, p. 8; 'The "Angel of Death" got a fright', *Truth* (Sydney), 21 February 1954, p. 12.

Chapter 11: A 'model housewife'

Bondi fall

'"Angel of Death" denies fall from window, *Central Queensland Herald* (Rockhampton), 20 January 1955, p. 27; '"Angel of death" won't talk', *Mirror* (Perth), 29 January 1955, p. 6; Davidson, *High Jinks at the Hot Pool*; Ron Davidson's is Frank Davidson's son. We talked in Fremantle in 2015 about his father's work and his professional relationships with Kate Leigh and other underworld figures.

Joe Shaw on Dulcie's fall

Joe Shaw, interviewed by Hamish Sewell, Forgotten Australians and Former Child Migrants oral history project, 2 sound files (c. 227 minutes), 2011, National Library of Australia, nla.gov.au/nla.obj-219414000/listen?searchTerm=dulcie markham, accessed 8 August 2018.

Sally-Ann Huckstepp

John Dale, *Huckstepp: A Dangerous Life*, Allen & Unwin, St Leonard's, 2000.

Bill Jenkings on Dulcie and 'angels'

Jenkings, *As Crime Goes By*, p. 135.

Changing nature of sex business

Frances, *Selling Sex*, p. 261–62.

Marriage to Martin Rooney

Jenkings, *As Crime Goes By*, p. 138; NSWBDM, 'Dulcie May Rooney', 9264/1976, reproduced death certificate in possession of the author. The death certificate names Martin Rooney as her husband.

Death of Dulcie's father

Death details from Reeves family tree, access to information and family records made available on ancestry.com.au by permission of Liz Reeves (this family tree includes family archival records).

Dulcie's death

NSWBDM, 'Dulcie May Rooney', 9264/1976; Jack Darmody, 'Dulcie, the Angel of Death, is dead', *Sydney Morning Herald*, 22 April 1976, p. 1, 4; Larry Writer, *Bumper: The Life and Times of Frank 'Bumper' Farrell*, Hachette, Sydney, 2017 (published 2011), p. 324–25.

Epilogue: 'What does it matter so long as you get the money?'

Dulcie's many convictions

SRNSW, State Penitentiary, Long Bay, 'Description card', 'Mary Eugene', NRS, 2494, 11/3127.

Notes

Bill Jenkings on Dulcie

Jenkings, *As Crime Goes By*, p. 135.

Greg Brown on Dulcie

Quoted in Writer, *Razor*, p. 133–34.

Toilet incident

Matthews, *A Fine and Private Place*, p. 11.

Femme Fatale exhibition

'Razor gangs and axe-wielding angels: Squalid Sydney on show', *Sydney Morning Herald*, 6 March 2009, smh.com.au/national/razor-gangs-and-axewielding-angels-squalid-sydney-on-show-20090305-8q1v.html, accessed 25 April 2018.

Dulcie as 'Angel of Death' in newspaper stories

'"Angel of Death" weds', *Courier-Mail* (Brisbane), 10 December 1951, p. 1; '"Angel of Death" hoodoo still haunts "Pretty Dulcie"', *Truth* (Brisbane), 27 April 1952, p. 2; '"Angel of Death's" husband shot in back', *Illawarra Daily Mercury* (Wollongong), 12 June 1953, p. 2; 'The "Angel of Death" got a fright', *Truth* (Sydney), 21 February 1954, p. 12.

Larrikins, flappers and modern women

Bellanta, *Larrikins: A History*, chapter 2; Melissa Bellanta, 'The larrikin girl', *Journal of Australian Studies*, vol. 34, no. 4, 2010, p. 499–512.

'There are ways of getting money…'

'Glamorous young underworld girl's amazing life story', *Truth* (Brisbane), 9 January 1944, p. 10.

Anne Summers and women's history

Anne Summers, *Damned Whores and God's Police*, Penguin Books, NewSouth Books, 2016 (first published 1975); Michelle Arrow,

'Damned Whores and God's Police is still relevant to Australia 40 years on – more's the pity', *The Conversation*, 21 September 2015, theconversation.com/damned-whores-and-gods-police-is-still-relevant-to-australia-40-years-on-mores-the-pity-47753, accessed 29 April 2018.

Women and crime

Shani D'Cruze & Louisa A. Jackson (eds), *Women, Crime and Justice in England since 1660*, Palgrave Macmillan, Basingstoke, 2009; Frances Heidensohn, *Women and Crime*, 2nd edn, Macmillan, Basingstoke, 1996, p. 194.

Bill Jenkings on Dulcie and 'angels'

Jenkings, *As Crime Goes By*, p. 135.

'Hoodoo Girl'

'Notorious woman pays us a visit', *Daily News* (Perth), 26 June 1946, p. 15; 'Hoodoo Girl's 3 lovers killed', *Daily Telegraph* (Sydney), 21 July 1940, p. 6.

Bill Jenkings and Dulcie movie

Jenkings, *As Crime Goes By*, p. 138.

Bibliography

J.S. Battye Library of West Australian History, Perth

Government Statistician's Office, *Statistical Register of Western Australia*, Perth, 1903–1939

Police Gazette, Western Australia, 1930–1957

Interviews and transcripts

Some of the content of this book has been informed by my conversations over the years with locals in Darlinghurst and Surry Hills.

Baker, Hal, interviewed by the author, 16 August 2013

Baker, Mary, interviewed by her granddaughter Jeannine Baker, 18 April 1998, transcript copy given to the author

Beahan, Mark, several conversations about Kate Leigh with the author, June–December 2015

Wilson, Wendy, interviewed by the author, 10 September 2015

Newspapers

Advertiser (Adelaide)

Advocate (Burnie)

Age (Melbourne)

Argus (Melbourne)

Arrow (Sydney)

Canberra Times

Central Queensland Herald (Rockhampton)

Courier-Mail (Brisbane)

Daily Advertiser (Wagga Wagga)

Daily News (Perth)

Daily News (Sydney)

Daily Telegraph (Sydney)

Evening News (Sydney)

Examiner (Launceston)

Farmer and Settler (Sydney)

Forbes Advocate

Gosford Times and Wyong District Advocate

Grenfell Record and Lachlan District Advertiser

Illawarra Daily Mercury (Wollongong)

Labor Daily (Sydney)

Leader (Orange)

Maitland Daily Mercury

Mercury (Hobart)

Mirror (Perth)

Morning Bulletin (Rockhampton)

National Advocate (Bathurst)

Newcastle Morning Herald and Miner's Advocate

Newcastle Sun

Northern Star

People (Sydney)

Scone Advocate

Shepparton Advertiser

Singleton Argus

Smith's Weekly (Sydney)

Star (Sydney)

Sunday Telegraph (Sydney)

Sunday Times (Sydney)

Sunday Mail (Brisbane)

Sun-Herald (Sydney)

Sydney Morning Herald

Telegraph (Brisbane)

Truth (Brisbane)

Truth (Melbourne)

Truth (Perth)

Truth (Sydney)

Tweed Daily

Watchman (Sydney)

West Australian

Western Champion (Parkes)

Oral histories

Blissett, Ray, interviewed by Stephen Rapley, 2 March 1988, NSW Bicentennial oral history collection, 3 sound cassettes (c. 140 minutes), recordings available online via Trove for the National Library of Australia, nla.gov.au/nla.obj-216363690/listen, accessed 1 February 2018

Hayes, Chow, interviewed by Margaret Throsby, 1990, ABC Radio, mpegmedia.abc.net.au/innovation/sidetracks/sydney_content/ mp3/ChowHayes/ChowHayes.mp3, accessed 1 November 2017

Mewjork, Richard, interviewed by Margo Beasley, 12 September 2011, City of Sydney Oral History Project, sydneyoralhistories. com.au/?s=surry+hills, accessed 1 July 2015

Ramsay, Anne, interviewed by Sue Rosen, 21 September 1994, 'City of Sydney Oral History Collections', s3.amazonaws.com/ media.cityofsydney/OralHistories/Our+City/AnneRamsay/ Ramsey,+Anne.pdf, accessed 5 February 2018

St Louis, J.E., interviewed by Chris Jeffery, 1988, Oral History
    Records Rescue Group, OH1978, State Library of Western
    Australia, catalogue.slwa.wa.gov.au/search~S2?/Xinterview+j+
    e+st+louis&searchscope=2&SORT=D/Xinterview+j+e+st+louis
    &searchscope=2&SORT=D&SUBKEY=interview+j+e+st+louis
    /1,2,2,B/frameset&FF=Xinterview+j+e+st+louis&searchscope=
    2&SORT=D&1,1, accessed 22 January 2018
Shaw, Joe, interviewed by Hamish Sewell, 2011, Forgotten Australians
    and Former Child Migrants oral history project, 2 sound files
    (c. 227 minutes), National Library of Australia, nla.gov.au/nla.
    obj-219414000/listen?searchTerm=dulcie markham, accessed
    8 August 2018
Stingemore (née Brophy), Joan, interviewed by Larraine Stevens, 22 June
    1999, oral history project, LHC OH/STI, Fremantle City Library

Police Gazette Archives

NSW Police Gazette, 1911–1938, digitised volumes, Archive CD
    Books Australasia
Queensland Police Gazette, 1943–1944, digitised volumes, Archive
    CD Books Australasia

Public Record Office, Victoria

State Coroner's Office, Inquest Deposition Files, 'Leslie Ernest
    Walkerden', 1946/1982, series VPRS 24, P0000, unit number
    1534
State Coroner's Office, Inquest Deposition Files, 'G. T. Walsh', 1951,
    series VPRS 24, P0000, unit number 2054

Registry of Births, Deaths and Marriages, NSW

NSW Government, Registry of Births, Deaths and Marriages
    (hereafter NSWBDM), 'Markham, Dulcie May', 516/1914,
    reproduced birth certificate in possession of the author

NSWBDM, 'Markham, John and Parker, Florence Millicent', 2988/1913, reproduced marriage certificate in possession of the author

NSWBDM, 'Dulcie May Rooney', 9264/1976, reproduced death certificate in possession of the author

Registry of Births, Deaths and Marriages, Victoria

Registry of Births, Deaths and Marriages, Victoria, 'Guido Caletti and Ellen Kelly', Marriage Certificate, online.justice.vic.gov.au/bdm/indexsearch.doj?viewSequence=200&language=en&trxId=IDX&commandAction_displayDetailsAction=F64D2DCD2215E931FB49EAD972D11361, digital copy obtained 11 June 2018

Reeves family records

'Reeves family tree', ancestry.com.au, access to information and family records by permission of Liz Reeves

State Archives and Records, New South Wales

'Darlinghurst Gaol Photographic Description Book 1913–1914', NRS 2138, 3/6083

Information and other papers, November 1939, [T105], R v Allan/Allen or Branch, Murder, NRS 13477

NSW Legislative Assembly, 'Select committee into the condition of the working classes of the metropolis', *Votes and Proceedings*, vol. 4, 1854–60, p. 68

Papers and depositions, Supreme Court, Sydney and on Circuit, November 1939, [9/7384] or [9/7385], R vs ALLAN/ALLEN or BRANCH, Murder, NRS 880

Register of Coroners Inquests and Magisterial Inquiries, 1834–1942, Inquest Deposition Files, 'McCormack, Cecil', NRS345, 2/10513-15

'Registers of Police 1913–1924', NRS 10945, 7/6213, 8/3259

State Penitentiary, Long Bay, 'Gaol Photographic Description Books, 1914–1960' 'Guido Calletti', NRS 2497, No. 29332, 17/1515

State Penitentiary, Long Bay, 'Photograph Description Book 1930–1970', 'Nellie Cameron', NRS 2497, No. 792, 14/3137

State Penitentiary, Long Bay, 'Photograph Description Book 1910–1930', 'Matilda Devine', NRS 2496, No. 659, 3/6007

State Penitentiary, Long Bay, 'Description card', 'Mary Eugene', NRS, 2494, 11/3127

State Penitentiary, Long Bay, 'Photographic Description Sheet', 'Mary Eugene', NRS 2497, 14/3142, photo no. 208/172

State Penitentiary, Long Bay, 'Photograph Description Book 1930–1970', 'Kate Leigh', NRS 2497, No. 155/92

State Penitentiary, Long Bay, 'Photograph Description Book 1930–1970', 'Kate Leigh', NRS 2497, No. 839, 14/3137

State Penitentiary, Long Bay, 'Gaol Photographic Description Books, 1914–1960' 'Cecil William McCormack', NRS 2467, No. 20967, 3/6114

State Penitentiary, Long Bay, 'Gaol Photographic Description Books, 1914–1960' 'Harry Pidgeon', NRS 2467, No. 20963, 3/6114

Transcripts of evidence of the various courts, 1939, Criminal, [6/2031], A-B, NRS 2713

State Archives, Queensland

Police Department, Police Service Commissioner's Office, Police Correspondence, VD Suspects and Prostitution, 1 January 1899 to 31 December 1932, Queensland State Archives, item no. 318632

State Records Office, Western Australia

Register of Local Prisoners (Female) – Fremantle Prison, Gaol Department Western Australia, Perth, WAS-678, Series 1809, 4186/1–2

Register of Local Prisoners (Male) – Fremantle Prison, Gaol
     Department Western Australia, Perth, WAS-678, Series 1809,
     4173/1–9

Books

Adams, Simon, *The Unforgiving Rope: Murder and Hanging on
     Australia's Western Frontier*, UWA Publishing, Perth, 2009

Allen, Judith A., *Sex and Secrets: Crimes Involving Australian
     Women Since 1880*, Oxford University Press, Melbourne,
     1990

Anderson, Hugh, *The Rise and Fall of Squizzy Taylor: A Larrikin
     Crook*, Pier 9, Sydney, 2009 (first published 1971)

Anleu, Sharyn L., *Deviance, Conformity and Control*, Pearson,
     Sydney, 2006

Bellanta, Melissa, *Larrikins: A History*, University of Queensland
     Press, Brisbane, 2012

Blaikie, George, *Wild Women of Sydney*, Rigby, Adelaide, 1980

Crotty, Martin & David Andrew Roberts (eds), *Turning Points in
     Australian History*, UNSW Press, Sydney, 2009

Dale, John, *Huckstepp: A Dangerous Life,* St Leonard's, Allen &
     Unwin, 2000

Daniels, Kay, *Convict Women*, Allen & Unwin, Sydney, 1998

—— (ed.), *So Much Hard Work: Women and Prostitution in
     Australian History*, Fontana Collins, Sydney, 1984

Darian-Smith, Kate, *On the Homefront: Melbourne in Wartime,
     1939–45*, 2nd edn, Melbourne University Press, Melbourne,
     2009

Davidson, Ron, *High Jinks at the Hot Pool*, Fremantle Arts Centre
     Press, Fremantle, 1994

Dawson, Christopher, *Intemperance and the Train of Evil: A Life
     on the Wrong Side of the Tracks in Colonial Brisbane*, Boggo
     Road Gaol Historical Society, Brisbane, 2008

D'Cruze, Shani & Louisa A. Jackson (eds), *Women, Crime and Justice in England since 1660*, Palgrave Macmillan, Basingstoke, 2009

Ditmore, Melissa Hope, *Prostitution and Sex Work*, Greenwood, Oxford, 2011

Doyle, Peter with Caleb Williams, *City of Shadows: Sydney Police Photographs 1912–1948*, Historic Houses Trust of New South Wales, Sydney, 2005

Dugan, Darcy, with Michael Tatlow, *Bloodhouse*, HarperCollins, Sydney, 2012

Durstan, Gregory, *Victims and Viragos: Metropolitan Women, Crime and the Eighteenth-century Justice System*, Arima Publishing, Bury St Edmunds, 2007

Emsley, Clive, *Crime and Society in England, 1750–1900*, Pearson Longman, London, 1987

——, *Crime and Society in Twentieth-Century England*, Pearson Longman, London, 2011

Fitzgerald, F. Scott, *The Crack-Up*, Scrivener, New York, 1945

——, *The Great Gatsby*, Scrivener, New York, 1925

Fitzgerald, Ross & Trevor L. Jordan, *Under the Influence: A History of Alcohol in Australia*, ABC Books, Sydney, 2009

Frances, Raelene, *Selling Sex: A Hidden History of Prostitution*, UNSW Press, Sydney, 2007

Fraser, Antonia, *The Weaker Vessel: Woman's Lot in Seventeenth-century England*, Random House, London, 1994 (first published 1984)

Godfrey, Barry, Paul Lawrence & Chris A. Williams, *History and Crime*, Sage Publications, London, 2008

Grabosky, Peter N., *Sydney in Ferment: Crime, Dissent and Official Reaction 1788–1973*, Australian National University Press, Canberra, 1977

Bibliography

Graycar, Adam & Peter Grabosky (eds), *The Cambridge Handbook of Australian Criminology*, Cambridge University Press, Cambridge, 2009

Heidensohn, Frances, *Women and Crime*, 2nd edn, Macmillan, Basingstoke and London, 1996

Hickie, David, *Chow Hayes, Gunman: Australia's Most Notorious Gangster*, Angus & Robertson, Sydney, 1990

Jenkings, Bill, *As Crime Goes by … The Life and Times of 'Bondi' Bill Jenkings*, Ironbark Press, Sydney, 1992

Jensen, Vicki (ed.), *Women Criminals: An Encyclopedia of People and Issues*, Volume 1, *Issues Related to Women and Crime*, ABC-CLIO, Santa Barbara, California, 2012

Keating, Christopher, *Surry Hills: The City's Backyard*, 2nd edn, Halstead Press, Sydney, 2008

Kelly, Vince, *Rugged Angel: The Amazing Career of Policewoman Lillian Armfield*, Angus & Robertson, Sydney, 1961

——, *The Shadow: The Amazing Exploits of Frank Fahy*, Angus & Robertson, London, 1955

Keneally, Thomas, *Australians*, Volume 3, *Flappers to Vietnam*, Allen & Unwin, Sydney, 2015

Knightley, Philip, *Australia: Biography of a Nation*, Jonathan Cape, London, 2000

Lake, Marilyn, *Getting Equal: The History of Australian Feminism*, Allen & Unwin, Sydney, 1999

Lomazow, Steven & Eric Fettman, *FDR's Deadly Secret*, PublicAffairs, New York, 2009

McCoy, Alfred W., *Drug Traffic: Narcotics and Organised Crime in Australia*, Harper & Row, Sydney, 1980

MacDonald, Robert (ed.), *Youth, the 'Underclass' and Social Exclusion*, Routledge, London, 1997

McHugh, Paul, *Prostitution and Victorian Social Reform*, Croom Helm, London, 1980

Mackrell, Judith, *Flappers: Six Women of a Dangerous Generation*, Pan, London, 2014

Mahood, Linda, *Policing Gender, Class and Family: Britain 1850–1940*, UCL Press, London, 1995

Manderson, Desmond, *From Mr Sin to Mr Big: A History of Australian Drug Laws*, Oxford University Press, Melbourne, 1993

Matthews, Brian, *A Fine and Private Place: A Memoir*, Picador, Sydney, 2001

Matthews, Jill Julius, *Good and Mad Women: The Historical Construction of Femininity in Twentieth-century Australia*, Allen & Unwin, Sydney, 1992 (published 1984)

Menzies, Robert, *Afternoon Light: Some Memories of Men and Events*, Penguin, Melbourne, 1969

Mizener, Arthur, *The Far Side of Paradise: A Biography of F. Scott Fitzgerald*, Houghton Mifflin, Boston, 1951

Moore, John Hammond, *Over-Sexed, Over-Paid and Over Here: Americans in Australia 1941–1945*, University of Queensland Press, Brisbane, 1981

Morton, James & Susanna Lobez, *Bent: Australia's Crooked Cops*, Melbourne University Press, Melbourne, 2014

——, *Gangland Australia: Colonial Criminals to the Carlton Crew*, Melbourne University Press, Melbourne, 2007

——, *Gangland Melbourne*, Victory Books, Melbourne, 2011

——, *Gangland Queensland*, Melbourne University Press, Melbourne, 2012

Mukherjee, Satyanshu K., *Crime Trends in Twentieth Century Australia*, Allen & Unwin, Sydney, 1981

Nowra, Louis, *Kings Cross: A Biography*, NewSouth Books, Sydney, 2013

——, *Woolloomooloo: A Biography*, NewSouth Books, Sydney, 2017

Park, Ruth, *The Harp in the South*, Michael Joseph, London, 1948

Riis, Jacob, *The Battle with the Slum*, Patterson Smith, Montclair, New Jersey, 1902

Robinson, Russell, *Khaki Crims and Desperadoes*, Pan Macmillan, Sydney, 2014

Saunders, Kay, *Notorious Australian Women*, HarperCollins, Sydney, 2011

Simon, Linda, *Lost Girls: The Invention of the Flapper*, Reaktion Books, London, 2017

Straw, Leigh, *Lillian Armfield: How Australia's First Female Detective Took on Tilly Devine and the Razor Gangs and Changed the Face of the Force*, Hachette Australia, Sydney, 2018

——, *After the War: Returned Soldiers and the Mental and Physical Scars of War*, UWA Publishing, Perth, 2017

——, *The Worst Woman in Sydney: The Life and Crimes of Kate Leigh*, NewSouth Books, Sydney, 2016

——, *Drunks, Pests and Harlots: Criminal Women in Western Australia, 1900–1939*, Humming Earth, Kilkerran, Scotland, 2015

Sturma, Michael, *Vice in a Vicious Society: Crime and Convicts in Mid-nineteenth-century New South Wales*, University of Queensland Press, Brisbane, 1983

Summers, Anne, *Damned Whores and God's Police*, NewSouth Books, Sydney, 2016 (first published 1975)

Swain, Shurlee (with Renata Howe), *Single Mothers and Their Children: Disposal, Punishment and Survival in Australia*, Cambridge University Press, Melbourne, 1995

Walkowitz, Judith, *Prostitution and Victorian Society: Women, Class and the State*, Cambridge University Press, Cambridge, 2001 (published 1980)

Wright, Alan, *Organised Crime*, Routledge, London and New York, 2011

Wright, Clare, *Beyond the Ladies Lounge: Australia's Female Publicans*, Melbourne University Press, Melbourne, 2003

Writer, Larry, *Bumper: The Life and Times of Frank 'Bumper' Farrell*, Hachette Australia, Sydney, 2011

——, *Razor: Tilly Devine, Kate Leigh and the Razor Gangs*, Macmillan, Sydney, 2009

Journal articles and conference papers

Auerbach, Nina, 'The rise of the fallen woman', *Nineteenth-Century Fiction*, vol. 35, no. 1, 1980, p. 34

Bellanta, Melissa, 'The larrikin girl', *Journal of Australian Studies*, vol. 34, no. 4, 2010, p. 499–512

Bland, Lucy, '"Purifying" the public world: feminist vigilantes in late Victorian England', *Women's History Review*, vol. 1, no. 3, 1992, p. 397–412

Bodington, G.F., 'On the control and restraint of habitual drunkards', *British Medical Journal*, 28 August 1875, p. 255–56

Doyle, Peter, 'Public eye, private eye: Sydney police mug shots, 1912–1913', *Scan Journal*, vol. 2, no. 3, 2005, scan.net.au/scan/journal/display.php?journal_id=67, accessed 2 January 2017

Doyle, Sue, 'The pyjama girl', *Journal of Australian Studies*, vol. 24, no. 64, (2000): p. 34–41

Evans, Richard, '"The police are rottenly corrupt": policing, scandal, and the regulation of illegal betting in Depression-era Sydney', *Australian and New Zealand Journal of Criminology*, vol. 48, no. 4, 2015, p. 572–87

Frances, Rae, '"White slaves" and White Australia: prostitution and Australian society', *Australian Feminist Studies*, vol. 19, no. 44, 2004, p. 189–90

Luckins, Tanja, '"Satan finds some mischief"? Drinkers' responses to the six o'clock closing of pubs in Australia, 1910s–1930s', *Journal of Australian Studies*, vol. 32, no. 3, 2008, p. 295–307

——, 'Pigs, hogs and Aussie blokes: the emergence of the term "six o'clock swill"', *History Australia*, vol. 4, no. 1, 2007, p. 1–17

McConville, Chris, 'The location of Melbourne's prostitutes', *Historical Studies*, vol. 19, no. 74, 1980, p. 90

McKewon, Elaine, 'The historical geography of prostitution in Perth, Western Australia', *Australian Geographer*, vol. 34, no. 3, 2003, p. 300–302

Nixon, Christine, 'The history of women in the police service', in Patricia Weiser Easteal & Sandra McKillop (eds), *Women and the Law: Proceedings of a Conference Held 24–26 September 1991*, Australian Institute of Criminology, Canberra, 1993

Petersen, Nick, 'Neighbourhood context and unsolved murders: the social ecology of homicide investigations', *Policing and Society*, vol. 27, no. 4, 2015, p. 372–92

Phillips, Walter, '"Six o'clock swill": the introduction of early closing of hotel bars in Australia', *Historical Studies*, vol. 19, no. 75, 1980, p. 261

Piper, Alana, '"A growing vice": the truth about Brisbane girls and drunkenness in the early twentieth century', *Journal of Australian Studies*, vol. 34, no. 4, 2010, p. 485–97

——, 'Women's work: the professionalisation and policing of fortune-telling in Australia', *Labour History*, no. 108, 2015, p. 37–52

Smith, Norris, 'The Shadow: an undercover pioneer', *Police Monthly*, April 2013, p. 21–23

Tennant, Margaret, '"Magdalens and moral imbeciles": women's homes in nineteenth-century New Zealand', *Women's Studies International Forum*, vol. 9, nos 5–6, 1986, p. 491–502

Welburn, A.C., 'The Singapore Strategy', *Australian Defence Force Journal*, no. 100, June 1993, p. 45

Williams, Marise, 'The gender politics of *Underbelly: Razor*', *Southerly*, vol. 17, no. 2, 2012, p. 9–22

Online resources

Allen, Judith & Baiba Irving, 'Devine, Matilda Mary (Tilly)', *Australian Dictionary of Biography*, National Centre of Biography, Australian National University, adb.anu.edu.au/biography/ devine-matilda-mary-tilly-5970, accessed 29 January 2017

Arrow, Michelle, 'Damned Whores and God's Police is still relevant to Australia 40 years on – more's the pity', The Conversation, 21 September 2015, theconversation.com/damned-whores-and-gods-police-is-still-relevant-to-australia-40-years-on-mores-the-pity-47753, accessed 29 April 2018

Australian Police, 'James Mitchell', australianpolice.com.au/nsw-police-history-index/police-commissioners-of-nsw/james-mitchell, accessed 9 October 2016

Baker, D.W.A, 'Mitchell, Sir Thomas Livingstone (1792–1855), *Australian Dictionary of Biography*, National Centre of Biography, Australian National University, adb.anu.edu.au/ biography/mitchell-sir-thomas-livingstone-2463, accessed 16 May 2018

Benjamin, Gerard, 'Florence and Les still telling the Village history', *Village News*, September 2011, p. 13, issuu.com/ newfarmvillagenews/docs/villagenewsseptember2011, accessed 10 August 2018

'Bronte', Dictionary of Sydney, dictionaryofsydney.org/entry/bronte - ref-uuid=ee57534b-6283-d20f-8e08-9075ae8d976b, accessed 4 February 2018

Cain, Frank, 'MacKay, William John (1885–1948)', *Australian Dictionary of Biography*, National Centre of Biography, Australian National University, adb.anu.edu.au/biography/ mackay-william-john-7381/text12829, accessed 30 August 2015 and 22 March 2018

Damousi, Joy, 'Female factory inspectors and leadership in early twentieth-century Australia', in Joy Damousi, Kim Rubenstein

& Mary Tomsic (eds), *Diversity in Leadership: Australian Women, Past and Present*, ANU Press, Canberra, 2014, p. 169–88, press-files.anu.edu.au/downloads/press/p292111/pdf/9.-Female-factory-inspectors-and-leadership-in-early-twentieth-century-Australia.pdf

Fairfax Syndication Photos, 'Sydney crime figures and former rivals, Kate Leigh and Tilly Devine, photographed on 20 August 1948', consumer.fairfaxsyndication.com/C.aspx?VP3=Search Result&VBID=2ITP1GQBFSELM&SMLS=1&RW=1440& RH=776, accessed 30 March 2017

Gamble, Beau, 'On this day: Australia at war', *Australian Geographic*, 2 September 2011, australiangeographic.com. au/blogs/on-this-day/2011/09/on-this-day-australia-at-war, accessed 15 March 2018

Gilchrist, Catie, 'Tilly Devine', Dictionary of Sydney, dictionaryofsydney.org/entry/tilly_devine, accessed 27 January 2017

Howson, Frank, 'Fawkner Street, St. Kilda', Frank Howson blog, frankhowsonblog.wordpress.com/2014/04/03/fawkner-street-st-kilda, accessed 16 November 2017

Lack, John, 'Coates, James (1901–1947), *Australian Dictionary of Biography*, National Centre of Biography, Australian National University, adb.anu.edu.au/biography/coates-james-5694, accessed 9 September 2018

McConville, Chris, 'Melbourne crime: from war to Depression, 1919–1929', *Australian Dictionary of Biography*, National Centre of Biography, Australian National University, adb.anu.edu.au/essay/6, accessed 3 April 2018

Metropolitan Cemeteries Board, 'Summary of record information – Ernest Alexander Ryan', www2.mcb.wa.gov.au/NameSearch/details.php?id=FB00020099, accessed 6 May 2015

NSW Government, *Police Offences Amendment (Drugs) Act*, NSW
    Legislation, legislation.nsw.gov.au/acts/1927-7.pdf, accessed 12
    February 2017
——, 'History of the NSW Police Force – significant dates', NSW
    Police Force, police.nsw.gov.au/about_us/history, accessed 1
    February 2017
——, 'Women of the NSW Police Force', NSW Police Force, police.
    nsw.gov.au/about_us/100th_anniversary_of_women_in_
    policing/women_of_the_nsw_police_force, accessed 24 March
    2017
Perkins, Roberta, chapter 2, 'Control, regulation and legislation',
    Working Girls: Prostitutes, Their Life and Social Control,
    Australian Institute of Criminology, Canberra, 1991, aic.gov.
    au/publications/previous series/lcj/1-20/working/chapter 2
    control regulation and legislation.html, accessed 13 June 2017
'Razor gangs and axe-wielding angels: squalid Sydney on show',
    Sydney Morning Herald, 6 March 2009, smh.com.au/national/
    razor-gangs-and-axewielding-angels-squalid-sydney-on-show-
    20090305-8q1v.html, accessed 25 April 2018
SRNSW, 'Tilly Devine & the Razor Gang wars, 1927–1931', records.
    nsw.gov.au/archives/magazine/galleries/tilly-devine-and-the-
    razor-gang-wars, accessed 2 June 2018
'Suburban Sydney', Dictionary of Sydney, dictionaryofsydney.org/
    entry/suburban_sydney - ref-uuid=ee57534b-6283-d20f-8e08-
    9075ae8d976b, accessed 4 February 2018
'Waverley', Dictionary of Sydney, dictionaryofsydney.org/place/
    waverley, accessed 2 February 2018

Theses

Beresford, Quentin, 'Drinkers and the anti-drink movement in
    Sydney, 1870–1930', PhD thesis, Australian National
    University, July 1984

Davidson, Raelene, 'Prostitution in Perth and Fremantle and on the Eastern Goldfields, 1895–September 1939', MA thesis, University of Western Australia, 1980

Farrell, Rita, 'Dangerous women: constructions of female criminality in Western Australia 1915–1945', Murdoch University, PhD thesis, 1997

Hammond, Robin, 'Young men with guns: crooks, cops and consorting law, Sydney 1920s–1930s', Master of Arts thesis, University of New England, 2009, e-publications.une.edu.au/vital/access/manager/Repository/une:3467?source=Advanced&field1=text&query1=young+men+with+guns, accessed 21 July 2018

Stella, Leonie, 'Policing women: women's police in Western Australia 1917–1943', Honours thesis, Murdoch University, 1990

Toole, Kellie Louise, 'Innocence and penitence hand clasped in hand: Australian Catholic refuges for penitent women, 1848–1914', Master of Arts thesis, University of Adelaide, 2010

Acknowledgements

When I started writing Kate Leigh's story a few years ago, I had a feeling I needed to tell Lillian Armfield's story too. They were, as we know, two strong women on opposite sides of the law but succeeding in the male-dominated worlds of crime and policing. It may well have ended with Kate and Lil were it not for the enthusiasm of publisher Katie Stackhouse, who contacted me after reading the Kate Leigh book and while I was already contracted to write the Lillian book for the great team at Hachette. Katie understood I had a plan for the Dulcie story that I wanted to tell. Since its early inception and the writing and shaping of this story, Katie's publisher colleague Mary Rennie has also put her heart and soul into supporting this book. Thank you to everyone at ABC Books and HarperCollins Australia for your commitment to seeing Dulcie's story published and brought to life for readers.

Early on in my research, Dulcie's nephew and his wife were incredibly supportive. Despite describing the Markham family story as fragmented and with many silences, they still gave me their early backing to tell Dulcie's story as I saw fit. I really appreciate this. I am hoping that the release of this book will prompt more of Dulcie's family to come forward and share their stories, adding to the complexities of what we already know about Dulcie.

So much of my research has been made possible by the availability of records through the State Archives and Records of New South Wales. I would like to thank Coleen Milicevic in particular for hunting down Dulcie's records for me with great enthusiasm and interest. Coleen also had to contend with my moments of excitement when I was so focused on seeing Dulcie's mug shot that I forgot to look through other archival records brought out for me. Thanks, Coleen, for reminding me of the other records and really going out of your way to assist with my research.

Staff at the NSW Department of Corrective Services were also a key part of my research into Dulcie's criminal record, providing access to restricted records.

There have been times when I've needed records and not been able to get to Sydney quick enough. Fellow historian, researcher and writer Catie Gilchrist assisted with my research at the NSW Archives, while Erik Nielsen located records for me at the State Library of New South Wales. I

Acknowledgements

know you took time out from your own work and research to do it, and I really appreciate it.

I am also grateful for the research services provided by the Public Record Office of Victoria, which gave me access to its criminal and inquest records. The State Records Office of Western Australia also made prison records available for me to widen my research around the crooks with convictions in other states.

I am grateful to Robin Hammond for contacting me about my research and reminding me of her uncle Clarence 'Clarrie' Thomas's life in eastern Sydney. Clarrie left behind a long criminal record when he died in 1937 aged only thirty-six. He was shot dead on the corner of Castlereagh and Park streets in the city centre. Clarrie was a standover man who knew all the lead players in Sydney crime in the 1920s and 1930s. He wrote a number of poems about Kate, Tilly and Dulcie in exercise books but they were thrown out. Robin has shared the pain of this loss of creative, important records of a Sydney gunman. Clarrie's life will make a fantastic story, Robin, so I'm hoping you do write it.

I would also like to single out one of my postgraduate students, Alexandra Wallis, who is currently undertaking a PhD under my supervision and has listened to me talking about Dulcie for some time. Your insights are greatly appreciated. You understand women's stories in

Australian history and make me very proud to be a part of your academic journey.

None of this would be possible without the love and support I receive from my family and friends. The book is dedicated to Kristina Kotua because she has brought so much love and support to my life over the last few years. We are both mothers of three kids, though Kris mixed it up and had two girls. I have three boys.

My thanks to all of our family and friends who have followed my books and sustained our friendships with their love, laughter and understanding. Beatons, Browns, Coyles, Leahys, McGregors, McMenemys, Mansons, Middlemass cousins, Tanks, Yettons – thank you. My nephew Lachlan Beaton gets a special mention. I am a very proud auntie knowing you love writing too. Lachlan, I became passionate about writing because your dad, my big brother, inspired me when I was a kid. Thanks also to my mate Gemma Spencer, who is always there at the end of a text when I have my 'writer' moments, and has looked after my biggest boy so well with his schoolwork. Amanda Wright has also followed my writing across cities and travelled to events. Thank you.

I would also like to thank my students at Notre Dame University, and the many others I've taught over seventeen years. I hope that some of my passion for history and telling stories inspires you to go out and tell your own.

Acknowledgements

Maisey, you also get a special mention, sweetheart. Be fierce, be intelligent, be proud, be tough, be sensitive, be emotional, be no-nonsense. Be all the myriad of things that makes every woman wonderful. I have now written about women who were crime bosses, police officers and prostitutes. It's probably best if you are not all of these, but take from their stories the things that make us women the inspiring, intelligent and tough people we are.

Those who know me well know that I carry the spirit of family members who have all contributed to my writing in their own ways. They are no longer with us, but it is important to me to thank my Granny Janet, Granny Esther, Granda John, Uncle Jim and Aunt Cath. My husband's grandparents also walk alongside our kids.

I dedicated my last book to Larry Writer, but this book is also a product of Larry's enthusiasm and support for my work. When I started turning the Dulcie idea over in my head and considering it as a book, Larry was the first person I went to. Just as he had with my Kate and Lillian projects, he spurred my interest on and gave me the confidence to know I had a good story to tell. Thank you, Larry. You're a great pal – and I love that you're a fellow Fitzgerald tragic.

As well as being a writer, I'm a lecturer in history at the University of Notre Dame, Fremantle. I would like to thank the Dean of the School of Arts and Sciences, Professor

Sarah McGann, for her unwavering support for my writing. Sarah is a great champion of research and understands the connections between my teaching and writing. My thanks also to my great colleagues across the university who have all been a part of the effort that go into all my books. I would especially like to mention Shane Burke, who has the office next to mine and has demonstrated the patience of a saint in suffering my banter and me asking, 'Shane, mate, do you have a second?' He always does. Thank you.

There is no way I could do my writing without the great support of my husband, Tony, my parents, James and Sandra, and my mother-in-law, Debbie. I put in many hours of writing in the evenings and weekends, but when I need to travel for research or attend book events, my family rallies around me to ensure our boys are looked after.

Finally, thank you to my boys, Jack, Lawson and Riley. My life for the last decade has been filled with more laughter, fun and special moments than I could ever have dreamed of. I am so very proud of the boys you are and can't wait to see the men you become. Be brave, independent and change the world for the better through each of your contributions. You will always make me proud, and I know you will back women's stories because you've grown up knowing their importance.

Acknowledgements

Picture Credits

Facing the Prologue

Dulcie Markham: photograph by Gordon F. De Lisle, Mitchell Library, State Library of NSW.

Picture section, page 1

Florence Markham: courtesy of the Reeves family.

Dulcie Markham: photograph by Gordon F. De Lisle, Mitchell Library, State Library of NSW.

Harmer and Palmer streets, Woolloomooloo, mid-1930s: NSW Police Dept., 31181, Caroline Simpson Library & Research Collection.

Picture section, page 2

Lilliam Armfield (both photos): courtesy of Norm O'Brien.

'Death Walks with the "Black Widow"': *Smith's Weekly* (Sydney), 7 August 1948, p. 1.

Picture section, page 3

Cecil 'Scotty' McCormack's charge sheet, 1925: NSW State Archives & Records.

Harry Pigeon, 1925: NSW State Archives & Records.

'Lurid Romance Crime Stiletto Behind': *Truth* (Sydney), 17 May 1931, p. 15.

Picture section, page 4

Dulcie Markham: photograph by Gordon F. De Lisle, Mitchell Library, State Library of NSW.

Guido Calletti, 1930: Special Photograph number 1912, Central Police Station, Sydney, NSW Police Forensic Photography Archive, Justice and Police Museum.

'For the men who love "Pretty Dulcie" – death takes no holiday': *Mirror* (Perth), 28 July 1945, p. 16.

Picture section, page 5

Tilly Devine, mugshots, 1934: Police Gazette, Western Australia, State Library of Western Australia.

Tilly Devine, 1953: News Ltd / Newspix.

Nellie Cameron, 1935: News Ltd / Newspix.

'Police seek mystery blonde': *Truth* (Brisbane), 26 December 1937, p. 7.

Picture section, page 6

Kate Leigh, 1953: News Ltd / Newspix.

'1101 bottles of liquor seized': *Herald* (Melbourne), 24 May 1943, p. 3.

Josie's Bungalow, 1929–30: State Library of Western Australia, 048405PD.

'Curly blonde "had" Perth': *Mirror* (Perth), 22 June 1946, p. 7.

Picture section, page 7

Dulcie Markham, 1951: News Ltd / Newspix.

Leonard 'Redda' Lewis and Dulcie Markham, 1951: *The Argus* (Melbourne), 10 December 1951, p. 3.

'Dramatic story of bedroom shooting; Two men to stand trial': *Truth* (Sydney), 14 October 1951, p. 7.

Picture section, page 8

Dulcie Markham's charge sheet (under the name 'Mary Eugene'), 1952: NSW State Archives & Records.

www.ingramcontent.com/pod-product-compliance
Lightning Source LLC
Chambersburg PA
CBHW060026030426
42334CB00019B/2198